DR. KNOX'S
MARITAL EXERCISE BOOK

Dr. KNOX'S
Marital
Exercise Book

DAVID KNOX, PH.D.

DAVID McKAY COMPANY, INC.
New York

Dr. Knox's Marital Exercise Book
Copyright © 1975 by David McKay Company, Inc.

LIBRARY OF CONGRESS CATALOG CARD NUMBER: 74-83693
ISBN 0-679-50499-0
MANUFACTURED IN THE UNITED STATES OF AMERICA

To Frances—
the ultimate answer
to a happy marriage

Acknowledgments

Marriage, the most intimate relationship, is a major source of human happiness. This book suggests basic ways of how to maximize that source. The ideas presented represent the thinking of many people. I am particularly indebted to Dr. Jack Turner for introducing me to a behavioral perspective, to Dr. Charles Madsen for specifying its implications for marriage counseling, to Dr. Jack Wright for his unique applications, and to former clients and current colleagues who have verified the efficacy of the behavioral approach.

I would also like to thank Dr. Turner, Dr. Thomas D'Zurilla, Dr. Buford Rhea, Tom Knox, and Frances for their careful reading and criticizing of the manuscript.

Special appreciation is also expressed to Dianna Morris, Louise Haigwood, Susie Gutknecht, Ray Brannon, and Kathy Moore—former students in our marriage counseling program who now teach me.

Finally, Dee Jackson, Jackie Joyner, and Mae Allen collaborated in typing the final manuscript. To them, I am grateful.

D.K.
Greenville, North Carolina

Contents

Introduction

SCHOPENHAUER, THE GERMAN PHILOSOPHER, told the story of two porcupines huddled together on a cold winter's night. The temperature dropped; the animals moved closer together. But then there were problems: each kept getting "stuck" by the other's quills. Finally, however, with much shifting and shuffling and changing of position, they managed to work out an equilibrium whereby each got maximum warmth with a minimum of painful pricking from the other.

Many husbands and wives have something in common with the huddling porcupines. They want to achieve and maintain a kind of equilibrium: warmth and closeness on the one hand, but without the unpleasant, sometimes agonizingly painful "pricking" that can be the result of continuous intimate interaction with another human being.

This book was written as an attempt to present practical, workable guidelines for coping with the "prickly" aspects of marriage. It is based on three assumptions:

First, that the attitudes and feelings one has about one's partner are based on the partner's *behavior* (a term which can be roughly defined for our purposes here as "words and deeds.") When pleasing behavior is demonstrated—when nice things are said and done—one thinks of one's partner as being a kind, *lovable* person. If you want to continue to have good, positive feelings about your partner—and if your partner values those good, positive feelings—pleasing behavior must be maintained. Right?

Next, all behaviors—pleasing and unpleasing, positive and negative, constructive and destructive—have been learned. People do and say things in response to, or as a consequence of, what's been done and said to them, and in this way behavioral patterns are established. Husbands and wives exercise an enormous influence on each other's marital behaviors. Showing affection, enjoying sex, sulking, nagging, yelling at the kids, forgetting to water the plants—all are to some degree influenced by the mate. In a very real sense, and whether they're aware of it or not, married people *teach* each other how to behave toward one another.

Third, behaviors can be changed or modified. Just as negative behaviors—those that make one feel angry or upset or sad or disappointed—have been learned, so they can be unlearned and replaced by more desirable behaviors.

All couples who marry have the same desire—to have a happy, productive, creative, spontaneous, and mutually satisfying relationship. Yet desire is not enough; each couple must specify the conditions under which their marriage achieves maximum enjoyment and must work toward achieving those conditions. This implies setting goals based on the couple's values and using behavioral principles to initiate or maintain the behaviors necessary to accomplish those goals.

Most of this book is taken up with an explanation of behavioral-change techniques and how husbands and wives can apply them to various specific problems that arise within their relationship.

I've done my best to eliminate scientific jargon wherever possible, but every now and then little bits of "behaviorese" have made their way into the following pages—mainly because the behavioral approach to problem solving is, in fact, "scientific," with a specialized vocabulary that sometimes does not lend itself to easy or precise translation into the more generalized and less specific (though usually more graceful and eloquent) language in which most people are used to expressing themselves. I urge the reader to bear with these lapses. Where they occur, it is because, unfortunately, no other terminology will do.

The reader will also undoubtedly notice the frequent use of doubled-up pronouns, such as he/she, him/her, himself/herself, etc. Like many others, my first impulse always is to use the masculine "he" or "his" or "him" unless I am thinking specifically of a "her." However, it was pointed out to me by some of my friends in the women's movement that almost all the techniques, guidelines, and suggestions presented here are equally applicable to both husband and wife and that it is perhaps discriminatory to assume a "he" when under the circumstances one could just as well assume a "she." So, after thinking about it a bit, it made perfect sense (though it did *feel* awkward at first) to use he/she, him/her, and so on in those many instances where the discussion is concerned specifically with neither men nor women but with married *people*.

I have illustrated many of the points I wanted to make with little "vignettes"—vastly trimmed case histories of actual marriages observed during the course of my work. The reader may detect an element of sex-role stereotyping in many of these vignettes. This is because so many of the marriages that come to my attention are what might be called "traditional" in structure: most of the wives expend most of their time and energy in the role of mother/housekeeper, while most of the husbands expend most of theirs earning their families' daily bread. It is not my intention to promote the "traditional" marriage and all that the term implies as the ideal or only workable arrangement. On the contrary, there are relatively few references to alternative life-styles because, as yet, relatively few people are experimenting with them. However, and this is the important point here, basic behavioral techniques apply to *any* marriage (or, more precisely, to any permanent or even semipermanent man/woman relationship) regardless of the division of labor and responsibilities in and out of the home.

When alcoholism, heroin addiction, or any indication of bizarre, unexplainable behavior patterns or other pathological disturbances enter the picture, I urge the reader to consult a professional psychologist, psychiatrist, or other trained professional for help.

Otherwise, as an ardent believer in do-it-yourselfism, I am hoping that this book will provide the means for couples to successfully work through their *own* problems—to function, in a sense, as marriage counselors to themselves. In fact, I am certain that you already have a number of your own "marital exercises" that you and your partner have found very effective. I invite you to share your experiences and techniques with me by writing to me at the following address: Department of Sociology, East Carolina University, Greenville, North Carolina 27834.

"Spouses are students and teachers of each other."

DR. KNOX'S
MARITAL EXERCISE BOOK

PART I

New Beginnings

CHAPTER 1

How to Begin

I HOPE YOUR MARRIAGE is a good one. And even if it has its ups and downs, I assume that you're committed to it if you picked up this book, and that you're looking for positive, practical ways to make it an even happier, more expanding relationship for both you and your partner. I'm convinced that by applying the behavioral-change principles that follow you can reach your goal and find more growth, excitement, and fulfillment in your partnership than you ever dreamed possible.

It is our *behavior*—what we say and do—that makes or breaks a marriage. We may have feelings of affection or gratitude or misery or resentment. But it is only when we communicate these feelings by acting upon them, by expressing them either verbally or nonverbally—in short, by translating them into *behavior*—that they have the power to influence our relationships with others. Husbands and wives feel happy and loved when their partners say and do things that please them. Unkind, thoughtless words and deeds evoke feelings of sadness or anger, and, often, the urge to retaliate.

We know that all behavior is learned and that it can also be unlearned—that with sufficient motivation (the carrot-

and-stick approach if you will) new behaviors can be taught that eventually will take the place of old. In a very real sense, husbands and wives can (and do) teach each other how to behave within the context of their marriage. How to teach positive, pleasing behavior—the kind that makes for real happiness in marriage—is what this book is all about.

Unfortunately, a few individuals will feel a bit uneasy about some of the teaching techniques outlined later in this section. They may flinch at the idea of making up lists and inventories, of charting their own and their partners' positive and negative behaviors, of drawing up precisely worded contracts with their mates, of penalizing themselves for not abiding by the terms of these contracts, of arranging "artificial" environments that encourage the frequency of certain behaviors. Too cold, they say. Too manipulative. What about human feelings and emotion? What about *love*?

What about love indeed? From time to time I hear comments such as "I want my wife to *want* to do nice things for me because she *loves* me and not just because we've exchanged pieces of paper telling each other how we can please one another better."

Think about this for a minute. Here is a man who admits to being unhappy because of certain things his wife says and does. And yet, he is implying that he would go right on being unhappy if she modified her behavior because he asked her to do so.

To this I can only respond by pointing out that husbands and wives either choose or do not choose to modify their behaviors according to their partners' expressed desires. But what better proof of love than choices made in favor of pleasing the mate?

I might also add that the dynamics of behavioral-change techniques are such that one often finds it is easier to *act* one's way into new modes of thinking and feeling than to think or feel one's way into new modes of action. In other words, when husbands and wives *behave* in new, positive ways (as defined by their partners) and when the new, positive behaviors are reinforced by self and partner (more about reinforcers later), these new ways of behaving tend to become established parts of the behavioral repertoire, and as such, influence future feelings, attitudes, opinions, etc.

The feeling of being loved is a direct response to expressions of love. Indeed, how else *can* one know one is loved?

> . . . how should one know that he is loved [but?] by the way people act toward him: what they say, how they look, how they touch, in a word, what they do? Attention, praise, spoken niceties, and physical contact have been demonstrations of love for years. Who cares if someone loves them if they never receive evidence through attention, contact, or the spoken word?[1]

But what if one partner doesn't know what behaviors the other might interpret as expressions of love? I remember one young couple whose problems arose primarily out of the fact that neither knew how to "read" the other's behaviors. For John, the husband, food and love had been inextricably tied together since early childhood. *His* mother had always attempted to make the dinner hour something of an occasion and demonstrated her love for her own husband and children by serving prompt, carefully planned and beautifully executed meals. For John, then, a "caring" wife was one who, like his mother, expressed love through cooking and other food-related behaviors. John's wife, Ellen, however, exhibited none of these behaviors. An indifferent cook who had little interest in food herself, and for whom eating was significant only in that it was a prerequisite for staying alive, she was for a long time unaware of John's real feelings in the matter. John did indeed complain about their meals from time to time, but in a way that led Ellen to believe he did so out of what she called "sheer fussiness."

These misunderstandings are more common than one might suspect, and this is only one of the reasons that I so strongly urge husbands and wives—as I did with Ellen and John—to specify exactly what behaviors can best express their love for one another.

The behavioral-change approach is *the* most loving, compassionate, humane way to treat an ailing marriage, or make a good one better. During the course of counseling in hundreds of cases, I have found that this approach encourages partners to communicate with one another, to express their desires and to define how and in what ways they can make each other happier. It offers plans—with built-in rewards and negative consequences—that can be immediately implemented and through which the desired changes are affected and eventually lead to the establishment of new ways of thinking and feeling about the partner. It offers hope.

I cannot help but think of the *alternative*—the clinging to vain hopes that somehow, some way, given enough love and understanding and sympathy, some magical "thing" will happen to improve a relationship and make the trouble go away—as being truly grim in that it is so often and so cruelly disappointing.

Making a Behavioral Diagnosis

Right now, or as soon as you can get your hands on a pencil, jot down on paper five things your partner presently says or does that *please* you. (I always like to begin by emphasizing the positive, but as we shall see, there's more to this than counting your blessings; the list of five pleasing behaviors will come in handy later on.)

I know that for those of you whose home more closely resembles an armed camp than the tranquil haven it could and should be, making up this kind of list may not be easy. Even so, think hard.

(One woman, convinced that this was an utterly impossible task, chewed the end of her pencil for a while and then finally came up with the following: "1. John takes responsibility for getting the children off to school in the morning. 2. Drinks only at parties. 3. Maintains an erection. 4. Remembers birthdays and anniversaries. 5. Mows the lawn every other week.") This wife, like so many other married people, was amazed to discover that her partner said and did so much that was "right and pleasing."

Once your list is completed, set it aside for a while.

At this point, I'm going to suggest a way for you to make a "behavioral" diagnosis[2] of your marriage. We're going to focus on defining problems, specifying the behaviors that "cause" the problems, and establishing behavioral goals that will modify or eliminate the problems.

On another sheet of paper, rule off four more or less equal columns. Column I should be headed Felt Dissatisfactions; Column II, Partner's Behavior; Column III, Behavioral Goal for Partner; and Column IV, New Feelings.

Felt dissatisfactions: In Column I, enter any uneasy feelings you may have about your mate or the nature of your relationship. You needn't be specific here. Many husbands and wives start out with rather vague statements such as "We're drifting apart," or "I feel trapped," or "He/she doesn't love me."

Partner's behavior: Here the idea is to relate felt dissatisfactions specified in Column I to *behavior* exhibited by your partner. You can do this by asking yourself "what does he/she *say* or *do* that makes me feel uneasy?"

Keep in mind that you must be able to describe your partner's behavior in terms of words and deeds. Avoid statements such as "seems to dislike intercourse"—which may be perfectly true but is not valid for our purposes here because the word "seems" is ambiguous and doesn't refer to an exhibited behavior, i.e., something that actually has been

BEHAVIORAL DIAGNOSIS AND GOALS

Spouse	Felt dissatisfaction	Partner's behavior	Behavioral goal for partner	New feelings
Wife	"I don't like him"	He lied to me	Tell me the truth	"I like him"
Husband	"She's a bitch"	She nags	Compliment me	"She's a pleasant person"
Wife	"He's mean"	He yells at me	Speak softly to me	"He's a kind person"
Husband	"She's never happy"	Frowns constantly	Smile	"She's a happy person"
Husband	"She doesn't love me"	Never hugs or kisses me	Hug and kiss me	"She cares about me"
Wife	"He hates sex"	Never approaches me for intercourse	Approach me for intercourse	"He likes sex"
Wife	"I'm frustrated"	He provides no foreplay	30 minutes of foreplay	"He's a good lover"
Husband	"Doesn't enjoy sex with me"	She has no orgasm	Orgasm	"She enjoys me sexually"

BEHAVIORAL DIAGNOSIS AND GOALS

Spouse	Felt dissatisfaction	Partner's behavior	Behavioral goal for partner	New feelings
Wife	"I can't depend on him"	Drinks too much	Be sober	"He's a dependable person"
Husband	"She's no fun"	Doesn't drink alcohol	Drink alcohol	"She's fun at parties"
Wife	"I'm afraid of him"	Hits me	Be gentle with me	"He's kind to me"
Husband	"She's a lush"	Drinks too much	Be sober	"She's a good woman"
Husband	"She doesn't care about me"	Complains about me to her mother	Tell her mother nice things about me	"She cares"
Wife	"He's still a baby"	Calls his mother daily	See mother once weekly	"He's mature"
Wife	"He doesn't appreciate me"	Compares my house-keeping to his mother's	Praise my housekeeping	"He appreciates me"
Husband	"She makes me mad"	Makes sarcastic remarks to my father	Speak kindly to my father	"She makes me feel good"

BEHAVIORAL DIAGNOSIS AND GOALS

Spouse	Felt dissatisfaction	Partner's behavior	Behavioral goal for partner	New feelings
Husband	"She is unsociable"	Ignores my friends	Speak to my friends	"She is sociable"
Wife	"He makes me feel trapped"	Nags when I am with my friends	Encourage me to spend time with my friends	"He is an independent person"
Wife	"He's a fool"	Loans money to his friends	Leave money in bank	"He is responsible"
Husband	"Can't keep her mouth shut"	Talks about my salary to her friends	Talk about things other than my salary to her friends	"She respects my wishes"
Wife	"He's self-centered"	Doesn't get involved in community	Go to meetings with me	"He's a good person"
Husband	"She's a do-gooder"	Spends too much time on volunteer work	Spend time with me	"She is reasonable about volunteer work"
Wife	"He's too cheap"	Never contributes to charity	Give $100 to charity each year	"He's a generous person"

BEHAVIORAL DIAGNOSIS AND GOALS

Spouse	Felt dissatisfaction	Partner's behavior	Behavioral goal for partner	New feelings
Husband	"She's messed up"	Goes to church 3 times per week	Go to church once per week	"She's not a fanatic"
Wife	"He works too hard"	Spends his evenings at the office	Leave the office at 5:00	"He is organized"
Husband	"She is irresponsible"	Doesn't pay bills on time	Pay bills on time	"She is dependable"
Husband	"She thinks I'm a bore"	Doesn't talk to me	Share ideas with me	"She thinks I'm interesting"
Wife	"He's very jealous"	Asks me about myself and other men	Tell me he trusts me	"He trusts me"
Wife	"He isn't fair"	Wants to be out twice each week but wants me to stay home	Encourage me to go out twice per week	"He is fair with me"
Husband	"She doesn't enjoy parties"	Refuses to go to parties	Go to parties with me	"She is fun to be with"

BEHAVIORAL DIAGNOSIS AND GOALS

Spouse	Felt dissatisfaction	Partner's behavior	Behavioral goal for partner	New feelings
Wife	"Blames me for things"	Expects me to know what he wants to eat	Tell me what he wants to eat	"He is a co-operative person"
Husband	"Tries to irritate me"	Is never on time	Be on time	"I can depend on her"
Husband	"I feel depressed"	Tells me I am fat	Encourage me to be trim	"I am happy"
Wife	"Makes me angry"	Tells me how to drive	Be silent when I drive	"He's fun to travel with"

Of course, each "Felt dissatisfaction" may have a number of behavioral causes which should be translated into behavioral goals.

Spouse	Felt dissatisfaction	Partner's behavior	Behavioral goal for partner	New feelings
Wife	"I don't like him"	He lied to me He drinks too much He yells at me He won't go to parties He provides no foreplay	Tell me the truth Be sober Talk softly to me Go to parties with me Provide 30 minutes of foreplay before intercourse	"He is an honest, sober, respectable person and a great lover"

BEHAVIORAL DIAGNOSIS AND GOALS

Spouse	Felt dissatisfaction	Partner's behavior	Behavioral goal for partner	New feelings
Husband	"She's a bad wife"	She frowns She avoids intercourse She nags me She coddles the children She never cleans the apartment	She smiles Approach me for intercourse Compliment me Ignore some of baby's demands Vacuum apartment	"She is happy, and a good lover, conversationalist, and mother who keeps a neat apartment"

FIGURE 1-1. Each spouse identifies the behavior or behaviors which cause the felt dissatisfaction. The desired behavior is then specified and, when developed, results in a new feeling.

said or done. What you're after is the *specification* of behaviors that lead you to believe your partner dislikes intercourse (assuming that this is your particular problem):
Does he *say* he's too tired for sex? Does she *wait* until you're
asleep before coming to bed?

Thus, one angry woman whose husband never lifted a
finger around the house expressed her gripe correctly in
behavioral terms when she wrote in Column II, "Sits and
watches TV while I do all the work."

Behavioral goal for partner: In this column, specify how
you want your partner's behavior to change. Be careful to
express these changes positively. Think in terms of what
you would like your mate to say or do, rather than what you
want him/her to stop saying or doing.

In Column III, for example, our friend, the angry woman
whose husband didn't help around the house, wrote,
"Vacuum house once a week and cook dinner on weekends,"
instead of "Stop being so lazy."

New feelings: In Column IV, enter the hoped-for result
of your mate's positive new behavior. Thus, the angry
woman who felt overburdened by the responsibilities of running her home and resented her husband because of it, felt
that as a result of her mate's sharing some of the housework,
she would regain a more positive feeling about her role in
their marriage. In Column IV she wrote, "We have a good,
equal relationship."

The following chart, which lists other examples of behavioral diagnoses, may be helpful.

The Pre-contract Inventory

Once you've made a behavioral diagnosis, you will not
only have gained a clearer understanding of *why* you feel
the way you do—i.e., you will have defined the relationship
between your own feelings and your partner's unpleasing,

unkind, or thoughtless behavior—but you will also have specified positive new behaviors for your mate.

You can use this information as the basis for drawing up what I call a "pre-contract inventory"—an admittedly high-flown name for an invaluable little document that serves the purpose of communicating your feelings and desires to your partner.

As a quick glance at the sample inventories below will indicate, part A is reserved for the listing of your mate's

PRE-CONTRACT INVENTORY

Name *Elise Bauman* Date *April 6*

A. Five things which you are already doing or saying which please me are:

1. You arrange to eat lunch with me twice a week.
2. You spend time with our children.
3. You provide for the material needs of our family.
4. You tell me that I look good.
5. You side with me rather than your parents.

B. One thing which I would like you to *do* more often (in the future) is:
Show me affection without trying to have intercourse with me.

C. One thing which I would like you to say or not to say more often (in the future) is:
Tell me that you love me.

Please give me a completed Pre-contract Inventory so that I will know what to do and say to make you happier.

NOTE: See Appendix for a list of goals other spouses have developed for themselves and each other.

positive behaviors: the five pleasing things he/she already does and says.

In parts B and C, you will enter the positive new behaviors specified in Column III of the behavioral diagnosis.

Make two copies of the following contract, one for yourself and one for your spouse. Give a completed inventory to your mate and ask for one in return.

Now you both have some idea of what behaviors please

PRE-CONTRACT INVENTORY

Name _Bill Bowman_ Date _April 6_

A. Five things which you are already doing or saying which please me are:

1. You dress neatly.
2. You compliment me on how nice the lawn looks.
3. You are a loving mother to our children (you spend time with them).
4. You are an exciting sex partner (you yell obscenities when we have intercourse).
5. You serve delicious meals (liver and onions is your best).

B. One thing which I would like you to *do* more often (in the future) is:

Be more independent (Do things without asking me).

C. One thing which I would like you to say or not to say more often (in the future) is:

Stop talking about the past.

Please give me a completed Pre-contract Inventory so that I will know what to do and say to make you happier.

the other. Each of you also knows what the other would like to happen in the future.

Some husbands and wives—and I hope yours is not one of them—may balk at the idea of putting it all down in black and white. Why make up an inventory, when it would be so much easier simply to verbalize one's desires?

Why indeed? If you're convinced that you and your partner will be able to discuss the need for making behavioral changes in a calm, dispassionate manner, you may very well decide to dispense with the paperwork.

My feeling, however, is that a document packs a bigger wallop: your partner will be more apt to take your requests seriously, and at the same time there will be less likelihood that your desires will be misinterpreted as criticism.

If, for example, Susan cozies up to Stanley and proceeds to inform him that she appreciates his help around the house and the fact that he cooks dinner on alternate Saturdays (etc., etc.) and then goes on to say that she wishes he would also spend more time with her in the evenings, Stanley *may* begin to get the feeling that he is being conned. In which case, their nice, calm discussion could easily degenerate into just another sniping session.

The point, of course, is that documents don't con—or at least not when they are properly worded—nor do they nag or cajole or threaten or whine or simper. They are merely pieces of paper clearly specifying what one partner can do in order to please the other better.

Fair Play: How You Can Resolve the Problem of Conflictin, Desires

It's possible, even probable, that when husbands and wives exchange completed pre-contract inventories, they will discover that one partner has requested behavior that the other considers inappropriate or unreasonable. (Two cases come immediately to mind: A sensuous young woman requested sex every single night; for various reasons, not altogether related to physical incapability, her husband felt he could not comply. I also remember a thirty-five-year-old man who specified that his wife approve of all his financial decisions; his wife thought this was an unfair request, especially in view of his penchant for investing in the stock market and almost always sustaining losses when he did so.)

One way out of this dilemma is for both husband and wife to define the behaviors that constitute his/her concept of a "satisfactory" marriage.[3] (I emphasize the word "satisfactory" here, rather than "perfect," or "ideal," because while it may be admirable to strive for the sublime, in practice, it's a state most of us are not likely to achieve.)

To illustrate your idea of what constitutes a satisfactory marriage, draw a circle and cross it with several horizontal and vertical lines. Then label the sections to represent your expectations regarding your partner's behavior. (You needn't fill in every section of the grid, but do be sure to note all that you feel are important.)

Now, rate each of these desired behaviors on a scale of 1 to 10. A behavior given a rating of 10 is one to which you attach maximum importance, while a rating of 2 or 3 indicates that while it may be desirable it is not necessarily crucial to your happiness. Behaviors not included in your circle would be considered as having little or no value to you with respect to your concept of satisfactory marriage.

Lucy, a suburban mother of three, identified and rated behavior important to her marital happiness thus:

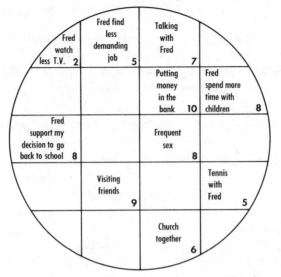

FIGURE 1-2. Lucy identifies and ranks on a 10-point scale the importance of various behaviors that make her happy. It is important to Lucy at a level of 10 that she and Fred bank some of their money. No other behavior is as important to her.

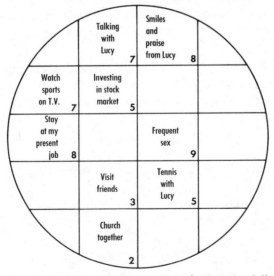

FIGURE 1-3. Lucy's husband, Fred, identified the following behaviors as important to his marital happiness.

Exchange completed diagrams with your partner, then sit down to discuss any discrepancies. Mutually exclusive behavioral goals will be immediately apparent. Wherever they occur, the partner with the low rating should defer to his/her mate.

Fred and Lucy, for example, had very different ideas about how their money ought to be managed. Fred enjoys investing in the stock market at a level of 5. Lucy, however, is miserable when there's no money in the bank and gives "saving" a rating of 10. Since Lucy feels more strongly about saving than Fred does about stock market speculation, it is fair that Fred give in to her wishes on this particular point. (In other words, the cost to Fred of discontinuing his behavior is less than the cost to Lucy if she were forced to yield.)

When two people are as honest as they know how to be in expressing the intensity of their desires—and, of course, there's not too much point in any of this if either partner is deliberately dishonest—the frequency of giving-in behavior usually averages out about equally for both husband and wife.

Lucy, for example, resented the "hours and hours" (or so it seemed to her) that Fred sat mesmerized in front of the television set. But she objected at a level of 2, while Fred gave a rating of 7 to TV watching. Thus, Lucy deemed it fair that she withhold her negative comments and allow Fred to sit back and enjoy his football games in peace.

Obviously, it will always be more difficult to resolve an issue on which partners disagree with *equal* intensity. Suppose Fred had given a rating of 10 to stock market speculation. (Lucy, remember, rated "putting money in the bank" at the same level.) Ideally, some kind of compromise would be reached. They might agree, for example, to revise their budget in such a way that each month a certain amount would automatically go into a savings account, with Fred reserving the right to use any funds left over for his ventures in the market.

Or they might decide to resolve the issue by flipping a coin—which at first thought may appear to be a rather irresponsible way to arrive at a solution to such a dilemma. But coin-flipping at least has fairness in its favor; it's more equitable and certainly no less satisfactory than allowing the outcome of the conflict to be determined by virtue of which partner is most adept at browbeating the other into submission.

When resorting to coin-flipping, it should always be with the understanding that the spouse who loses is the automatic winner the next time husband and wife disagree with equal intensity on a particular issue.

Now, both you and your partner have a fistful of documents—love letters, in a sense, and potentially among the most important missives you will ever exchange.

Each of you knows beyond doubt—because it's all down in black and white—what the other considers to be pleasing, positive behavior. You have taken the first step toward greater happiness in marriage.

CHAPTER 2

Collecting
"Baseline Data"

IF YOU WERE a scientist working on a project, you would need to keep records in order to measure the results of your work. Otherwise you'd have no way of knowing just how things were progressing.

As a husband or wife, it's unlikely that you feel any very pressing need to keep records (other than those for income tax or insurance purposes), and yet I am going to suggest that you do just that: that you mark down on paper the number of times desirable behaviors—the ones you established as behavioral goals in Chapter 1—actually do occur.

I suggest you begin to count desirable behaviors as they occur and *before* you implement any plans to increase their frequency. Scientists call the process of amassing information about a particular phenomenon before modifying or experimenting with that phenomenon collecting "baseline data." This is what I want you to do.

Is spending more time with your partner one of your behavioral goals? Then begin now to keep a record, expressed in terms of minutes and hours, of the time you *presently* spend together.

Do you want more frequent sex? Then keep track of the number of times per week intercourse now occurs.

Do you want a more equal distribution of the work load? Then note the present frequency of who does which jobs.

The data you collect now will give you a better picture of your present situation, and weeks or months hence you'll be able to use this information to measure any changes that have taken place.

Records have a way of keeping people honest. If my bank doesn't keep a record of the checks I write, it might be easy for me to deceive myself about how much I spend. But the bank's record forces me to face the facts, to realize that what I might *think* I do, and what I *actually* do, may be two very different things.

So it was with Tina and Reed. Tina really believed that she kissed and hugged Reed "a lot." In fact she swore to it. Reed, on the other hand, said she "never" did. They decided to keep a record, and as it happened the truth of the matter lay somewhere in between their two versions of it: Tina kissed and hugged Reed when he left for work each morning and during intercourse (which is hardly "a lot," but not exactly "never," either).

What to Record

Keep in mind that the idea is to record *behavior*—words and deeds. Personalities and character traits cannot be measured or counted. Words and deeds can. For example, if you want your partner to be "more considerate," you must define for yourself what specific behaviors constitute "consideration" (or whatever other quality you are seeking in your mate). These may vary from marriage to marriage, but the important point is that you clarify the definition.

Ann, for example, defined "consideration" in terms of

Richard's (1) being home in time for dinner (or calling when he knew he would be late), (2) consulting her about any major purchases, (3) informing her of his plans for a particular evening at least two or three days in advance (they were both active in a number of different community groups, and she needed this information to know when it would be necessary to call a baby-sitter), and (4) making some of the baby-sitting arrangements himself. For Ann, these behaviors added up to "consideration." She kept a record of each time Richard did any of these things.

Who Records

Ideally, both you and your partner should keep independent records indicating the frequency of behaviors each of you wants to see increased. Though it was Reed who wanted Tina to show more affection—i.e., hug and kiss him more often—both recorded the number of times she actually did these things. (Tina, in turn, wanted Reed to spend more time with their children, but both kept track of the number of hours he spent with their two young daughters.)

Occasionally a couple will report discrepancies in the records they keep. One husband recorded almost twice as many desirable behaviors as his wife. When this kind of thing happens, it's important to develop some sort of "cue system." It was suggested that this man give his partner a red poker chip every time she told him she had noticed a desirable behavior that either of them were engaging in, and a blue chip each time she overlooked one. Their records soon became congruent.

When to Record

Count desirable behaviors *as they occur*. Don't wait until you have a minute to sit down with paper and pencil; it's too easy to forget. It may be helpful to carry a pencil and a 3x5 card with you. I know one man who made it easier for himself by clicking a golf counter each time a desirable behavior occurred, and another who switched pennies from one pocket to another.

At the end of each day, transfer the information you've collected to a graph. Make it a habit. If you tend toward absentmindedness try to relate the act to something you do each evening. (A good idea is to put a rubber band on your toothbrush; when you brush your teeth, you'll feel the rubber band and be reminded to bring your graph up to date.)

How Long to Record

I think it's wise to continue keeping records until you notice a pattern developing, or until you feel you can predict with a fair degree of accuracy how often specific behaviors are likely to occur.[1] In other words, if Reed spends four hours with the children one week, five the next, and four on the following week, in all likelihood he will spend between four and five hours with the kids on the fourth week. A pattern has been established and there's no real need for further record keeping at least insofar as this particular behavior is concerned.

What Next?

For the time being, nothing. You and your partner should both concentrate on collecting baseline data until, as was noted previously, some sort of recognizable pattern becomes clear. This may take a few days, a week, a month or longer, during which time I hope you will go on to read and think about the techniques discussed in the following chapter.

However, no matter how anxious you may be to apply appropriate behavioral-change techniques to your own situation, don't. If you neglect accumulating accurate data now, you will not be able to evaluate what happens later on.

The following sample graph demonstrating the collection of baseline data may be helpful.

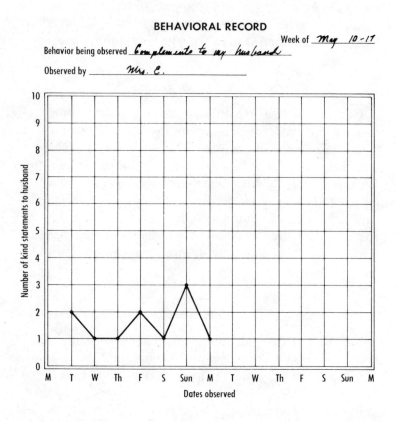

FIGURE 2-1. Mrs. E. made 11 positive statements to Mr. E. during one week.

CHAPTER 3

*The How-to of
Behavioral Change*

BEFORE IMPLEMENTING THE procedures in this chapter, you should make a record of how often the behaviors that you want to increase presently occur. (Make up a chart to record behavior that you want to increase.)

If someone you've just smiled at smiles back at you, you're likely to smile again at that person the next time you meet. If you get nothing in return for your smile, you may simply nod or perhaps ignore—or even turn your face from—that person at your next meeting. In any case, the consequences of your smile will influence your future behavior.

So it is in marriage, only more so. The way husbands and wives respond to each other's present behavior has a tremendous impact on how they will react to one another in the future. Much of the rest of this book is concerned with behavior-change techniques and how you and your partner can use them to cultivate those pleasing behaviors that make you feel good about yourself and each other and thus strengthen the very foundations of your marriage.

Reinforcers

Marital behaviors, like all behaviors, are learned—or, rather, taught—according to their consequences. A reinforcer is a consequence that increases the probability that a specific behavior will recur.

Let me cite an example: Under certain circumstances, a simple "yes" answer might be a reinforcer. As a wife, suppose you ask your husband to go with you to the theater. If he answers in the affirmative and you do in fact go to the theater together, your "asking behavior" has been reinforced. You're more likely to ask again than if his answer had been a resounding "no!" As a husband, imagine asking your wife to fix you a bedtime snack. If she nods, goes into the kitchen and comes back with milk and a sandwich, your behavior has been reinforced. If, on the other hand, she mutters something about how you're an able-bodied adult and tells you to go make your own snack, you may hesitate before asking again. Your behavior has not been reinforced.

Actually, there are two basic kinds of reinforcers: negative and positive.

A negative reinforcer is anything which stops something unpleasant. The normal response is to act in a way that turns off or terminates the unpleasantness.

Jane, for example, was constantly after Harry to fix the leaking faucet in the bathroom. Finally, to put an end to the unpleasantness (nagging), Harry angrily jammed new washers into the faucet. His faucet-fixing behavior was negatively reinforced; he acted in order to stop the unpleasantness.

Jane's nagging behavior, however, was positively reinforced; she got what she wanted. She was, in a sense, "rewarded" for nagging, and as a consequence, she may resort to nagging more often in the future.

Positive reinforcers, then, make us feel good or bring

about some desired response. They fall into a number of rather general categories:[1]

Personal reinforcers are your own good thoughts and feelings about something you've done. When you paint a picture, play a good game of tennis, mow the lawn, or wash the car, you're apt to give yourself a mental pat on the back —assuming, of course, that you've done a fairly competent job. You like yourself, and this good feeling increases the probability that you'll engage in the behavior again.

Interpersonal reinforcers are the things you do and say that influence the behavior of others. Smiling, "yes" answers, compliments, praise, attentive listening, touching, and expressions of affection and gratitude are just a few examples. Regardless of whether we're consciously aware of it, we all use interpersonal reinforcers as a means of eliciting desired responses from others—and in turn, are enormously swayed by others.

Reinforcing activities are behaviors that you enjoy, such as eating desserts, going to the movies, watching TV, reading, yoga, needlepoint, playing an instrument, photography— whatever your particular thing happens to be. In the section on developing contracts, we shall see how reinforcing activities can be used on a contingency basis to reward desirable behaviors.

Tokens are symbols, or stand-ins, for other reinforcers. Money is the classic example. With it, you can get other things that you want—a car, a new suit, tickets to a show, etc.

Life-maintenance reinforcers are the basics—air, food, sleep, etc.—and of all the different kinds of reinforcers, their influence is most potent.

Reward Desirable Behavior

A reinforcer, remember, increases the probability that a specific behavior will occur more often. When your goal is to increase the frequency with which your partner engages in a particular behavior, the reinforcer should be something in the nature of a "reward." Consider the rather simplified example of Fred and Judy:

Judy doesn't smile much. In fact, her face is set in an almost habitual frown. Judy's expression makes Fred feel depressed and anxious. He'd be happier if Judy smiled more often. Thus, Fred, catching Judy in a rare smile, says, "Your whole face lights up when you grin like that. You're beautiful." This makes Judy feel good. It's her reward for smiling. She begins to smile more often. Fred feels better.

How you choose to notice and reinforce, or "reward," your partner's desirable behavior is almost entirely a matter of personal choice. In some homes, a big smile goes a long, long way. In others, compliments, praise, and other expressions of verbal appreciation are more to the point. You may feel it's a good idea to reinforce by touching—with hugs, kisses, caresses. (This can be a particularly valuable technique for couples who are not ordinarily very "physical" in their day-to-day approach to one another.) Another possibility is to relate the desirable behavior to some activity your partner especially enjoys by asking, immediately after the behavior has occurred, whether he/she feels like going to the movies later on (or making love, or playing chess, or visiting good friends, or buying that new record, or going out to dinner, etc.).

Keep in mind, however, that a reinforcer is valuable only insofar as it actually does tend to influence the frequency of the desired behavior in the desired way. Sometimes it's necessary to experiment a bit. Doug, for example, may feel that by smacking Karen on the rump, he is rewarding her for baking cherry pie. However, if Karen doesn't respond with more cherry pies in the future, his reinforcer has missed the mark. If he enjoys smacking Karen's backside and Karen doesn't mind especially, he may continue to do so. But he will have to try some other means of influencing the frequency with which she bakes those pies. (Perhaps, a "Thank you, that pie was fantastic," and a suggestion that they go out to a movie after dinner would be more effective.)

In any case, regardless of what reinforcers are employed to cultivate pleasing behavior, it's important to establish a firm connection between the two by making sure that the reward occurs as an immediate consequence of the behavior. The more time that elapses between behavior and reinforcer, the less forceful the link between the two, and the less effective the reinforcer. (To go back to Karen and Doug, Karen may appreciate Doug's movie suggestion under any circumstances, but unless the timing is appropriate, she may not associate it with cherry pies.)

You must watch out for one factor, once you are aware of how to reward behavior in order to make it happen more often. That is the tendency to say, "Rewarding my spouse for what I want him/her to do is manipulation—it's too mechanical. My partner is not an animal in a cage that I throw meat to; he/she is a human being." Rewarding positive behavior and using other behavioral procedures are both essential for helping to achieve your goals. Since Doug's goal is to have Karen fix him cherry pie more often, he must reinforce Karen for doing so. Otherwise, he relies on luck that Karen will enjoy cooking the pies and do it for herself, that one of her friends will compliment her for the tasty pastry; or some other happenstance event. The beauty of behavioral techniques is that we can use them to bring about the behaviors occurring in our marriage that make us happy. Not to use the procedures that we know are effective is to leave our marriage—and happiness—to chance.

In the beginning, when you and your mate first start to use behavioral-change techniques to achieve specific behavioral goals, you probably should reward new desirable behavior each and every time it occurs. Later on, when it occurs more frequently (and you'll know for sure if you're keeping records, as suggested in Chapter 2), you can reinforce on a now-and-then basis so that your partner never knows for sure just when to expect a reward. (It's been demonstrated beyond doubt that once a behavioral pattern is established, it is more likely to become a permanent part of the individual's behavioral repertoire if it is rewarded only once in a while—say 30 to 40 percent of the time.)

Shaping

It sometimes happens that one partner does what the other wants only rarely, if at all. In which case, reinforcers can be used to "shape" new behaviors. "Shaping" (this is a term used by behavioral scientists) refers to the technique of rewarding successive small units of behavior that approximate the ultimate goal.

As a wife, suppose you'd feel less resentful, and your life would be freer of mindless drudgery, if your husband were neater. But he's a slob. To "shape" new, neater behavior, you would reward him for being just a *little* more orderly than usual. You could, for example, watch for a time when he left the bathroom only *slightly* less messy than is his wont, and then make some appropriate comment ("I really appreciated your hanging up the towel, dear"—or some such), thus rewarding him for *approaching* desirable new behavior, while at the same time ignoring the uncapped toothpaste, hair in the sink, bathrobe draped over the tub, puddles on the floor, etc. You would continue to watch for signs of improvement and reward them as they occur.

Actually, you needn't wait for concrete evidence of emerging new behavior in order to use the shaping technique. There are ways to prime the pump. You could, in other words, say something such as "I like it when you put the cap back on the toothpaste"—even though he hasn't done it in years. A remark like this communicates to your mate the possibility that you may say or do something exceedingly pleasant if and when he actually does remember to leave the bathroom in some semblance of order, and is far more effective in the long run than "Why can't you put the cap back on the toothpaste, you son-of-a-bitch. Were you raised in a barn or something?"

Ignore Undesirable Behavior

Our society frequently emphasizes the negative. Attention is paid to carelessness and mistakes, while what is done ably and well is too often taken for granted.

This is the unfortunate state of affairs in many unhappy marriages. Where blame and criticism predominate, feelings of disappointment and resentment grow up to take the place of love. Conversely, happiness and good feelings are encouraged when "pleasing" behavior is noticed and reinforced, while "bad" behavior is ignored.

I realize that while the idea of ignoring "bad" behavior may look fine on paper, it is not an easy concept—indeed may require a great deal of effort and self-control—to put into practice. I can only say that behaviorists have demonstrated its validity, and that those of you who are sufficiently motivated to carry it through will eventually be rewarded.

The wife who wants her husband to stop shouting at her and the children (or, put in more positive terms, who wants to cultivate nonshouting behavior) can stop reacting to all the noise and instead be on the lookout for a situation that would normally have him bellowing, but doesn't. If and when such an occasion arises, she can tell him how much she admires and appreciates his restraint. (She might follow up with a kiss and/or a suggestion that they make love later on.)

Reinforcing what pleases and ignoring what doesn't is

the most effective way of extinguishing undesirable behaviors. By ignoring what you don't like, you are in effect
withdrawing whatever reinforcement you have—probably
unwittingly—been giving your mate's "bad" behavior. Yelling, nagging, crying, being late, forgetting, and anything else
that might be lumped under the heading of "undesirable behavior" are maintained by various reinforcers in much the
same way that desirable behaviors are encouraged by other
reinforcers.

A husband may yell at his wife because she has taught
him to do so; he knows from past experience that if he yells
long enough and hard enough she will "reward" him by
doing what he wants.

The dynamics of nagging are similar. Husbands and wives
who do what is being nagged about are actually teaching
their partners to be bigger and better naggers.

People who engage in crying or sulking behaviors are
frequently "rewarded" by reassurances of love ("There,
there, everything's okay . . . you know you're the whole
world to me," etc.) and the at least temporarily undivided
attention of their partners. In fact, men and women who sulk
or cry a lot often do so because they get so little attention
otherwise.

In the same way, late behavior is also an attention-getting
device. When you're late, you automatically loom large in
the consciousness of whoever is doing the waiting.

Forgetfulness is still another manifestation of behavior
that husbands and wives tend to teach each other. When one
partner is continually being reminded by the other to do
something (call relatives, pay bills, buy soap, etc.) what
he/she is actually learning is that there is no real need to
remember. The reminding partner does the remembering.

When the object is to terminate undesirable behavior,
then, that behavior must be totally and consistently ignored.
The husband of a wife who shouts can make it clear by

not responding, ever, that shouting will *never* get him to do what she wants. If he responds even once in a while, he is reinforcing her shouting behavior at the very highest level. (Remember, behaviors that are rewarded only occasionally are "learned" most permanently.)

In the same way, the wife of an absent-minded husband can simply stop reminding him of his responsibilities and allow him to suffer the possibly embarrassing or troublesome consequences of his forgetfulness. Again, to remind only once in a while is to encourage absent-mindedness.

By ignoring these, or any other, undesirable behaviors, you are in effect withdrawing the reinforcer. When the reinforcer is withdrawn, the behavior tends to occur with less frequency.

Establish Behavioral Consequences[2]

We live in a cause-and-effect world. As we've already seen, all behaviors have consequences—and the consequences attached to a specific behavior always have some bearing on whether or not and with what frequency that behavior will be repeated.

It's possible to set up a situation whereby positive consequences are attached to behavior you want to cultivate, either in yourself or in your partner. In regard to positive consequences, the "Premack Principle"[3] states that of any two behaviors, the more pleasurable one can be used to reinforce, or reward, the less pleasurable. Which means (roughly translated for our purposes here) that an enjoyable activity, such as playing tennis, might be made contingent on engaging in a less enjoyable one, such as washing the car. Or that reading a novel might be contingent on shopping for groceries. And so on.

Each of these examples implies a pact, or contract, made with oneself—i.e., no tennis until the car is washed.

The following is an example of an individual contingency contract based on the Premack Principle.

INDIVIDUAL CONTINGENCY CONTRACT

Desirable behavior: exercise (walking 1 mile)
Present frequency of behavior: 1 day per week (as indicated by previously collected baseline data)
Desired frequency of behavior: 7 days per week

Reinforcers:	Behavior	Frequency of Behavior
	Dinner	Each evening
	Movie	1 day per week

CONTRACT I: First week

I agree to walk one mile per day on Sunday, Tuesday, and Friday. I also agree that I will eat dinner on Sunday, Tuesday, and Friday only after I have walked one mile. In addition I agree to go to a movie on Saturday only if I have exercised on the specified days. I understand that failure to exercise as outlined in this contract results in no food and no movie on the specified days.

Goal for first week: 3 exercise days

Signed _____

Date _____

CONTRACT II: Second week

Contract II would be executed only if the goals of Contract I had been accomplished. The terms of Contract II might require an additional day of exercise with dinner and a movie as the positive consequences.

CONTRACTS III, IV, V

For each of these new contracts, add one additional day of exercise.

In contracts such as this one, based on the Premack Principle, one behavior becomes a reinforcer for another and increases the probability that the rewarded behavior will occur more often. Contracts like these can help you and your partner to work toward, and ultimately achieve, the behavioral goals you specified in Chapter 1.

Consider Ellen, for example. She has a full-time job and two children. Her work and the kids (both under six) keep her very busy and there are times when she feels guilty about neglecting her husband. She developed the following contract with herself.

Desirable behavior: spend 30 minutes with John each day for a week
Present frequency of behavior: twice a week

Reinforcers:	Behavior	Frequency of Behavior
	Read	Each evening
	Go out on the weekend	Once a week

CONTRACT:

I agree to spend 30 minutes with John each day. The positive consequence of doing so is the right to read before bedtime each evening and to go out one night on the weekend. The negative consequence of failing to do so is forfeiting the right to read each evening and to go out one night on the weekend. The terms of this contract are fixed for one week only. After one week this contract may be extended or another contract developed.

Of course, Ellen must keep an accurate daily record of her behavior to make sure she has earned the privilege of reading and going out on the weekend.

Ellen's husband, John, wanted to learn to be neater and to get into the habit of picking up after himself. He developed the following contract with himself.

Desirable behavior	Positive consequence Daily / Weekend	Negative consequence Daily / Weekend
Pick up after myself (hang up coat, dirty clothes in hamper, shoes in closet, towels on towel rack, shaving stuff in medicine chest, cap on toothpaste) daily	Watch TV Fishing	No TV No fishing

CONTRACT:

I agree to pick up after myself as specified every day. The positive consequence of doing so is the right to watch TV daily and go fishing on the weekend. The negative consequence of failing to do so is loss of the right to watch TV and go fishing on weekend. The terms of this contract are fixed for one week only. After one week this contract may be extended or another contract developed.

John, too, must keep an accurate daily record of his behavior to determine if he has earned the privilege of daily TV and weekend fishing.

Notice that in the preceding contracts each partner is responsible for providing her/his own positive or negative consequences. Using them as a guide, establish a contingency contract with yourself that has a positive consequence attached to a behavior you want to increase and a negative consequence for failure to engage in that behavior. (See Appendix for blank individual contracts.)

When you've been successful with two or three individual

contracts like the one Ellen made with herself and John with himself, try a contract that includes a reward from your partner as one of the positive consequences.

Bob, for example, wants to increase his "affectionate" behavior toward Marilyn. Together, they set up the following:

Desirable behavior	Positive consequence Self / Mate		Negative consequence
Put arms around Marilyn and kiss her on two surprise occasions each day for one week	Daily shower Golf Saturday	Back rub and massage Thursday night	20 push-ups (daily); no shower; no golf; no back rub and massage

CONTRACT:

I agree to put my arms around Marilyn and kiss her on two surprise occasions each day during the next week. The positive consequences for doing so are taking a shower each morning, playing golf on Saturday and a back rub and massage from Marilyn on Thursday night. The negative consequences of failing to do so are 20 push-ups each evening at bedtime, as well as forfeiting daily showers, golf on Saturday and the back rub and massage on Thursday. The terms of this contract are fixed for one week only. After one week this contract may be extended or another contract developed.

As noted for previous contracts, Bob must keep an accurate daily record of his behavior in order to make sure he has earned the privilege of showering, golfing, and the back rub and massage from Marliyn.

Admittedly, contracts like the ones we've been concerned with here have a touch of gimmickry about them. But they're *good* gimmicks. They work. Many couples enter into them in a spirit of fun—play, almost—while others approach the whole matter with a rather grim seriousness. Either way, it makes no difference. Assuming a basic honesty and a fair degree of motivation on the part of the people involved, contracts can be enormously influential in encouraging the frequency of new desirable behavior.

Contracts can also be instrumental in changing one's attitudes. The wife who seethes with anger when her husband spends the greater part of each Saturday afternoon glued to the television set might find it worthwhile to develop a continuing contract with herself whereby she would do something *she* particularly enjoys (like swimming at the Y, or visiting friends) *only* if her husband watches Saturday afternoon TV. Thus, she begins to think of his TV-watching behavior not so much as a colossal waste of time (whether it is or not is not the question here), but as the contingency by which she gains the opportunity for doing something she finds pleasurable. She'll be happier, he'll be happier, everybody wins.

In the same way, the husband who dreads visiting his wife's parents might enter into a similar contract with himself, in which he agrees that he will engage in some enjoyable activity (playing basketball, or whatever) *only* after a visit with his in-laws. So, though he may continue to have negative feelings about his wife's mother and father, being with them becomes less trying because the consequences of the visit (basketball, etc.) are pleasant.

Contingency management (which is what we've been talking about here) can be used to good advantage in many life situations. Let me give just two examples: Suppose you have a friend who is always, or almost always, late. You can manage (gain some control over) this contingency by establishing a consequence: the next time he is late, you will simply leave without him. Of course, you would tell your friend ahead of time that you will leave without him.

Or, suppose that your mother is in the habit of making unkind remarks to your children ("You look like a sissy with all that long hair, Jack"). To avoid subjecting your kids to her put-down, you can tell her outright that you will continue to bring the children to visit her if she will compliment, rather than criticize them. "If you make positive remarks to the children, Mother, we will continue to visit you once a week. If you make critical remarks, we will come only once a month."

Exchange Contracts[4]

Up until now we've been concerned with "individual" contracts—agreements or pacts that you make with yourself and in which *you* provide the positive or negative consequences of a particular behavior. I hope you will already have set up several of these individual contracts before going on to developing exchange contracts which specify desirable behavior—pleasing words and deeds—that you and your partner can trade with one another.

Most husbands and wives behave toward each other on the basis of a set of rarely articulated but mutually understood "rules of exchange."

For example: Charles and Leslie, a couple in their late twenties, operate within the framework of what might be described as a "traditional" marriage. Leslie is considerate of and expresses her affection for Charles, takes primary responsibility in caring for the children, prepares meals, and keeps an orderly house. When asked why she does these things, she replies, "Because I love Charles."

Leslie may indeed love Charles, but she engages in these behaviors in exchange for certain other behaviors from Charles: He is considerate of her and expresses his affection for her, he provides their income, makes household repairs, and takes care of the garden.

Many husbands and wives spend their married lives together without ever having specified to one another the particulars of the rules of exchange upon which their relationship is based—the "I do this for you, because you do that for me" part of it. However, in the happiest marriages each partner has a good understanding of what the other expects to give and to get in return. A wife's pleasing behavior reinforces pleasing behavior in her husband. And vice versa.

Unhappiness begins when a relationship ceases to be reciprocal—when the rules of exchange become confused or forgotten (or when they were only dimly understood in the first place), and when, as a result, one or both partners expect always to be on the getting end of pleasing behavior without ever having to give in return.

Exchange contracts can help to clarify the rules of exchange within a relationship. They are based on the assumption that neither partner does—nor should be expected to do—something for nothing—and further, that if you want your mate to modify certain behaviors in order to please you better, you must be willing to make certain changes of your own. Fair is fair.

Thus, Charles, who likes nothing better than getting up early on Sundays and driving out to the lake for a few hours of fishing—preferably with Leslie (who has never been particularly enthusiastic about fishing)—suggested the following exchange contract:

> *Charles*: I agree to spend every Saturday afternoon from 1:00 to 5:00 with the children, and to prepare supper on Saturday evening if, in return, Leslie will go fishing with me every Sunday morning, weather permitting.

> *Leslie*: I agree to go fishing with Charles every Sunday morning, weather permitting if, in return, Charles will spend every Saturday afternoon from 1:00 to 5:00 with the children, and prepare supper on Saturday evening.

Another young couple, Dwight and Maxine, felt their marriage was "going under in a sea of negativity." "Dwight is critical of almost everything I do," Maxine complained. Dwight said essentially the same thing: "I never hear a kind word from her." After much discussion they were able to specify two major areas of dissension. Dwight felt Maxine was a careless housekeeper and an indifferent cook, while Maxine felt that Dwight spent far too much money on cameras, film, and photographic equipment—so much, in fact, that there was never anything left over for things she wanted for herself.

They set up the following exchange contract:

Dwight: I agree to limit the amount of money I spend buying photographic equipment, film, and other supplies to $25 per month if, in return, Maxine will keep the living room straight (newspapers off floor, ashtrays empty, *TV Guide* near armchair, kids' toys away) four nights per week and serve other than TV dinners five nights each week.

Maxine: I agree to keep the living room straight (newspapers off floor, ashtrays empty, *TV Guide* near armchair, kids' toys away) four nights per week, and serve other than TV dinners five nights each week if, in return, Dwight will limit the amount of money he spends buying photographic equipment, film, and other camera supplies to $25 each month.

Using the above examples as a guide, develop an exchange contract with your partner.

YOUR CONTRACT

Husband
    I agree to _____ if, in return, my wife agrees
    to _____.

Wife
    I agree to _____ if, in return, my husband
    agrees to _____.

Exchange contracts can be drawn up in any number of different ways. Consider the following contract drawn up by Ralph and Mary Lou:

	Ralph	*Mary Lou*
Desirable behaviors	Compliments to wife	Serve dinner on time (7:00 P.M.)
Present frequency of behaviors	1 per week	1 per week
Desired frequency of behaviors	7 per week	7 per week
Reinforcers	Reading, smoking pipe daily	Using phone daily

CONTRACT I: First week

Ralph agrees to compliment Mary Lou on Monday, Wednesday and Friday by 7:00 P.M. Mary Lou agrees to serve dinner at 7:00 P.M. on Monday, Wednesday and Friday. Each partner's performing the desired behaviors allows him/her to engage in the reinforcing behaviors for the rest of the evening and during the following day. Failure to perform the desirable behaviors results in forfeiting the reinforcing behaviors for the rest of the evening and during the following day. The terms of this contract are fixed for one week only. After one week, the contract may be extended or another contract developed.

Goal for first week: 3 desirable behaviors

Husband _____

(Signed)

Wife _____

(Signed)

Date _____

CONTRACT II: Second week

Contract II is to be executed only if the goals of Contract I are accomplished. The terms of Contract II require one additional desirable behavior, with reading and smoking for Ralph, and using the phone for Mary Lou as reinforcers.

CONTRACT III, IV, and V.

One desirable behavior (compliment and dinner on time) added at the conclusion of each successful week.

An exchange contract, when it is realistic and fair (as it will be if both partners are satisfied that it provides the means for each to get as much as they give) sooner or later outlives its usefulness. It is only a tool, after all—a teaching device that encourages each partner, through reinforcement and rewards, to engage more frequently in behaviors that please the other. When these behaviors are more or less permanently learned—that is, when discontinuation of the contract has little or no effect on the frequency of the new, pleasing behaviors—then the contract has served its purpose and there's no point in going on with it. You and your partner have succeeded in teaching each other new behavior. On the other hand, if removing the contract results in a decrease in the frequency of pleasing behavior—if it puts you right back where you started—then it should be extended. It may take several weeks or even months, but I urge you to stay with it. In time, the lessons will be learned.

Modeling

Edgar A. Guest once wrote, "I can soon learn how to do it if you'll show me how it's done. Fine counsel is confusing, but example is always clear." He might well have been referring to the technique of "modeling," which, under certain circumstances, can be an invaluable aid in helping you achieve your goals.

Partners may be "models" of behavior to one another. A

sullen, gloomy partner elicits a sullen, gloomy response
from the mate. (Who, after all, can maintain a modicum of
cheerfulness and good spirits in the presence of one who is
habitually down?) Even the normally optimistic and expansive personality is influenced by continuous contact
with a melancholic and mirthless spouse.

Married people, then, should consider the effect they have
on each other. Perhaps more important in this context, they
must consider the effect *others* have on *them*.

Socializing, either as a couple or independently of one
another, with people who are unhappy in their own marriages—with men and women who criticize, nag, complain,
drink to excess, get over their heads in debt, boast about
extramarital love affairs, etc.—encourages an attitude of
tolerance toward these negative behaviors. ("X is my friend,
and it's too bad she's got so much to complain about, but,
wow! stop to think of it, *I* have a thing or two to complain
about, too.") In other words, being with husbands and wives
who complain (or nag or spend too much or drink too
much) can increase the frequency of complaining (or nagging or spending too much or drinking too much) in one's
own situation.

Conversely, seeking out those couples and individuals
who engage in behaviors you and your partner want to cultivate in your own relationship, spending time with them,
observing them, watching them interact with one another,
can have a positive effect, since, again, one tends to accept
as the norm the behavior that one sees demonstrated by
others most often.

Reed, for example, a young husband whose wife wanted
him to spend more time with their children, was encouraged
to cultivate the acquaintance of other husbands in the neighborhood who spent much of their time with *their* children
and who seemed to enjoy doing so. A couple of these men
were people Reed especially liked and admired, and as their

friendship grew, Reed's attitude about spending time with his children began to mirror theirs.

The "Stop-Think" Technique

This behavioral-change strategy can be very useful in those situations where negative or disturbing or unwanted thoughts and feelings—the kind that are incompatible with expressed behavioral goals—keep cropping up and threatening to overthrow the partner's resolve to engage in new positive behaviors.

In the stop-think technique, encouraging thoughts and ideas are jotted down on 3x5 index cards, which are carried in purse or pocket or kept in some handy place in the house.

When negative thoughts arise, the individual yells "STOP" (subvocally if he/she is in a social situation), takes out one of the index cards and reads what's been written on it. By yelling "STOP," the negative thought pattern is interrupted. By focusing one's attention on the message written on the card, new positive thoughts take the place of undesirable ones.

I remember one woman—let's call her Amy—whose use of this technique was especially effective. Her husband, Dan, is a salesman. Part of his job includes making a number of short overnight trips. Amy suffered greatly when he was out of town. Though they lived in a safe neighborhood (as safe as any neighborhood can be these days), and though locks had been installed on all the doors and windows of their house, she was obsessed with the idea that when Dan was gone someone would break into the house while she slept. She also worried incessantly Dan's being killed or injured in an automobile accident during one of his trips, even though she knew he was a careful driver.

Amy and Dan had specified as one of their mutual behavioral goals that Amy learn to be more at ease when he went out of town. The stop-think technique was suggested as part of her behavioral-change program. The messages on Amy's index cards were reassuring and optimistic in nature —"We'll have fun in Paris next summer," "We're both healthy and strong," "Dan loves me and I love him and we enjoy being together," etc.—and whenever Amy began to feel anxiety about his absence, she would yell "STOP," take out one of her cards and focus her attention on positive new feelings and thoughts.

Amy is still a worrier, but she now has the means for controlling and modifying her worrying behavior and is no longer obsessed with thoughts of burglars, rapists, and crashed cars.

The Summing Up

Now you know a little bit about the basic behavioral-change techniques. You know how to identify problems and the behaviors that contribute to them. You know how to specify goals for new behaviors—the ones you want your partner to engage in more frequently. You know the whys and wherefores of collecting baseline data and are aware of the importance of record-keeping in any behavioral-change program.

You've also learned something about reinforcing desirable behavior, shaping new behavior, ignoring undesirable behavior, and establishing consequences by developing individual and exchange contracts. In addition, you've seen how modeling and thought-control fit into the picture.

In short, you've come a long way.

In the next section, we will see how these basic techniques can be varied and elaborated upon, modified and altered, so that they may be applied to an almost unlimited number of different situations. In addition, new techniques, applicable to specific problem areas—a lack of communication skills, frigidity, impotence, to name just a few—will be introduced and discussed, and we will explore in greater detail how the behavioral-change approach can be used to encourage the good, warm, positive feelings that make for real happiness in marriage.

PART II

Behavioral Techniques in Action

CHAPTER 4

When Communication
Is a Problem

"WE NEVER TALK anymore . . ."

"We live in the same house, sleep in the same bed, go to the same parties, and yet I feel I know him less well now than before we were married . . ."

"We're drifting apart. She's there on the sofa with her needlepoint and I'm there with my book, but she might as well be off in California and me in New York. We've lost that wonderful feeling of closeness we used to have . . ."

When communication is a problem, it's a BIG one. And many other problems stem directly from it. Husbands and wives who don't talk, don't get their feelings and attitudes and emotions across to one another, lose *contact*, in the most literal sense of the word. They feel unloved. Unappreciated. Alone. Unhappy. Resentful about being made to feel unhappy.

I feel very strongly that *the* most important thing partners who are committed to each other and to their marriage can do is to learn—or, more often, to *relearn*—how to communicate with one another.

Think back to the days before your marriage. Probably you spent a great deal of time communicating. You wanted to be together. You wanted to know more about one another. You wanted to tell each other how you felt. (If you hadn't, perhaps you wouldn't have married.) When you did these things, you had good feelings. "He really understands me." "She cares about me." Communicating now, as you did then, can help keep those good things going for you.

I am going to make a suggestion that may seem rather odd at first, but it is one that could make all the difference in your marriage. I am going to suggest that you and your partner arrange to have a fifteen-minute "date" each day, during which time you will devote your exclusive attention to one another. This means phone off the hook, TV off, newspaper down, dog fed, and baby asleep.

I am also going to suggest that you engage in the following behaviors on your date.[1]

1. *Look into each other's eyes.* Poetry and the romantic tradition hold that the eye is the mirror to the soul. Perhaps. It is certainly true that by looking deep into each other's eyes, you and your partner will gain the kind of awareness of one another's moods and feelings that engender warmth and closeness.

2. *Hold hands.* Just as, during courtship, the touch of your partner's hand was a source of good feeling, so it will be now. Physical contact is an important part of communicating feelings of affection, and hand-holding has always had a special significance for lovers. Gently squeeze or press your partner's hand and stroke the back of it with your thumb.

3. *Ask open-ended questions.* (Up until now, no words have been exchanged, and yet you have said a great deal to your partner; we do not hold hands with, nor look deep into the eyes of, people we do not care about.) Now is the time for talk, which is best begun with what is called the

"open-ended" question. An open-ended question is feeling rather than fact-oriented. "How was your day?" is a rather prosaic but serviceable example of an open-ended question. It gives your partner the opportunity to tell you what's happening inside his/her head—to express feelings about experiences. It is the opposite of the "dead-end" question—the one that can be answered with a simple "yes," "no," or statement of fact. Dead-end questions serve a purpose ("Did anybody call?" "Did you get the milk?" "Where's the *TV Guide*?") but don't promote closeness. Try to avoid them on your dates.

By the same token, try to avoid dead-end answers to your partner's open-ended questions. "How was your day?" could be answered with, "Okay, how was yours?" and this would hardly be conducive to the kind of communication we're concerned with here.

4. *React in a non-evaluative way.* Don't criticize when your partner tells you how he/she honestly feels. I remember one wife who complained that when her husband asked, "How do you feel today?" and she replied (with a sigh), "Kind of lazy," he went into a long diatribe about how if she really appreciated all the money he spent on buying her this and that labor-saving device, she'd get busy and do something productive. And so on. The wife was greatly angered by this response—and justly so, under the circumstances. A better answer would have been, "You feel like you just couldn't get going today—huh?" This simple reflection of her feelings constitutes an example of a non-evaluative reaction, and the conversation could have gone on from there.

5. *When possible, be positive.* Expressions of sympathy and approval and pride are positive. But complaining, nagging, and criticizing might all be lumped together under the heading of "negative conversational behaviors." They are turn-offs. They are discouraging, rather than encourag-

ing, to further communication—which, after all, is the point of dates with your partner.

During courtship, there was great excitement and anticipation prior to a date because each expected the other to have positive and interesting things to say. Good communication will occur within a marriage for the same reason it did when you were really dating. If talking reinforces itself, it will recur with greater frequency.

Establishing contracts is a good way to make sure that you and your partner continue to engage in communication behaviors that foster feelings of being loved and cared for. The following samples may be helpful.

INDIVIDUAL CONTRACT: WIFE

PART I

To show my willingness to do my part in making our marriage happier, I agree to engage in the specified behaviors below. It is clear that engaging in the desirable behaviors below result in a positive consequence, just as failure to engage in the behaviors has a negative consequence. The terms of this contract are fixed for one week only. After one week, this contract may be extended or another contract developed.

Desirable behavior	Positive consequences Daily / Weekend		Negative consequences Daily/Weekend	
1. Spend 15 minutes daily with my spouse	Use the dish-washer	Saturday night movie	No dish-washer	No movie
2. Look into his eyes				

Desirable behavior	Positive consequences Daily/Weekend	Negative consequences Daily/Weekend
3. Hold his hands		
4. Ask open-ended questions		
5. React in a non-evalua-tive way		
6. Be positive		

PART II

To demonstrate how often the above desirable behaviors occur, I agree to keep a daily record of my behaviors for the next seven days.

Behaviors to occur (1-6)								
6	Y	Y	Y	Y	Y	Y	Y	
5	Y	Y	Y	Y	Y	Y	Y	
4	N	N	Y	Y	Y	Y	Y	Y=Yes
3	Y	Y	Y	Y	Y	Y	Y	N=No
2	Y	Y	Y	Y	Y	Y	Y	
1	Y	Y	Y	Y	Y	Y	Y	
	1st	2nd	3rd	4th	5th	6th	7th	

Days of week

A "Y" (Yes) should be marked to indicate that the behavior (1, 2, 3, 4, 5, or 6) occurred on each of the seven days. A "N" (No) should be marked to indicate that the behavior (1, 2, 3, 4, 5, or 6) did not occur on each of the seven days. It is clear that all of the behaviors occurred on five of seven days.

PART III

To practice observing good behavior in my husband, I agree to keep a daily record of his behavior for the next seven days.

a) The behavior my husband has agreed to engage in more often is to *Communicate effectively as defined in* part I.

b) The daily record of these behaviors is as follows:

Behaviors to occur (1-6)		1st	2nd	3rd	4th	5th	6th	7th	
	6	N	Y	Y	Y	Y	Y	Y	
	5	Y	Y	Y	Y	Y	Y	Y	
	4	N	Y	Y	Y	Y	Y	Y	Y=Yes
	3	N	Y	Y	Y	Y	Y	Y	N=No
	2	Y	Y	Y	Y	Y	Y	Y	
	1	Y	Y	Y	Y	Y	Y	Y	

Days of week

INDIVIDUAL CONTRACT: HUSBAND

PART I

To show my willingness to do my part in making our marriage happier, I agree to engage in the specified behaviors below. It is clear that engaging in the desirable behaviors below result in a positive consequence, just as failure to engage in the behaviors has a negative consequence. The terms of this contract are fixed for one week only. After one week, this contract may be extended or another contract developed.

Desirable behavior	Positive consequence Daily / Weekly		Negative consequence Daily / Weekly	
1. Spend 15 minutes daily with my spouse	Do the crossword puzzle in the *Times*	Attend Jets football game	No crossword puzzle	No Jets football game
2. Look into her eyes				
3. Hold her hands				
4. Ask open-ended questions				
5. React in a non-evaluative way				
6. Be positive				

PART II

To demonstrate how often the above desirable behaviors occur, I agree to keep a daily record of my behaviors for the next seven days.

Behaviors to occur (1-6)		1st	2nd	3rd	4th	5th	6th	7th	
	6	N	Y	Y	Y	Y	Y	Y	
	5	Y	Y	Y	Y	Y	Y	Y	
	4	N	Y	Y	Y	Y	Y	Y	Y = Yes
	3	N	Y	Y	Y	Y	Y	Y	N = No
	2	Y	N	Y	Y	Y	Y	Y	
	1	Y	Y	Y	Y	Y	Y	Y	

Days of week

A "Y" (Yes) should be marked to indicate that the behavior (1, 2, 3, 4, 5, or 6) occurred on each of the seven days. A "N" (No) should be marked to indicate that the behavior (1, 2, 3, 4, 5, or 6) did not occur on each of the seven days. It is clear that all of the behaviors occurred on five of seven days.

PART III

To practice observing good behavior in my wife, I agree to keep a daily record of her behavior for the next seven days.

a) The behavior my wife has agreed to engage in more often is *Communicate effectively as defined under* part I.

b) The daily record of these behaviors is as follows:

	6	Y	Y	Y	Y	Y	Y	Y	
Behaviors	5	N	Y	Y	Y	Y	Y	Y	
to	4	N	Y	Y	Y	Y	Y	Y	Y=Yes
occur	3	Y	N	Y	Y	Y	Y	Y	N=No
(1-6)	2	Y	Y	Y	Y	Y	Y	Y	
	1	N	Y	Y	Y	Y	Y	Y	
		1st	2nd	3rd	4th	5th	6th	7th	

Days of week

It is clear that all of the behaviors occurred on five of seven days.

Communication Basics

As we've seen, communication is more than just talking. One communicates not only by what one says (verbal communication) but also by what one does (nonverbal communication).[2] Both are important. And ideally, one should match the other. Too often, though, a husband or wife says one thing and behaves contradictorily. When this happens, the partner, quite naturally, is confused.

Let me cite an example: A wife (let's call her Pat), tells her husband (Sid) she doesn't care a bit if he's late for supper. But her behavior indicates otherwise—she doesn't speak when he comes in, slams a plate of cold food in front of him and then stomps off to watch TV while he eats alone. Verbal and nonverbal communication do not match. Sid was led to believe one thing, while very obviously the truth was something else indeed.

Whenever there are discrepancies between verbal and nonverbal behaviors, an attempt should be made to identify the *real* message. In the example above, Sid would be wise to indicate that he is aware of his wife's anger, and Pat, in turn, should acknowledge that, yes, his being late without calling really *does* make her angry. Only when the message has been thus clarified can the couple work toward either getting Sid regularly home on time or on changing Pat's responses to his being late. Otherwise, the problem continues.

It's important to say what is *meant* and to make sure actions are consistent with words. Husbands and wives make a mistake when they assume that their mates just somehow "know" how they feel. Rather, feelings should be communicated clearly and directly. Saying you don't mind not playing tennis next weekend when in fact you've been eagerly looking forward to it isn't a noble gesture. It's foolish and may culminate in feelings of resentment toward your partner that are entirely undeserved.

Express Desires Clearly

When verbal and nonverbal behaviors match and also correspond with true feelings, then one is saying what one means. Sometimes, one also needs to express how *strongly* one feels about what one says.

Usually, words are used. I have nothing against words, of

course, but expressions such as "I like this (or that) *a lot*," or "I *guess* I want to go" or "No, I don't feel *quite* up to that today" are not very precise. Back in Chapter 1 I suggested rating the intensity of one's preferences, feelings, and desires on a scale of 1 to 10 as a way of resolving conflict. Because a numerical rating can be more explicit than words, and because letting one's partner know the intensity of one's feelings is a part of good communication, the technique is worth discussing again here.

The phone rings. One partner—the husband—answers. It is a friend calling to invite the couple to dinner that evening. The husband asks his wife how much she wants to go. Her answer is "9." He, himself would like to go at a level of "4" (in other words, he's slightly more inclined to stay home). But the invitation is accepted because "9" implies more enthusiasm for going than "4" implies desire not to go. Likewise, on another occasion, when the husband wants to go to a movie at "8" and the wife wants to go at "5," they go to the movies.

If partners disagree at the same level—i.e., if the husband wants to go to the opera at a level of "9", while the wife rates her desire *not* to go at "9," they flip a coin. The loser gets to do what he/she wants the next time they conflict at the same level.

When desires and preferences are numerically defined, there can be no misunderstandings about who feels which way about what—and how strongly. Couples who learn this technique have at their disposal an objective and non-emotional way of settling disagreements as well as a basis for compromise.

Honest and Dishonest Questions[3]

Married people ask each other many kinds of questions. Let's consider two of them here: Honest questions. And dishonest questions.

An honest question is one to which *any* answer will be accepted without provoking a negative response. A husband who asks his wife if she would like to have intercourse is asking an honest question if she can say "no" without angering him. Similarly, a wife who asks her husband if he would rather fish or go shopping with her is asking an honest question if he can tell her he prefers fishing without her taking offense.

A dishonest question has only one right answer. If the husband is angry when his wife refuses intercourse, his question was dishonest. If the wife is offended when the husband says he'd rather fish, her question was dishonest.

Dishonest questions are unfair and misleading. I believe both partners have the right, when in doubt, to ask—*before* answering—whether a particular question is honest or not. If the answer is "no," no answer is necessary since the asking partner has already decided there is only one right answer.

Direct and Indirect Questions[3]

There is yet another category of questions: Direct questions, which ask for specific information. And indirect questions, which are asked in order to obtain unspecified information. The wife who asks her husband, "Are you tired?" is asking a direct question if she is truly concerned about his need for sleep. It is an indirect question if what she really wants to know is whether or not he is in the mood for sex. In the same way, the husband who asks, "Do you want me to go bowling with you tonight?" may really be asking, "Do you love me?" or "Do you enjoy being with me?"

Indirect questions, like dishonest questions, are devious and unfair. Husbands and wives who want to improve their mode of communication should concentrate on asking and answering honest and direct questions, avoiding the kind that are dishonest and/or indirect. Partners must first know what they are being asked before they can possibly know how to answer—and what the consequences of that answer will be.

Truthfulness

Some husbands and wives get into the habit of being evasive, or dishonest—of not being truthful about where they've been, what they've been doing, who they've been with, how long they were there, etc. Good communication demands that partners who fear asking honest questions or giving honest answers commit themselves to resolving these negative feelings.

The past can never be recaptured, nor can it be corrected. "Things without remedy should be without regard; what's done cannot be undone." (Score another one for Shakespeare.) Since regrettable past experiences "cannot be undone," the untruthful husband or wife can decide to modify future behavior so that dishonesty is no longer necessary. In the same way, the suspicious partner—the one who has been lied to in the past and thus fears honest answers to honest questions in the present—must decide that his/her mate is to be trusted. Honest behavior is encouraged within a framework of trust.

The most difficult application of the honesty/trust principle is in the sexual area. The wife, for example, who has been having an affair which, if discovered, might have disastrous consequences for her marriage, can decide either to terminate the affair—and thus remove the need to be dishonest as to her whereabouts, etc.—or keep on lying and take the chance that her husband will not find out about the affair. (Although a large proportion of the population engages in extramarital sex—see Chapter 5, "When Sex Is a Problem"—an affair, though it may be gratifying to the individual is almost always in the marriages I have observed damaging to the marriage, and the husband or wife who values mate over lover ought to end the affair.)

Assuming there have been affairs, and they have been terminated, the suspicious husband or wife must try to develop behaviors indicative of trust. Trusting means *not* asking questions such as "Where have you *really* been?" or "Where are you *really* going?" Trusting is accepting the partner's stated reason or excuse for being late. Our expectations of what a person is, or will be, or will do, can influence that person's behavior. The partner who is expected to be honest probably will be. The partner who is expected to be dishonest probably will be.

In addition to refraining from asking questions designed to "trap" the partner suspected of dishonesty, the attempt to develop behaviors indicative of trust probably should also include telling one's mate that his/her honesty is appreciated. (Such verbalizations may have the greatest impact when accompanied by hugs, kisses, and other expressions of affection.) Husbands and wives who are expected to be honest, and are also *reinforced* for being so, more easily fall into patterns of truthfulness.

Though free, honest, open communication is the ideal, there is one circumstance under which honesty is perhaps not the best policy. Many partners are unable to adjust to new information about their mates' previous sexual behavior. People who are married to one another want to feel that they and they alone—and not someone else in the deep, dark past—are responsible for their partners' greatest happiness. Questions such as "How many people did you sleep with before we met?" or "Who was the best lover you ever had?" or "Were you ever tempted to have an affair with X?" are neither necessary nor productive and are best left unasked. Nevertheless, they *do* get asked. I suggest the consequences of the answer be carefully considered.

Sex

Many husbands and wives are uncomfortable talking with one another about their own sexual behaviors—often because their respective parents indicated embarrassment, confusion, or self-consciousness whenever sex entered into a conversation. On the other hand, though there may be feelings of reluctance or uneasiness, most partners want to maintain open channels of communication in regard to sex.

Spouses who have never spoken openly about sex should acknowledge their lack of communication and resolve to overcome it. There are a few relatively simple techniques by which married people can ease their way gradually into more open and honest sex talk:

Each partner should list all the sexual words he/she can think of and then combine their two lists into one "master" list. Scientific words, because of their neutral connotations, should be included along with slang variations. The list may be expanded with new words culled from the indices of books offering information about sex. *Human Sexuality,* by James McCary, is an excellent resource book.

With the list as a guide, each partner can practice saying the words alone. This, to become accustomed to the sound of them. After a while, the couple should say them together, in unison, and finally, repeat them after each other. Embarrassment fades with familiarity.

When both feel comfortable pronouncing these sexual words, partners can take turns defining them to one another and explaining how they relate to human—hence, their own —sexuality. ("The clitoris is the erectile organ of the vulva and plays an important role in female orgasmic response," etc.)

Once the words are known and can be used without embarrassment, the couple may find lengthy discussions on an array of sexual topics both enjoyable and enlightening. Both partners might want to read and then talk about a variety of books on sex—from marriage manuals to volumes of erotica to the Kinsey and Masters' studies. *The Art and Science of Love,* by Albert Ellis is excellent.

The Touch-and-Ask Approach

Undoubtedly, frank and open sexual discussion adds a new dimension to many marriages. And once the partners feel free and easy about discussing sex in the abstract, they will feel freer and easier about discussing sex as it applies to them personally.

It's important to be able to tell one another which sexual behaviors are pleasurable, which are turn-offs, and which they would like to experiment with. The "touch-and-ask" agreement can be helpful in ridding partners of any residual embarrassment in this regard. The principle of touch-and-ask is that with each caress (or stroke, or nibble, etc.) an honest question is asked—"How do you like this?" or "How does this feel?"—and then answered. In this way, each becomes more aware of what is most pleasurable to the other and more comfortable about expressing possibly heretofore repressed sexual preferences and desires. (I remember one husband who enjoyed gentle tickling of his scrotum but couldn't bring himself to tell his wife. Touch-and-ask got the message across.)

Expressing Positive Emotion

As human beings, we are creatures of emotion and feeling. Some of us make decisions based on emotion—what we feel—rather than on reason—what we think. There are times when, as Spinoza so aptly put it, "We want things not because we have reasons for them, we have reasons for them because we want them."

Yet, though emotions play an enormous role in governing much of what we say and do, some of us experience great difficulty expressing those emotions.

This is thought to be particularly true of many males, but I've known quite a few females, too, who had trouble in this area. At any rate, some married people cannot bring themselves to express emotion and feeling—or perhaps believe that these expressions are not necessary—while at the same time, their partners may crave and enjoy such expressions. It's particularly frustrating for the volatile, expansive, affectionate personality who is married to someone whose cool and impassive exterior would make good CIA material.

I think it's important for partners to discuss the issue of expressing positive emotion. People who care about one another's happiness need to know how to make each other happy. Obviously. And if more "I love you's" and "you're wonderfuls," and more kisses and hugs will bring more happiness into the relationship, then it's a goal worth working toward.

In behaviorese, one can achieve greater facility in expressing emotion by focusing on increasing the frequency of positive expressions. Positive expressions of emotion may be verbal (the "I love you's") or nonverbal and physical, expressed by gestures, tone of voice, facial expression and even posture.

When greater frequency of expression of positive emotion is the goal, the husband or wife should (1) make a conscious effort to express positive feelings *as they occur* (and sometimes they pop up at rather odd moments—while taking a bath, or driving along in the car, or in the middle of dinner) and (2) make an agreement with him/herself that treats and other enjoyable activities are contingent on expressing positive emotion (either verbally or nonverbally) a specified number of times each day or week.

At the same time, the partner of the spouse who is bent on developing ease of emotional expression should of course systematically reward those expressions—again, *as they occur*—with reciprocal smiles, hugs, kisses and/or other indications of appreciation.

Negative expressions of emotions may be valuable and have very good consequences if they get the message across that certain behaviors are desirable (thereby implying that certain other, opposite behaviors are disturbing or unpleasant). In other words, Bob is making a constructive negative statement when he says to Sally, "It would be nice if you could go easy on the charge accounts for a while." A destructive negative statement, on the other hand, might go something like this: "My God, Sally, why in hell do you have to go out and spend every blessed penny I earn every blessed month." Or some such. Griping, nagging, and complaining are all expressions of negative emotion, but the response they elicit is rarely the hoped-for response.

Anger

Righteous anger can be a liberating emotion, and no one who is concerned with the general welfare of human beings would wish to see it sublimated or made over into feelings of depression or despair or hopelessness.

Even in the happiest marriages, husbands and wives get angry at each other. Only a fool would deny it, or deny them the feeling that it is sometimes right and good to express their anger. However, it seems reasonable that partners who rage out of control and express their hostility by physically abusing their mates (by beating, slapping, kicking, etc.), or their enviroments (by throwing or breaking things), or by brooding and refusing to speak for days on end, or by habitually saying hurtful, spiteful, vicious things unrelated to the issue at hand and inevitably regretted later on when the storm has passed should learn how to be angry in less destructive ways.

The Card Game.[4] One way to control such destructive interaction is to learn to play the Card Game. In the Card Game, the written, rather than the shouted word (or dead silence) is used to express anger or disapproval of the partner's behavior.

To play the Card Game, you need a packet of white 3 x 5 index cards. Twenty cards should be marked with red lines and twenty more with blue. The remaining cards (you will probably have about ten of these) should be left unmarked. Cut each card in half so that it can be conveniently carried in pocket or purse.

Distribute the cards so that the husband has twenty red-marked cards and five white cards. The wife gets the twenty blue-marked cards and also five white cards. They should each carry a supply of cards and a pen with them wherever they go. When at home, both partners should make sure their cards are in a convenient, easy-to-reach place.

The rules of the game are as follows:

1. When your partner does or says something that pleases you, indicate your pleasure and the behavior from which it resulted by jotting down this information on one of the color cards (red if you're a husband, blue if you're a wife) and give it to your mate, expressing verbal appreciation as you do so.

For example: Bonita was surprised and delighted when Russ remembered to clean out the car. She wrote on a blue-marked card, "Wonderful!!! You cleaned the car!" gave it to Russ with a smile and said, "Thanks for cleaning out the car."

2. When your partner does something you do not like— something that disturbs you or makes you *angry*—take out a white card and indicate on it not only the upsetting behavior but also how you would wish your partner to modify

his/her behavior in the future. Do not *tell* your partner you are angry or upset. Do not *say* anything. Simply hand over the card and walk away.

For example: Russ ate the last piece of chocolate cream pie, the one Bonita was planning to savor, along with coffee, as soon as the kids were in bed. A trifling matter? Perhaps. But it had happened much too often in the past and Bonita was, as they say, hopping mad. She took out a white card and wrote, "Dear Russ: In the future please check with me before eating the last piece of chocolate cream pie (or the last piece of *any* pie, but especially chocolate cream, because I am unnaturally addicted to that particular kind). Love, Bonita." She handed the card to Russ and then curled up on the sofa with her current book. Russ now knows not only what has made Bonita angry but also how to behave so that her anger will not recur.

The purpose of the Card Game, of course, is to make each partner aware of the effect certain behaviors have on the other. And, just as important, to specify new, pleasing behaviors.

The pen is mightier than the sword, but slower than the tongue (or fists) and therein lies its advantage. With the Card Game, knock-down, drag-out fights are next to impossible since the explosive feelings which trigger explosive behavior are written down and not acted out.

Actually, Card Game or not, it is probably always a good idea for partners who have difficulty controlling negative verbal behaviors—who cannot master the impulse to utter those words of hate, mistrust, and irritation that have a way of permanently lodging in the partner's consciousness and echoing there long after storm clouds have cleared—to express their anger on paper first, and then edit the manuscript for truthfulness and "tone." In this way, verbal barbs are not allowed to prick the ears of the spouse and thus do possible and perhaps irreversible damage to the relationship.

Develop a Cue System. The Cue System is another procedure that may be used to forestall physical or verbal violence. The idea here is for one partner to alert—or "cue" the other when he/she is approaching anger-to-the-point-of-no-return. The cue is followed, hopefully, by the withdrawal of the potentially violent spouse, or, failing that, the retreat of the intimidated spouse.

For example: The couple in which one partner habitually exhibits uncontrollable behavior when angry—let's say it's the wife and her name is Marjory, and she has a tendency to throw dishes—should discuss the matter and come to an agreement. When Marjory's husband first begins to notice behavior that indicates she will soon be hurling the china, he will say to her, calmly and quietly, "Marjory, you are getting angry." This is the cue.

At that point, according to their agreement, Marjory should go into the bathroom and smile or make goofy faces at herself in the mirror. In this way, the build-up of anger is interrupted by an incompatible behavior—going into the bathroom and grimacing.

Marjory's husband, of course, should encourage her to control her tantrums by noticing and praising her willingness to go into the bathroom and grimace. If and when she is unsuccessful and she does indulge her penchant for throwing crockery, however, he should leave the house, quietly and without comment. Marjory, herself, can make some of her enjoyable activities contingent on reacting to the cue in the agreed-upon way. Thus, making faces in the mirror could mean a visit to the hairdresser, while broken dishes could mean no novels for a month.

One more point here: Marjory and her husband should take time out to identify just what it is he says or does that so arouses her ire, and then set up contingencies to modify *his* behaviors.

Cursing, Screaming, Bellowing, and Nagging

Cursing, screaming, bellowing, and nagging are not forms of communication. They are . . . well . . . cursing, screaming, bellowing, and nagging. None of them is pleasant. None accomplishes any real purpose in the sense that they encourage behavioral change; or promote feelings of closeness, empathy, and understanding; or make anyone feel any happier about the marriage relationship. On the contrary. These negative verbal behaviors tend to have an opposite effect.

The frequency of cursing, screaming, and bellowing can be decreased by (1) collecting baseline data, (2) rewarding attempts to control the negative behavior, (3) ignoring these behaviors when they do occur, (4) developing contingencies (a contingency is the relationship between a behavior and its consequence), and (5) using the stop-think technique.

Assuming, for example, that a couple have as their goal decreasing the frequency of the husband's cursing behavior, the first step is to collect baseline data by keeping a record of just how often and under what circumstances he does curse.

The wife can then begin to notice and reward him on those occasions when he might be expected to curse, but doesn't. (Initially, she should tell him she is aware of—and appreciates—his not cursing every time she notices his success in controlling the behavior. After a while, she should make appropriate comments every third time he controls the behavior.)

When cursing does occur, it should be utterly and completely ignored. No laughing. No drawing-in of startled breath. No reciprocal cursing. Nothing. If the wife has trouble ignoring the undesirable behavior, she should quickly and quietly leave the room.

To speed up the development of better verbal control, the husband can make an agreement with himself whereby some of his enjoyable activities (pipe smoking, reading, movies, etc.) are contingent on his *not* cursing.

(A point system was suggested to one husband who admittedly cursed "continually." He earned one point for every half hour that went by without his engaging in the behavior. X points earned him the privilege of eating dessert, XX points allowed him to play golf, and so on. In this way, he reinforced himself for not cursing.)

Finally, the stop-think technique. When the husband experiences feelings of stress, frustration, or hostility that usually presage the urge to curse, he can yell "stop" (quietly, to himself, if he is in a social situation) and pull from his pocket an index card on which he has previously written, "A rose by any other name would smell as sweet. Don't curse," or some other similarly distracting nonsense. His attention is thus focused away from the original feelings that might have led to engaging in the undesirable behavior.

Nagging, though definitely a negative verbal behavior without much communicational value, should be approached from a rather different angle. Most husbands and wives experience nagging in terms of being continually reminded to *do* something. Husbands are typically nagged to take out the garbage, pick up their socks, or cut the grass. Wives are nagged to keep shampoo in the shower, take shirts and suits to the laundry and dry cleaner, serve dinner on time. Nagging usually has no effect on the speed or frequency of taking out the garbage, or getting suits to the dry cleaner. Most often, it has an opposite effect: the dynamics of nagging have a way of encouraging the partner to continue to engage in the very behavior he/she is being nagged about.[5]

A first step in modifying nagging behavior is for the couple to sit down together in order to define and clarify responsibilities for each partner. (Just whose job is it, for

JOB RESPONSIBILITIES

Job	Spouse	When	Positive consequences
Take out the garbage	Jan	Each evening by 8:00 P.M.	Taking a bath
Cut the grass	Doug	Every 3rd Saturday by 6:00 P.M. beginning April 1	Fishing
Car maintenance	Jan	Owner's manual to be followed specifically	Golfing

example, to take out the garbage? To keep the car in running order? To prepare meals? To take shirts to the laundry? Etc.) Ideally, chores should be divvied up equally and in such a way that they fit conveniently into each partner's normal schedule (i.e., if the wife is responsible for meal preparation and cleaning up afterward, then the chore of taking out the garbage should probably fall to her, since she knows better than her husband when the garbage bags are full).

Each partner should be given total responsibility for those jobs assigned him/her and there should be no overlap in function. Explicit in this kind of agreement is the idea that not only is each spouse responsible for certain jobs but also for remembering when they need to be done. It might be helpful to make up a chart/timetable similar to the one illustrated here:

Job	Spouse	When	Positive consequences
Clean living room (papers off floor, chairs arranged, floor clean, ashtrays empty)	Jan	By 6:00 P.M. daily	Reading
Bathe and dress children for bed	Doug	Each evening by 8:00 P.M.	Watching television
Appliance repair	Doug	24 hours after appliance failure (husband knows how to repair appliances)	Watching television

FIGURE 4-1. Spouses decide who is responsible to perform what job, when, and assign a consequence. Only by taking out the garbage can the wife earn the privilege to take a bath. Only by cutting the grass can the husband earn the privilege to fish, etc.

The division of labor indicated on the sample chart might be a good one for many households, but by no means do I wish to imply that it is "ideal." In a family where the wife has an office job, for example, while the husband works at home as a free-lance something or other (writer, editor, illustrator, etc.), chores might be assigned in an exactly opposite way. The point, of course, is that *who* takes out the garbage—or *who* is responsible for any of these (or any *other* jobs one might add to the list)—is not important. What is important is that individual responsibilities are understood and do not overlap.

Once jobs have been assigned, consequences can be established according to whether or not they actually are carried out. Thus, in the family who made up the illustrated sample chart, the wife earns the privilege of a long soak in a hot tub only if she has disposed of the garbage by 8:00 P.M., while the husband can look forward to an occasional day's worth of fishing only if he has cut the grass every third Saturday by 6:00 P.M., as per their plan.

Neither spouse should comment on the other's failure to do his/her job (that would be "nagging" wouldn't it?). The partner's own sense of responsibility and the built-in positive and negative consequences of self-management are what make this plan work. (And in my experience it *does* work.)

On the other hand, it's always important for each partner to notice and reward the mate for engaging in the desired behavior. The husband can comment on how neat and orderly the house looks and follow it up with hugs, kisses, etc. The wife might say something about how their lawn "is so well cared-for, the neighbors must think we're paying a gardener," or some such, and accompany it with appropriate nonverbal expressions of delight and approval. Remember, behavior that is rewarded can be expected to increase and eventually become an established part of one's behavioral repertoire. Good partners are taught to be so.

CHAPTER 5

When Sex Is a Problem

"WHEN THE SEX is wrong, how can anything else be right?" one young man asked not too long ago. He professed to have "good feelings" about his wife. They were, he said, compatible in many ways and on many different levels. And yet, they "just couldn't seem to make it sexually," and they were contemplating divorce. "What other choice do we have?"

This last was asked rhetorically. Truly, he thought, there were no choices. Or, more precisely, that the choices were limited to two: (1) settle for a marriage where there was little chance of ever achieving real and consistent sexual gratification, or (2) dissolve the marriage. He was expressing what I sometimes call the "either you have it or you don't" point of view. If you have it (good sex), fine. If you don't, see if you can get it with someone else.

A similar attitude is hardly ever expressed in reference to other areas of marital discord. It is somehow assumed by couples whose problems arise out of disagreements over religion, or how the money should be spent, or the children raised, or the housework divided, that with diligence and a certain willingness to compromise, differences can be resolved. And yet, there is a great throwing up of hands over the idea of "working" toward sexual harmony. As though good sex is a gift from the gods. A subject apart and one over which we human beings have little or no control. "Either you have it or you don't."

As a human being, I know that the sexual experience, perhaps more than any other, is inextricably tied up with one's most ungovernable feelings and emotions and that these feelings and emotions dictate one's sexual behavior. But as a behaviorist, I also know that sexual behaviors—like all other behaviors—are subject to modification and that, as I've indicated once or twice before (and probably shall indicate again before this volume is ended), one can sometimes "act" (behave) one's way into new modes of feeling sooner than one can "feel" one's way into new modes of behaving.

So, to the husband who felt his choices were limited to two—and anyone else disturbed by the nature of the sexual relationship—I should like to suggest a third alternative, one that seems to me to offer the possibility of far more positive consequences: that husband and wife use behavioral techniques in a conscious effort to improve their lovemaking.

Sex is more than intercourse. It includes, in my definition, a whole range of behaviors—from brief touchings of hands, and smiling, and gazing deep into each other's eyes, to actual penetration by the penis. Some wives say they "hate sex," and yet they enjoy being kissed and caressed by their husbands. Some husbands may think of sex purely in terms of penetration and behave accordingly. Problems arise when the sexual behaviors of husbands and wives are not mutually gratifying—and it is unlikely that they will be when one or both partners are unaware of what the other "expects," or "wants," or in some cases "needs."

In Chapter 4, I suggested a few ways in which couples can learn to communicate better, along with methods by which they can accustom themselves to thinking and talking about sex, their bodies, and their feelings in a more open manner. Couples who can bring these techniques to bear on the sexual part of their relationship should be able to go on from there to teach each other how to be better lovers.

The Good Lover

There are no magical, mystical qualities attached to being a "good lover." A good lover is simply one who does what his/her partner enjoys.

A wife may want her husband to shower before making love, to massage rather than nibble at her breasts, to manipulate her clitoris in a certain way, to engage in more foreplay before pentration, and to be affectionate afterward.

A husband may want his wife to come to bed in a sexy nightdress (or, fully clothed, so that he can undress her), to bite him gently on various parts of his body, to stroke his penis in a special manner, to murmur endearments, or moan, or shout obscenities.

Couples should certainly verbalize their likes and dislikes (see Chapter 4, p. 67 for a discussion of the touch-and-ask method of improving your physical relationship) and it is often a good idea for each partner to make a list of sexual behaviors he/she wishes the other would engage in more (or less) often. These lists could become the bases of exchange contracts.

For example:

SAM AND SANDY'S CONTRACT
PART I

Since keeping happiness in marriage involves doing things for each other, I, Sam, agree to shower before coming to bed for Sandy if, in return, she agrees to come to bed wearing the black-lace nightie I bought for her birthday. The terms of this contract are fixed for one week only. After one week, this contract may be extended or another contract developed.

PART II

. To demonstrate how often I do what I agreed to do, I will keep a daily record of my behavior for the next seven days.

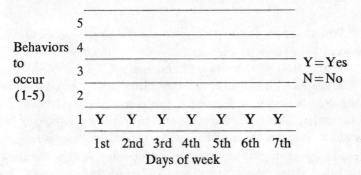

A "Y" (Yes) should be marked to indicate that the behavior(s) (1, 2, 3, 4, or 5) occurred on each of the seven days. A "N" (No) should be marked to indicate that the behavior(s) (1, 2, 3, 4, or 5) did not occur on each of the seven days.

PART III

To practice observing good behavior in my mate, I will keep a daily record of Sandy's behavior for the next seven days.

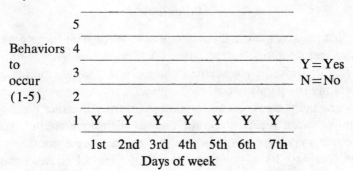

A "Y" (Yes) should be marked to indicate that the be-
havior(s) (1, 2, 3, 4, or 5) occurred on each of the seven
days. A "N" (No) should be marked to indicate that the
behavior(s) (1, 2, 3, 4, or 5) did not occur on each of the
seven days. It is clear that each partner did as he/she
agreed on seven of seven occasions.

Perhaps more to the point, however, is to reward desirable
sexual behaviors *as they occur*—and, conversely, to withhold rewards for undesirable behaviors.

The wife who is concerned about how her husband fondles
her breasts should indicate her preference *during* the sexual
encounter. She can guide him by putting her hand on his
and leading him through the motions. Or show him what she
wants by manipulating herself. When he does something
that she likes, she can express pleasure and approval by
saying, "Yes . . . that feels good," or by audible sighs or
moans. When he does something that "turns her off," she
should let him know by moving away slightly and by saying,
"No," or "Not that." She should then move closer to him
and show him what she does like: "Don't suck my breasts;
nibble at them."

Of course all of this applies equally as well to the husband
who wants to teach his wife how to please *him* better.

Foreplay

Many wives want their partners to engage in more foreplay before actual intercourse. (Although this wish is most
often expressed by women, some men, too, would prefer to
prolong the pleasures of stroking and fondling their partners
—and being stroked and fondled in return.) If either partner
thinks more foreplay would add to their lovemaking, the
couple may agree *together* to make intercourse contingent
on foreplay, by stipulating (ahead of time, of course) that

penetration shall not occur until either wife or husband has stated *three times* that she (or, he, as the case may be) is ready for intercourse.[1]

Afterplay

Some partners get the feeling that they have been "used," sexually, when there are no post-coital expressions of affection. Again, it is most often the wife who craves hugging and kissing after intercourse, but husbands certainly are not exempt.

As a matter of fact, in one marriage that came to my attention, it was the wife, who, following intercourse, turned immediately away from her husband, switched on the bedside lamp and reached for whatever book she was currently reading. Her husband would have preferred that she lay in his arms for a while instead, and interpreted her behavior to mean she was all too happy to "get the sex bit over and done with," and that she preferred reading to caressing him. (This was not quite the case; this particular woman said she was deeply in love with her husband, but upon achieving orgasm quickly lost interest in further affectionate behavior.)

As a first step, it was suggested that the husband communicate his feelings to her. She, in turn, was encouraged to make an agreement with herself whereby she would lie with him for as long as his penis remained inserted and kiss and hug him as many times as she wanted to read pages in her book. (In a more typical instance, where it was the husband who neglected post-coital expressions of love, it was suggested that he make an agreement with himself to keep his penis inserted for as long as possible after ejaculation and to hug and kiss his wife once for every hour he wanted to spend on the golf course the following weekend.)

Yes . . . I know. There is a comic element in all of this, but humor aside, it's a valuable procedure because it works.

Frequency of Intercourse

Most newlyweds—especially those who have not had much premarital sex—assume that they will spend many long, sensuous hours alone together on their honeymoon; that in fact their lovemaking will be continuous and interrupted only briefly for meals, or a stint of sightseeing, or a brief dip in the pool. One or both partners may be embarrassed and wonder "what went wrong," if he/she (or *they*) do not want frequent intercourse during this time.

As the years go by, loss of desire ceases to be a source of *embarrassment* and may become a source of great *conflict*, instead. I'm thinking specifically now of those marriages where one partner consistently wants more sex than the other.

The following procedure[2] has been proven helpful in overcoming some of the problems that arise when partners disagree over the frequency of intercourse. In the step-by-step guide below, let's assume that it's the husband who wants frequent sex—say, three times a week—while the wife would be satisfied with once-a-week intercourse, or less. (Let's *not* assume, however, that the "sexier" partner is always the husband; very often it works the other way around—in which case, read "husband" for "wife," and "wife" for "husband" in the following.)

1. The wife should make an attempt to seduce her husband *five* times during the course of a week. She should make herself as alluring as possible—perfume, provocative nightdress, the works. She might even resort to such devices as calling her husband at the office to tell him—in a breathy voice, full of emotion—that she is aroused and to please hurry home.

2. The husband should *refuse* his wife's first two attempts to seduce him. Under no circumstances should he give in, regardless of how much he (or she) wants intercourse.

3. The husband should refuse intercourse on *one* of the remaining three times she approaches him. Thus, out of five attempts at seduction, intercourse will occur *twice*.

4. The husband should hug, kiss, fondle, and caress his wife on two surprise occasions each day. These expressions of affection are *never* to be followed by intercourse.

This procedure should be used only by couples who have a good out-of-bed relationship. Otherwise, it is difficult to reverse the roles and have the necessary humor to carry it off successfully. For couples who do try it, some good, positive things have a way of happening. The procedure encourages in both partners new attitudes and feelings about sex and often has the effect of shaking each out of his/her accustomed role (i.e., in this case, husband as dogged pursuer, and wife as reluctant pursuee). At the very least, the wife learns that her husband is capable of affectionate behaviors for their own sake and that each kiss and hug need not necessarily be interpreted as an expression of desire for intercourse. She also learns that her husband is in control of himself and that he can, if he chooses, withstand her best attempts at seduction; she sees that since he is capable of refusing her (something he probably never has done before), he is in truth not the "insatiable sexual beast" she might have imagined him to be. Finally, the wife, by play-acting the temptress, may find that she has "behaved" herself into a newer, sexier way of feeling, and this may add greatly to her future enjoyment of sex.

Who Makes the Approaches?

Once in a while I am asked (usually by women, though occasionally some men express uncertainty about the matter) whether it is appropriate for a wife to approach her husband for intercourse. It's a question that always surprises me because though at one time, very long ago, a woman's

sexual needs were seldom discussed (let alone acknowledged), and as a result many "nice" women perhaps did not
dare to indicate much enthusiasm for the sexual act, times
have changed. Women *do* have sexual needs and *should* attempt to gratify them, and it is the rare man who doesn't
welcome his wife's sexual advances.

Let me suggest another marital exercise for the problem
of who approaches whom: *either* spouse may approach the
mate at *any* time. However, penetration should not take place
unless preceded by at least fifteen minutes of foreplay, after
which the spouse who was approached has the option of
either refusing or proceeding on to intercourse.

With this kind of agreement, either spouse is at liberty
to approach the partner at any time and—just as important
—neither need feel guilty if after fifteen minutes of foreplay
he/she is not sufficiently turned on to want to engage in
intercourse.

The point, then, is that couples who want to teach each
other to be more exciting lovers must first make clear to
one another their individual sexual desires (as well as those
behaviors that are "turn-offs," or "no-no's"), and then to
go on from there to commit themselves to *mutual* goals. The
behavioral approach to solving sexual problems is very
similar in nature to the techniques that may be brought to
bear on other kinds of marital conflict: reward desirable
behaviors; ignore or refuse to reinforce undesirable behaviors; and, where appropriate, establish contingency or
exchange contracts to further encourage the ultimate realization of those mutual goals.

Frigidity

Everyone's heard of the "frigid" wife (or woman), but
even among sexologists there is some disagreement as to
just what attitudes and behaviors constitute "frigidity."

Many define it as an infrequent desire for sex, while others maintain that the frigid woman is one who achieves only clitoral, as opposed to vaginal, orgasms. (Masters and Johnson vigorously assert that there is no physiological difference between the two, but some women report an emotional or psychological distinction.)

In the following discussion, I shall use the term "frigidity" in its broadest sense—as referring to a state of having little interest in or enjoyment of sex, regardless of the reason.

From a behavioral point of view, a woman may be "frigid" because the consequences of the sex act, as practiced within her particular marriage, are not positive. I have heard many, many wives say they enjoy being kissed, hugged, and fondled by their husbands, but that the ultimate positive reinforcer—the orgasm—is somehow missing.

Although most men interpret their orgasmic experiences in similar terms, one woman's account of what orgasm feels like may be surprisingly different from another's.

Some do not identify an orgasm while it is occurring and recognize it only in retrospect.[3] Others report what might be termed a "crescendo" orgasm, characterized by a gradual build-up of tension that eventually culminates in a sort of "explosion" of intensely pleasurable feelings. Still others define their orgasms as a gentle, throbbing sensation, rather like a soft and lovely melody with a begining, a middle, and an end, but with no identifiable "peaking" of sensation. This last is sometimes referred to as the "violin" orgasm.[4] Some women consistently experience either one or the other. Many women have both.

Theoretically, all women can and should experience orgasm. The wife who is "frigid," who is literally left "cold" by the idea of sex because the ultimate positive reinforcer, the orgasm, is not forthcoming, *must* communicate the fact to her husband. She owes it both to herself and to him. There are ways to remedy the situation, and a mutual commitment should be made to do so.

Before deciding on a course of action, however, I think

it is always a good idea to check with a gynecologist in order to make sure that the problem is not due to a hormonal deficiency, neural malfunction, maldevelopment of vaginal muscles, or the presence of genital lesions. A doctor will also be able to ascertain whether a lack of sexual response is caused by dyspareunia, or vaginismus.

In dyspareunia, the vagina is so abnormally dry or tight that intercourse causes real pain. Physical pathology—such as an inflamed uterus—is often associated with dyspareunia, and a physician may prescribe treatment.

Vaginismus is characterized by involuntary spasmodic constriction of the outer portion of the vagina, making it all but impossible for the penis to penetrate. (Though in the vast majority of cases, frigidity cannot be blamed on vaginismus, the condition is common enough to merit some discussion later on.)

In most instances, a failure to achieve orgasm with a beloved partner is a direct result of never having learned to appreciate and enjoy sexual behaviors. One *can* learn, however.[5] And the following discussion is concerned with how to encourage pleasurable responses to *new* sexual behaviors.[6]

I want to touch on just one or two points before we go on to the specifics of learning these new behaviors. First, since tension and anxiety inhibit one's capacity to respond orgasmically, it is important to be able to relax. Uptight people (both men and women), who can never quite let themselves go, are the ones most apt to have sexual problems. If this sounds like you, I suggest you turn to page 275 for a rundown of relaxation techniques.

Next, and although this may seem almost too obvious to mention, truly enjoyable sexual experiences depend on one's positive attitude toward one's partner. The wife who harbors deep resentments against her husband—because he lies, or because he's been unfaithful, or because he drinks too much

—for *whatever* reason, will carry these resentments with her to bed and frigidity will continue to be a problem (and, in a sense, a weapon) until negative attitudes are resolved. I strongly urge any woman who is not satisfied in her own mind that her feelings for her husband are basically warm and loving to work with him to encourage positive new behaviors that will result in the good feelings necessary for good sex.

How to Encourage Orgasmic Behavior

The following step-by-step, week-by-week program encourages orgasmic behavior—partly through masturbation, but also by manual and/or oral stimulation by the husband and the use of an electric vibrator.

In regard to masturbation, a study done in the late 1960s indicated that 100 percent of all males and 85 percent of all females in the sample group had masturbated.[7] The behavior, apparently, is on the upswing. In a previous study, completed more than twenty years ago, 94 percent of the males and 58 percent of the females admitted to masturbating.[8] If we are to place any faith in such studies, we must assume that an increasing number of women masturbate, and that it is quite likely that many of your female friends do, and do so regularly. Masturbation is common and "normal."

Another rather interesting statistic having to do with masturbation: On the average, women achieve orgasm in 95 out of 100 masturbatory attempts—this, in contrast to the average married woman's 73 percent probability of reaching orgasm through intercourse.[9]

Though some few women may choose not to cultivate masturbatory behaviors, when they are to be included as one of the techniques for overcoming frigidity, it is important for the husband to know of and to encourage his wife's self-stimulation. (One way to indicate his approval would be for him to discuss with his wife his own masturbatory experiences. If he does so, it's all right for her to discuss hers too.) Thus, the self-stimulation may be dissociated from any lingering feelings of guilt.

Now, for the program itself: I suggest you set aside three private sixty-minute time periods each week to engage in the suggested behaviors.

First week. Examine your nude body. After taking a warm bath, dry off and lie down on a bed. Place a hand mirror between your legs and closely examine the whole genital area. Look at and touch the major and minor labia (vaginal lips), the vaginal opening itself, and the clitoral shaft and hood. For the time being, the point is not self-arousal, but merely to become better acquainted with the look and touch and feel of these (possibly unfamiliar up till now) parts of your own body.

Second and third weeks. Locate and stroke pleasure zones. Discover what feels best—i.e., what produces orgasm. Use your fingers to thoroughly explore the major and minor labia, the vaginal opening, the clitoris and the area surrounding it. Stroke, press, rub; try various pressures and rhythms. Don't be too anxious to have an orgasm. Relax, and as you are relaxed, explore the right combination of place (where does it feel best?), pressure (hard or soft?), and rhythm (fast or slow?) for your orgasm. (You many want to use a sterile jelly—K-Y is a good one—both to enhance pleasurable sensations and to prevent soreness.)

Fourth and fifth weeks. Involve your husband. By now you should have a good idea of how to produce pleasurable sensations for yourself. At this point, tell your husband what you've learned about your own body and explain to him —either verbally or by demonstrations of self-manipulation —how he can stimulate you to orgasm. (Since it's rather doubtful that many of you are contortionists, it's unlikely that you could have learned how to stimulate yourself orally. Nevertheless, you may want to sugget to your husband that he try oral manipulation of those areas you have found to be prime pleasure zones.)

Sixth and seventh weeks. Try an electric vibrator. If orgasm has not yet occurred—either through masturbation or manual or oral stimulation by your partner—I suggest you invest in one of these small, motor-driven machines. (You may want to have one in any case, since, properly used, it produces intensely pleasurable sensations.)

Vibrators have been around for a long time now, and the fact that they can be enormously effective in encouraging orgasm is not a newly discovered one. In his book, *Everything You Always Wanted to Know About Sex* (etc.), Dr. David Reuben notes, ". . . the device is a small electric motor which attaches to the back of the hand with an elastic strap. As the motor operates, it sets up strong vibrations in the hand which are then transmitted to the muscle [*sic*] of whatever else the hand is touching . . . one orgasm [may] follow another in swift succession. As many as sixty orgasms an hour are possible with this electronic assistance."

Although Dr. Reuben may be overstating the case for the vibrator, the fact remains that it can be an extremely useful aid in initiating orgasmic behavior, and for this reason I think it's probably a good idea to discuss in some detail the various kinds of vibrators and how to use them.

There are four basic types. The electric hand vibrator, described by Dr. Reuben, above, is the kind used in many barber shops. They cost anywhere from about $7 to $40. Inexpensive models may be purchased in most drug stores, while the more costly ones are sold in department and specialty stores.

Another kind—the Panabrator, made by Panasonic—is notable for the intensity of its vibrations. While there's certainly no guarantee that this particular model will result in the same highly pleasurable sensations for any and all users, some women have commented on the "explosiveness" of the orgasmic experiences it produces. The Panabrator costs about $25.

A third type, Prelude II, was developed "to provide intense stimulation on and around the clitoris" by Sensory Research Corporation (2800 Springfield Avenue, Vauxhall, New Jersey, 07088). It is grasped in the hand and costs $20.00.

None of these machines is to be confused with the penis-shaped, battery-operated models which are sold in nearly all drug stores for about $5. Although they are sometimes effective, they are far less powerful than the others and thus do not produce the intense vibratory sensations some women may require for orgasm.

Since a vibrator is sold as a "massager" and not as an instrument of sexual pleasure, the instruction sheet that comes with it makes no mention of how to use it for encouraging orgasm. There are several things you and your partner should keep in mind when attempting to "turn on" with one of these machines.

Be careful. A vibrator is powered by electricity and as with all appliances care should be taken never to use it in such a way that it comes into contact with water. To do so might produce a deadly shock. For obvious reasons, then, those women—and there are many of them—who experience an uncontrollable tendency to urinate at orgasm should consider only those vibrators that are guaranteed "waterproof."

Relax. A vibrator, helpful as it may be, is not a miracle cure for frigidity. Once before in this chapter I mentioned the importance of being able to relax. Vibrator or not, the tense, anxious woman is always far less likely to achieve orgasm than her less uptight sister. If relaxing is a problem, again I refer you to the relaxation techniques described in the Appendix, page 275.

Get comfortable. If you're using the vibrator on yourself, then of course you know best how to position your own body. But if your husband is using it, remember that many men complain that holding the vibrator becomes a strain after the first few minutes. To make it easier for him, I suggest that he lie on his side, with your head resting on one of his arms, while he rests his other elbow on his side, with his hand (and the vibrator) over your vaginal area.

Give directions. Obviously, if it's going to be effective, the vibrator has to be used where it feels best. A husband can't possibly know that he's holding it too high, or too low, or exerting too much pressure, unless his wife tells him. (Incidentally, often, when the vibrator is in direct contact with the clitoris, the extremely intense sensations it produces are interpreted as pain.)

Stay with it. Be patient if you do not experience immediate and regular climaxes with the vibrator. Women respond to it in widely varying ways. Some climax within seconds, while it may take forty-five minutes to an hour for others. Also, keep in mind that the vibrator will *not* induce orgasm every time it is used. As a matter of fact, statistics indicate that it is somewhere between 85 and 95 percent effective—which implies of course that there may be times when no amount of vibratory stimulation will produce orgasm.

Most women, after discovering (sometimes to their overwhelming surpirse and delight) that they can and do have frequent orgasms when the vibrator is used—or when their husbands stimulate them manually or orally—are anxious to come to climax during intercourse.

This may be done by starting out as usual with the vibrator, or the husband's manual and/or oral stimulation. Then, as orgasmic tension builds, the husband—at a signal from his wife—inserts his penis.[10] In this way, climax occurs with the penis penetrating the vagina. This technique may not be successful the first two or three times, and when it isn't,

I suggest that the wife wait until she is on the very verge of orgasm before allowing penetration.

After experiencing orgasm in this way on several occasions, the vibrator may be gradually withdrawn so that manual and/or oral stimulation provides the basis for orgasm. Still later, manual and/or oral stimulation may be withdrawn and, if desired, replaced by "straight" intercourse. ("Straight" in the sense that the vibrator and masturbatory techniques though still possibly an important part of the sex act, are not absolutely necessary for inducing orgasm.)

Many men and women are hesitant about using a vibrator ("It's a *machine*; it's too artificial," they say), while some few may be reluctant even to rely on the husband's manual and/or oral stimulation of the wife's clitoris and vaginal areas. Unfortunately, many of us were brought up to believe that simple penetration and subsequent thrusting of the penis in the vagina is the only "real" (or "natural" or "normal") way to have sex and that it is somehow wrong to explore other means of achieving gratification. I can only urge couples who harbor such feelings to remember that though the vibrator is a comparatively new invention, cunnilingus and masturbation have been around for a long, long time and that the sexual myths and attitudes of our particular society impose unfair restrictions on free and joyous love-making. (In this respect, I'm in wholehearted agreement with the young who proclaim so loudly and often that "if it feels good, *do it*.") Indeed modern sexologists are often quick to point out that the only real sexual perversion is to insist that there is only one "right" way to achieve gratification. Husbands and wives may deprive themselves of some wonderfully rich and fulfilling new sexual experiences by insisting to themselves and to each other that straight intercourse is the only "legitimate" way to sexual enjoyment.

Self-exploration, masturbation, manual and/or oral stimulation by the husband and the use of an electric vibrator all help to set up patterns of orgasmic response, and it's often remarkable how, once the patterns are established, a woman almost automatically develops a greatly heightened interest in sex. Orgasm becomes the reinforcer, and whereas in the past, lovemaking might have been a bore and a chore, associated with frustration, irritation, and feelings of a distinctly nonpleasurable nature, it becomes—usually within a matter of just a few months—a delightfully exciting and enriching new experience to share with one's mate.

Vaginismus

A few pages back, the condition known as vaginismus was mentioned as one of the possible causes—though by no means the chief one—of frigidity. In vaginismus, remember, the outer part of the vagina constricts spasmodically in response to the attempted insertion of any object—including the husband's penis. The reaction is involuntary and usually unaccompanied by organic pathology.

A young woman I shall call Joan suffered from the condition. She and Steve were married in April and by the end of July, the marriage still had not been consummated. Joan's gynecologist found no anatomical dysfunction to account for the spasmodic constriction of her vagina. Thus, the plan outlined below was suggested as a possible antidote to the condition.

The excercises, as described, were to take place on three different occasions during each week.

First week. In Steve's absence, Joan was to insert her clean index finger (lubricated with K-Y Jelly) into her vagina and to keep it there for several minutes while she attempted to relax. Having successfully accomplished inserting one finger, she was to insert two fingers and relax.

Second week. With Steve beside her, Joan was to repeat

the procedure for the first week, with the following additions: after she had inserted one of her own fingers, she was to relax, and then guide one of Steve's fingers into her vagina. Next, she was to insert two of her own fingers, relax, and follow by inserting two of Steve's fingers.

Third week. The second week's exercises were to be repeated. But after Steve had inserted two of his fingers into Joan's vagina, he was to remove them and gently insert only the head of his penis, keeping it there for several minutes while Joan attempted to relax.

Fourth week. Again, the procedure for the third week was to be repeated. However, instead of inserting just the head of his penis, Steve gradually and gently penetrated deeper, waited a few seconds, and then—just as gradually and gently—partially withdrew. After waiting a minute or so he again penetrated and withdrew. Finally, full penetration was achieved, followed by partial withdrawal. The exercise was repeated several times with the ultimate result that Joan and Steve were having "real" intercourse for the first time in their marriage.

It's important to note that the couple had agreed beforehand that Joan could stop whatever was happening if she became overly tense and anxious. Joan was thus assured that at no point would she be pressured into intercourse. The agreement undoubtedly contributed greatly to their success with this method.

Impotence

"Impotence" refers to a man's inability to achieve and maintain an erection. There are two basic types: physiological and psychological. Physiological impotence is caused by physical defects, metabolic dysfunction, and occasionally by medication or drugs (including barbiturates and alcohol). Any man troubled by impotence should see a urologist in order to rule out the possibility that the problem is of a physiological nature.

Psychological impotence is quite another thing. What many husbands don't realize is that *most* men suffer from this kind of impotence at some point in their lives. Stress of one kind or another is the chief cause of psychological impotence: an extramarital affair, for example, with its distractions and concomitant load of guilt, or intense feelings of frustration or pressure on the job may cause temporary psychological impotence.

Impotence also is often the result of other problems that exist within a marriage. Like the frigid wife, the impotent husband may be unable to function because of dissatisfactions or conflicts with his partner. Until these other problems are resolved (and as we have seen, they usually can be by employing the appropriate behavioral procedures discussed elsewhere throughout this book) and good, warm, positive feelings take the place of hostility and resentment, it's likely that the ability to achieve and maintain an erection will continue to be affected.

However, impotence can exist even within a loving relationship where both partners are happy and have no major cause for complaint (other than the impotence). This is sometimes the case where the wife's sexual needs far exceed her husband's.

I know of several marriages where the wife wanted to make love approximately twice as often as the husband, and her continued references to sex, coupled with aggressive behavior in bed, caused him to doubt his virility. In all of these relationships, the husband had swallowed whole the myth that "real" men are *always* ready for sex, and that since he, himself, did not conform to this mythical image of what a real man is or should be, he was, in his own mind, something less than a man.

The dynamics at work in this kind of situation are self-perpetuating. Once the husband fails to achieve an erection —for whatever reason—his worst fears are confirmed. He becomes even more doubtful about his masculinity, and in the effort to *will* himself to have an erection, may fail miserably. Stress imposed by feelings of obligation—that one *must* perform—decreases the probability that one will be *able* to perform. The problem grows and feeds on itself and patterns of impotency are established.

To reestablish behaviors associated with potency, feelings of anxiety and concern over failure to achieve an erection *must* be diminished. And, just as a husband must work with his wife to overcome frigidity, the wife plays an important role in helping her husband with the problem of impotency. With her cooperation, it is often only a matter of weeks before lovemaking becomes the joyous and fulfilling experience that it can and should be.

(One word of caution here: Though the problem obviously must be initially discussed if both partners are to work together toward its solution, a wife should never, under any circumstances, mention again or berate her husband for his failure to achieve an erection.)

The following two techniques for reestablishing patterns of potency work because of the way in which they tend to decrease the husband's feelings of anxiety.

The first might best be called the "approach-refuse" method. Here, I suggest that the husband approach his wife for intercourse several (three? four? five?) times weekly, the wife consistently *refuses* him. If this method is to be effective, it is absolutely imperative that intercourse *not* occur. (Though, if the wife is aroused, her husband may bring her to climax manually or orally or by using an electric vibrator.)

New behaviors begin to be established here: The husband becomes the aggressor, since he is attempting to initiate intercourse. More important, he learns that he is under no obligation to "perform" with his penis and that his wife may experience pleasure through some means other than intercourse. So, in effect, the anxiety associated with achieving an erection is removed and it is this very cessation of pressure that often results in erection.

I've known many couples who were reluctant to use this method. Some wives, for example, are interested in intercourse only. However, as was pointed out in the section on frigidity, self-stimulation, manual and/or oral manipulation by the partner and the electric vibrator are all valid and pleasurable ways to achieve orgasm—and statistically speaking, orgasm actually occurs *more frequently* with self-stimulation or the use of a vibrator than by means of simple penetration and thrusting of the penis. So, I can only urge those wives who hesitate to rely on anything but their husbands' penises for gratification to at least experiment for a while with the suggested alternatives—to, as they say, "try it. You'll like it." (And even if you don't, it's most important to communicate to your husband during this retraining period that you experience sensual pleasure even though his penis is not involved.)

Some husbands, too, object to using a vibrator because they feel it's a "cop-out" device. I always try to remind these men that the most masculine and virile males are the ones who can satisfy their partners in a *variety* of ways, that many of the great lovers of history did not always rely only on their penises to bring their wives and mistresses to orgasm, and that in fact some of them were particularly adept at the use of various "devices."

Let me give an example of how the approach-refuse procedure was used in a marriage which, according to the husband, had "turned into a nightmare because I just couldn't get it up."

Wally and Sherrill had been married for six years and had two children. According to Wally, "one night, about four years ago, I couldn't get an erection. It had never happened before and I don't know why it happened that time, but it did, and ever since then I've had erections only when we were on vacations."

Sherrill expressed her disappointment in Wally, but, even more disturbing, was her feeling that the problem was somehow *her* fault. "I wondered what was wrong with me," she said. "It seemed he no longer found me sexually attractive or exciting."

Both said they were happy in all other areas of their marriage, but at the same time stated that they would separate if the problem continued.

Since Wally had already consulted a urologist and there was no physiological basis for his impotence, the following plan was suggested:

First week

1. Wally was to bring Sherrill to a climax—either manually, orally or by using a vibrator—on five different occasions. He, not Sherrill, was to initiate these interactions. (However, they were instructed that under no circumstances should intercourse occur—even if Wally *did* have an erection.)

2. So there would be no misunderstandings about who was seducing whom, Sherrill was to respond reluctantly to Wally's approaches.

3. Sherrill was instructed to provide Wally with "positive feedback"—to tell him what she wanted him to do with his hands, mouth, and the vibrator and how it felt, and at the point of climax to indicate her pleasurable feelings either verbally or with moans and sighs.

4. Neither was to mention Wally's past failure to maintain an erection.

During that first week, Wally brought Sherrill to a climax, orally and with a vibrator, on four separate occasions. On three of these occasions, Wally maintained a stiff erection.

"At one point," Sherrill reported with glee, "I thought he was going to rape me. Literally."

Second week

1. Wally was instructed to approach Sherrill for intercourse on five different occasions and to bring her to climax by means other than penile penetration.

2. Sherrill was instructed to submit to Wally three out of the five times she was approached. (I had given her a slip of paper indicating when and how often to refuse intercourse.) Wally, however, was told that Sherrill might refuse him all five times or that she might submit on one or two or three of these occasions. Thus he never knew beforehand whether or not intercourse would take place after he had initiated their lovemaking.

3. Sherrill was not to indicate in any way whatever whether intercourse was a possibility on any given occasion.

4. To let her know of his urgent desire for intercourse, Wally was to say "now," or "I'm ready," three times before Sherrill would allow penetration.

The couple adhered strictly to the plan for the second week, with the result that Wally maintained "fantastic" erections on all five occasions. Intercourse occurred on the second, third and fifth approaches. They were both elated.

Third through eighth weeks

Wally was directed to approach Sherrill for intercourse five times a week during the next five weeks. Sherrill was told to refuse on the 2nd, 4th, 8th, 12th, 18th, 24th, and 25th occasions. Thus, Wally still never knew for sure when • intercourse was a real possibility. By this time, however, his anxiety was greatly diminished and he was impotent on only two occasions. This, after a six-year period of consistent failure.

Sherrill was instructed to repeat the same refusal sequence for another five weeks, during which Wally maintained an erection on all twenty-five occasions. I'm delighted to report that except for a card at Christmas I have not heard from them since.

There is another very effective technique for overcoming impotence. This one involves the husband's rating his anxiety about intercourse and achieving an erection on a scale ranging from zero to ten. At zero, for example, he experiences no anxiety to speak of, while at ten, he is extremely concerned and tense about the prospect of performing.

Since, as we already know, it is difficult if not downright impossible to maintain an erection when one's anxiety level is high, the husband should not attempt intercourse on any occasion when he feels nervous or anxious above a level of *two*. In this way, he never allows himself to be caught in a situation where failure is inevitable. He can, in a sense, control his anxiety, simply by withdrawing from the situation that causes it.

When this method is put into practice, the couple should make an agreement whereby it is understood that the husband will bring his wife to climax orally, manually, or with a vibrator on any and all encounters when he feels anxious about maintaining an erection.

Premature Ejaculation

Again, as with frigidity, interpretations vary as to just what constitutes "premature" ejaculation (as opposed, I assume, to "mature" ejaculation). Certainly, ejaculation that occurs before penetration may be considered premature. But otherwise, one man's "premature" ejaculation may appear to be a miracle of control to another. For our purposes here, then, I think it best to define the term simply as "ejaculation that takes place before either partner wants it to."

Ejaculation occurs as a response to friction against the nerve endings of the penis, and, in some cases, as a response to that old arch-enemy of sexual enjoyment, anxiety. So, when premature ejaculation is a problem, the resolution lies in decreasing the friction on the one hand and/or decreasing anxiety on the other.

Some of the more well known ways to combat the condition include the application of a local anesthetic to the head of the penis (this, to partially deaden sensation), attention-distracting ploys, such as counting or holding one's breath during intercourse, and total cessation of movement after penetration.

Occasionally, one or a combination of these methods does the job, though in general, results are rather disappointing. There is another technique developed by Masters and Johnson that has proven consistently successful.[11]

As when any new sexual behavior is the goal, husband and wife must first be open enough with each other to discuss an existing problem and then go on from there to make a mutual commitment to do something about it.

When an understanding has been reached, the first step is to collect "baseline data" by noting in terms of minutes (or perhaps seconds) the amount of time that elapses between penis contact with the vaginal lips and ejaculation. I suggest you do this on at least three occasions of intercourse (four or five would be better) so that you will have some basis for evaluating the results of the following procedure:

Phase I

1. The wife sits on the bed with her legs spread and her back against the headboard, while the husband lies on his back, his head at her feet, his pelvis between her legs, and his legs over hers.

2. The wife begins manual manipulation of the penis. When a full erection is attained, she should place her thumb on the underside of the penis (the frenum)—which, in this position, is facing her—and her first and second fingers on either side of the ridge formed by the head of the penis (glans) on the top side. She then squeezes the penis—*hard*

—between thumb and first two fingers for three or four seconds.

3. This "squeeze," if it is hard enough, will result in a diminution of the husband's urge to ejaculate, and he will probably lose some of his erection. After a pause of about thirty seconds she should again begin to manipulate the penis until full erection is regained, and then repeat the "squeeze" technique as described above in Step 2.

4. After repeating this procedure three or four times, the husband may desire stimulation to the point of ejaculation, or the couple may choose to have intercourse. There need be no concern about delayed ejaculation at this early point. Ordinarily there are no discernable results after only one such session.

The whole procedure, however, should be repeated regularly—i.e., as part of the foreplay involved in each of the couple's sexual encounters—until the husband can experience continued manual stimulation without ejaculation for as long as each partner would like.

Phase II

Once the desired ejaculatory delay has been achieved through manual stimulation, the couple is ready for the second part of this procedure.[11] Here's how it works:

1. While the husband lies, relaxed, on his back, the wife stimulates him manually and then applies the squeeze technique as above. After she has done this two or three times, she shifts position so that she is sitting astride her husband with his penis inserted in her vagina. Initially, she should not move her hips at all, but remain still so that her husband becomes accustomed to vaginal containment without movement. As before, when the husband begins to experience the first hint of nearing ejaculation, he should tell his partner, who will dismount and again squeeze his penis until the urge to climax disappears. After a pause of thirty seconds or so, she again stimulates him manually until full erection

is regained, then once more shifts position so that she is sitting astride with the husband's penis inserted.

2. At this point, the wife may want to introduce some slight pelvic movement. This must be done very slowly and gradually, and again, she should dismount and apply the squeeze technique when her husband indicates that he is about to ejaculate. Thus, the husband experiences gradually increased vaginal friction while climax is delayed.

The main idea here, of course, is to remember to use the squeeze technique at the slightest hint of readiness to ejaculate. Eventually—usually within a matter of just a few weeks —new ejaculatory behaviors are established and there is less and less need to resort to "squeezing" as the husband becomes more and more adept at delaying his climaxes.

Clearly, with this method, the wife's cooperation is crucial. She must be willing to interrupt intercourse even though she may be approaching her own orgasm. Obviously this is going to be frustrating, especially at the beginning, and many women may feel at first that the price they have to pay in terms of their own pleasure is not worth the effort. But believe me, it is. I strongly urge any wife who is reluctant to go along with this procedure to remember that when the problem of premature ejaculation is resolved—as it can be —lovemaking will be all the more delightful for both partners.

Admittedly, however, the program just described is an intensive one and there is another option open, which though it doesn't alter the husband's ejaculatory behavior, can result in pleasurable sexual experiences for both partners and helps to relieve any guilty feelings the husband may have as a result of climaxing immediately upon penetration. (My personal opinion is that the "squeeze technique" is preferable because it encourages the development of new sexual behaviors, but for those couples who are interested, the alternative program is outlined below:)

1. Allowing at least thirty minutes for foreplay, the husband brings his wife to climax through manual manipulation, oral stimulation, or a vibrator.

2. The wife indicates when she is on the verge of climax, at which point the husband penetrates. Thus, by inserting his penis *during* his wife's orgasm, he is under no pressure to delay ejaculation and both partners are satisfied.

Keeping the Past Buried

Some husbands and wives take great delight in recounting to their partners—often in graphic detail—their past sexual exploits. It's "bragging," really, a word which, for most of us, is loaded with extremely unpleasant (perhaps "repugnant" is a better term) connotations.

Bragging is detrimental to a good relationship. Most men and women want to feel that they and they alone are responsible for their mates' happiness. Without exception, no one likes the idea that unforgettable ghosts from the past continue to lurk on in the minds of their partners and that indelible memories of "what was" keep rising up to compete with the very real "what is." The husband or wife of a bragging mate cannot help but have doubts that, had circumstances been different, the braggart might have chosen that mysterious and much discussed "other" as a lifetime partner.

Where either partner is disturbed by his/her mate's compulsive references to past affairs, an agreement should be made to overcome this obnoxious habit. This will involve a program designed to eliminate this negative behavior.

It's always helpful in such instances to record not only how often references to past sexual involvements occur, but also to note down what events precede and follow these references. For example, are remarks made monthly? weekly? daily? more often? Are they mumbled during intercourse? Screamed out in arguments? Intoned in times of stress or frustration (as when the children have been particularly difficult to manage, or when nothing seems to go right on the job)? And how does the partner respond? With anger? Sulking? Tears? When these questions are answered, the couple has a basis for understanding and changing the frequency of the behavior.

As we know, all behaviors are learned and become an established part of our behavioral repertoires through reinforcement of one kind or another. It's reasonable to assume that one learns to talk about past sexual adventures in the same way one learns to nag, or to forget, or to be late most of the time, and that the same techniques that work to diminish the frequency of these other undesirable behaviors can be used to modify boasting about past love affairs.

Let me use the case of Matty and Carol as an example: Matty had been something of a "ladies' man" (he used this term himself) before marrying Carol almost four years ago. Although he professes to be deeply in love with her and says that their four years of marriage have been the happiest of his life, there are times when the day-to-day sameness of their existence throws him into depression.

"On the one hand I like waking up with Carol every morning, going off to work and knowing that she'll be there to talk to and love when I get home in the evening," he told me. "But sometimes I can't help thinking about the old days, the times when there were two or three different women in my life, the excitement of going out with them and then later getting them into bed. Those are good memories and I try not to talk about them, but then something will set me off—like maybe Carol will start to nag, or the basement is flooded, or I don't pull off a big sale—and I remember how it used to be all fun and games with no responsibilities, and I start running off at the mouth about this girl and that girl. And then Carol gets terribly upset and cries and runs into the bedroom and won't speak to me for two or three days. I don't blame her. I wouldn't like it if she started telling me about every Tom, Dick, and Irving she'd gone out with before we got married."

Because Matty seemed to be engaging in this undesirable behavior more and more often as time went by, and because Carol was suffering more and more on account of this constant dragging up of his past, and—most important—because they love each other and want to stay married, the following plan was suggested as a way of modifying Matty's habit of bragging about former sexual exploits:

1. Because behavior that is rewarded can be expected to increase in frequency, Carol was instructed to notice, by making appreciative comments, whenever Matty talked positively about *their* relationship "I really get turned on when I think about what *we* do in bed," was typical of the remarks she reinforced).

2. They had kept a record of the frequency of Matty's bragging behavior and found that it occurred on approximately two occasions each week. It was suggested to Carol that she make periodic comments about his *not* mentioning past sexual experiences at the rate of four times a week (or, in other words, to notice nonbragging behavior twice as often as the bragging was likely to occur).

3. Carol was told to ignore (and when possible go off to another room) any of Matty's references to his old girl-friends—in other words, to meet his remarks with apathy and indifference, never with anger or tears. (As we already know, ignored behaviors can be expected to decrease in frequency.)

4. Matty was encouraged to curb the impulse to verbalize his thoughts about the past by first jotting them down on paper. (Usually, after several minutes of writing up his feelings, the urge to talk about them disappeared and the paper got torn up and thrown out with the garbage.)

5. Finally, Matty established a contingency contract with himself. It went something like this:

MATTY'S NONBRAGGING CONTRACT
PART I

To show my willingness to do my part in making our marriage happier, I agree to engage in the specified behaviours below. It is clear that engaging in the desirable behavior(s) below results in a positive consequence just as failure to engage in the behavior(s) has a negative consequence. The terms of this contract are fixed for one week only. After one week, this contract may be extended or another contract developed.

Desirable behavior	Positive consequence Daily / Weekend		Negative consequence Daily / Weekend	
1. Make no statements to Carol about my past love life	Watch TV	Golf	No TV	No golf Clean out basement
2. Tell Carol that she is a fantastic lover				

PART II

To demonstrate how often the above desirable behavior occurs, I agree to keep a daily record of my behavior for the next seven days.

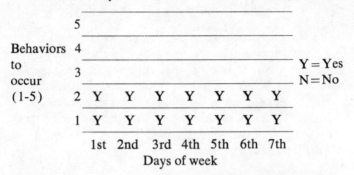

Behaviors to occur (1-5)							
5							
4							
3							
2	Y	Y	Y	Y	Y	Y	Y
1	Y	Y	Y	Y	Y	Y	Y
	1st	2nd	3rd	4th	5th	6th	7th

Y = Yes
N = No

Days of week

A "Y" (yes) should be marked to indicate that the behavior(s) (1, 2, 3, 4, or 5) occurred on each of the seven days. A "N" (no) should be marked to indicate that the behavior(s) (1, 2, 3, 4, or 5) did not occur on each of the seven days. (Matty engaged in both behaviors every day for the first week.)

Mistress or Lover?

Some men and women crave new experiences more than others, but in all of us there is a kind of built-in desire for variety, and it is the rare married person—husband or wife —who does not from time to time consider the possibility of a fleeting or prolonged relationship with someone new. These thoughts are normal and probably inevitable. The extramarital affair, however, while common, is *not* inevitable, and though some of the more fashionable thinking of our day may imply otherwise, there are many reasons to believe that outside sex does not contribute to a happy, satisfying marital relationship.

About 45 percent of all married men and 20 percent of all

married women are unfaithful to their partners at least once. Some of these outside relationships—the so-called one-night stands—are purely physical in nature and often the result of a fortunate (or perhaps unfortunate, depending on one's point of view) convergence of circumstances: the right time, the right place, plus two people who are for the moment strongly drawn to one another. And so, why not?

It almost always hurts to find out one's partner has been unfaithful, but the one-night stand often goes undiscovered —or, when finally confessed (or otherwise revealed) weeks, or months or maybe years later, the consequences are not always irreparably damaging to a marriage that is on a good, sound footing otherwise.

But what about the full-blown affair, with its overtones of emotional as well as physical involvement? Although there are exceptions,[12] such extramarital arrangements are almost always destructive. A good marriage, remember, is firmly based on mutual trust, and except in those still rare instances where husband and wife decide *together* that affairs are "okay"—that the freedom to pursue outside relationships will be a part of their particular life-styles—the concept of trust is violated when either or both partners make a private commitment of time, energy, and emotion to someone other than their spouse.

If the affair is discovered (perhaps I should say "when" the affair is discovered, because the prolonged liaison usually comes to light), the "injured" partner almost always experiences great difficulty coping with the information; the response may range anywhere from immediate initiation of divorce proceedings, to retaliation (a deliberate attempt to find a lover of his/her own), to grin-and-bear-it forgiveness (which on the one hand tends to reinforce the straying partner's inclination to continue the affair, and on the other is absolutely necessary, since to get the affair behind you and get on with your marriage, you must forgive and forget).

But even when an affair is not discovered, the partner who is caught up in a prolonged outside emotional and physical involvement inevitably reaches a point where he/she must choose between spouse or lover, and the decision—especially where there are children to be taken into consideration—is an agonizing one.

I'm not concerned here with whether affairs are "good" or "bad" for the individual. Some are *very* good in that they can be sources of wonderfully enriching new personal experience—while others are merely guilt-provoking exercises in frustration. But there is no doubt in my mind that affairs are "bad" in terms of maintaining a mutually satisfying and fulfilling marriage, and since the primary business of this book is to suggest ways in which marriage can be made better, not worse, I must express the opinion that husbands and wives who want to stay together will have an easier time of it if sex is something they share with one another only.

For many, this undoubtedly reads like a prescription for a very bitter medicine indeed. The spouse represents security, companionship, respectability, but rarely—especially after the passing of several years—excitement. I think the comments of a thirty-two-year-old woman who had been sexually active before her marriage, ten years ago, sum up the feelings of many: "I love Stanley," she said. "I really do. I can't imagine life without him. But it depresses me something awful when I think that maybe I'll never, ever again have the thrill of sleeping with someone new."

This desire for the excitement of a new experience is what most often sets up the circumstances leading to an affair. In a culture that values excitement, novelty, and youth over stability and maturity, as ours does in many ways, the scales are easily tipped in favor of outside sexual experimentation.

There's also the fact that many men and women getting on into their late thirties and forties become keenly aware of and concerned about the aging process. The feeling that life is somehow passing them by deepens with every line that turns up on their faces and every gray hair newly sprouting on their heads. In an effort to reassure themselves that they "still have what it takes" (as one forty-five-year-old father of three expressed it), they actively seek out an extramarital partner.

As mentioned before, retaliation is still another reason for carrying on an affair. When one partner learns that the other has been "playing around," he/she may want to even the score. Retaliatory affairs are more often ignited by the desire for revenge than by any burning passion for the new sex partner. One wife told me she felt "If I had an affair of my own, I think I could more easily get over my husband's having one." She did have the affair, and it did not help her marriage.

If one is to successfully manage an extramarital involvement one must have mastered the art of compartmentalization so that the one relationship does not affect the other. Most normal people find this exceedingly difficult, since the tendency is to integrate—rather than partition off—the many feelings and experiences that make up the whole of their lives. Prostitutes and psychopaths are good at compartmentalization.[13] The prostitute makes the distinction between sex for business and sex for love, while the mind of the psychopath operates in a way that separates his/her actions from their logical consequences. I mention this not by way of comparing the man or woman who carries on an affair to the prostitute or psychopath, but rather to point up the fact that normal, healthy people usually lack the ability of the more deviant personality to compartmentalize their experiences.

Except in those wide-open marriages where each partner encourages the other to engage in sexual experimentation, the "successful" affair (if there is such a thing) is successful only so long as it remains a "secret." Once the cat is out of the bag, so to speak, a whole new and overwhelmingly negative element is introduced into the marital relationship. One partner is hurt and suffers feelings of inadequacy, while the other assumes a burden of guilt—and none of these emotions is conducive to the harmony of their interaction.

Some men and women enter into an affair confident that there is very little chance of being found out. Yet, feelings about the outside relationship cannot help but affect behavior within the marriage. The signals may be ever so slight and subtle—an inability to concentrate, a fleeting and mysterious smile as thoughts of the lover flit through the mind, periods of inattentiveness to the spouse followed by unusually fierce demonstrations of affection—but the perceptive partner will mark these new behaviors and in time begin to wonder. As one woman expressed it: "He just started acting . . . *differently*. Nothing I could really put my finger on, but it bothered me and then suddenly the thought jumped into my mind, 'He's having an affair!' When I asked him about it he told me the truth and my whole life came crashing down around me. I thought we had so much going for us and then I came to this hideous realization that the person I *thought* I was married to wasn't the person I was *really* married to at all."

Immediate feelings of pain and anger usually result in the stipulation that the straying mate either end the outside involvement—or leave, though occasionally, a husband or wife will attempt to "adjust" to the partner's affair. "She's a good wife and mother, otherwise," one man told me. "And maybe I haven't the right to insist that she stop seeing the guy she sleeps with, since it doesn't seem to affect *our* relationship all that much." But in a later conversation with this same man, he confessed that "It just can't work. I go to the office every day and I sit there wondering whether she's with him. I imagine them in bed together. It's torture."

Everything taken into consideration, then, affairs make very little sense in those marriages where partners value each other, their children, and their lives together. And I will make the rather flat-footed statement that if you are presently involved in an affair, but are at the same time committed to your marriage, the affair should be terminated. This means no more communication with mistress or lover—no phone calls, no letters, no secret meetings. Nothing.

Good feelings between husband and wife inevitably deteriorate when one or the other invests much energy, time, and emotion in an "outsider." We might wish it differently, but for most of us it cannot be any other way.

Now, let's assume that either you or your partner has had an affair and that an agreement was made to terminate the involvement. Can the marriage regain anything of its former stability? Can new feelings of trust and affection replace resentment and hostility? I would have to answer with a qualified "yes."

To put a relationship back together again, it's necessary that neither partner discuss the past affair ever again. Talking about it only keeps the old, bad feelings alive. And while it may not be possible to *forget* what's happened, it *is* possible to keep one's mouth shut. The stop-think technique discussed in Chapter 3 may be helpful when there is difficulty in controlling one's thoughts about the past.

Next, both partners must identify those pleasing behaviors they want their mates to engage in more often, and the appropriate behavioral techniques should be used to make sure the new behaviors really do occur. One husband told me, after receiving a long, detailed list from his wife outlining what he would have to say and do to improve their relationship, that it was simply "too much trouble. Why should I have to go through all of this when my secretary will have me on my own terms?" Apparently, he valued intercourse with his secretary over making any efforts to improve his marriage, and a divorce ensued. Other husbands (and wives) beat a hasty retreat to their spouses and are successful in rekindling positive feelings for each other.

Swinging

"Swinging" is attracting much public attention as an alternative to the clandestine affair. It has been called an "honest" form of adultery, since both partners know what's happening. Swinging couples meet, usually have a few drinks, then undress and switch partners for intercourse.

I think it is extremely important for husbands and wives to communicate to each other their true feelings about swinging. It often happens that one partner goes along with the idea in order to be considered a "good sport," or in a "with-it" attempt to accommodate the mate's desire for sexual experiences with others.

Even communicating your "true feelings" regarding swinging does not insure that you can keep the situation from getting out of hand. There is a tremendous gap between rational, logical thought, and the emotions that well up in us when certain events actually happen. Ray and Olivia talked about the honesty of swinging, the possible necessity of experiencing others sexually to avoid marital boredom, and the irrationality of jealousy. They discussed all the angles and decided to give swinging a try. They "recruited" from among their friends another couple who had been thinking along the same lines. A year later, Ray and Olivia were divorced and not on speaking terms with their "friends." Olivia said, "It's not what you think it is. When Ray was behind a closed door with another woman, I was eaten alive with jealousy and guilt at ever agreeing to my husband having sex with another woman."

Unless both partners are in rational and emotional agreement that swinging will have positive consequences for each spouse and for the marriage (and according to Robert Rimmer,[14] it sometimes does) the ultimate outcome can be just as devastating to a good marriage as the results following the discovery of an affair. When in doubt, don't do it.

CHAPTER 6

When Hard Liquor[1] or Soft Drugs Are a Problem

WHEN IS LIQUOR a problem? I would say that in general a person may be considered to have a problem with alcohol if drinking interferes with his economic, social or physical well-being. In other words, when it impedes one's ability to get or keep a job, when it disrupts interpersonal relationships, when there are actual physical consequences—weight loss, headaches, agitation, confusion, hallucinations, gastrointestinal inflammation, and liver disorders—drinking must be considered a negative behavior: a *problem*.

Problem drinking, almost by definition, has a negative effect on one's economic, social, and physical well-being and as such has the potential to undermine marital happiness in any number of different ways. It may impede the ability to get or keep a job; thus, financial difficulties arise. It almost always disrupts communication and the free and easy exchange of thoughts and feelings necessary to a warm, loving relationship. The actual physical consequences—frequent headaches and hangovers, not to mention the confusion, hallucinations, gastrointestinal inflammations, liver disorders, etc.—associated with real alcoholism, can make good sex difficult, if not impossible. And, though this book was put together with the idea of suggesting how behavioral techniques can help maintain happiness within a marriage, it's worth noting that the effects of problem drinking extend far beyond one's relationship with one's partner; Skid Rows across the country offer all too tragic testimony.

As you may know, alcohol is not a stimulant but a depressant, which acts on the cortical center of the brain, reducing anxiety and producing a temporary feeling of well-being. Despite the many and varied explanations offered to account for the *cause* of alcoholism, there is little evidence to indicate a chemical, genetic, or physiological base. Therefore, no one is locked into an uncontrollable drinking pattern because of inheritance. Another rather interesting fact: the effect of alcohol varies according to the amount consumed (obviously), its proof level, the presence of food in the stomach, the rate at which it is consumed, and the weight of the consumer. A thin person with no food in his stomach, gulping down a quart of 100-proof whiskey will experience a reaction quite different from that of a heavy person with a full stomach, who nurses a fifth of 80-proof whiskey over a six-hour period.

Alcoholism?

I've seen many people who have had some vague awareness that they, or their partners, were drinking more than they used to and that their weekly expenditure for whiskey (or whatever it is they like best) had risen over the years, or months, but who did not feel that they had a drinking problem. Certainly, they did not consider themselves "alcoholics." However, there are several specific and objective signals that spell out the existence or the beginnings of alcoholism. Anyone who engages in all, or some, of the following drinking behaviors should acknowledge the fact that drinking *is* a problem and take steps to control it:

1. *Morning drinking.* Do you or your partner begin the day with alcohol?
2. *Solitary drinking.* Do you or your partner spend much time drinking alone?
3. *Absenteeism.* Do you or your partner tend to skip work on a Monday after a weekend brimful of alcohol?
4. *Blackouts.* Do they occur? Do you or your partner experience loss of memory after a drinking bout?
5. *Binges.* Do you or your partner drink for long periods of time and/or stay drunk for several days on end?
6. *Anxiety obliteration.* Do you or your partner automatically reach for the bottle in stressful or frustrating situations, or when social relationships become strained?

One cannot begin to extinguish problem drinking behaviors without first acknowledging that the problems do in fact exist. Neither can one begin a treatment program unless one has decided unequivocally that nondrinking is a positive, worthwhile goal. Finally, when one partner has a drinking problem while the other does not, the nondrinking spouse must observe and perhaps modify his/her behavior to make sure that it does not help perpetuate the other's drinking. The wife who continues to criticize her husband for being a "drunken louse" when he has successfully refrained for a week, may be the very factor that drives him straight back to the bottle. Nondrinking partners *must* encourage and praise their spouses for demonstrating control, and at the same time do everything within their power to ignore drinking behaviors when and if they recur.

Assuming the problem is acknowledged, then, and that a

decision has been made to take steps to control it—and also that one's partner is anxious to cooperate—one is ready for a treatment program. This should always begin by consulting with a therapist trained in treating alcoholism. The specific procedure may vary according to the individual and the therapist, but the problem drinker can expect some or all of the following to enter into the program.

1. *Detoxification*: This is the process by which alcohol is cleared from the system. The person who has been drinking for several days or weeks will need detoxification and a ten-to-fifteen-day stay at a detoxification center may be suggested.

2. *Antabuse* (*Disulfiram*): Usually in pill form, Antabuse (which is administered only under the direction of a physician) causes a violent physical reaction—vomiting, flushing, rapid pulse and breathing, pain around the heart—if drinking occurs within ten days after ingestion. Because it results in such severe negative consequences, Antabuse encourages the development of nondrinking behavior patterns.

*3. *Alcoholics Anonymous*: A therapist may encourage the problem drinker to join this well-known organization. More than 400,000 A.A. members in 140,000 A.A. groups help each other overcome alcoholism. The only membership requirement is the desire to stop drinking. The program is based on the belief that a former alcoholic is the best person to help another drinker with his/her problem. Each new member accepts a former alcoholic as "sponsor," and close, nondrinking friend who may be called upon for support and encouragement whenever the urge to drink is felt. Frequent meetings provide additional social support for not drinking.

---

* For further information about Alcoholics Anonymous, consult the Yellow Pages of the telephone directory. If you find no A.A. chapter listed in your area, write to General Service of Alcoholics Anonymous, P.O. Box 459, Grand Central Post Office, New York, N.Y. 10017.

4. *Other procedures*: Some people have negative feelings about A.A. because of the religiosity of its approach and/or because its stated goal for its members is that they stop drinking *forever*.

While A.A. may be the best and only solution for some, many therapists are investigating the usefulness of training the individual to *control* drinking rather than to think in terms of total lifetime abstinence. When total abstinence is the treatment goal, "one little drink" becomes the source of enormous guilt and disappointment, often creating the additional anxiety and feelings of defeatism ("I just don't have what it takes") that send the drinker off on another binge.

Some therapists utilize a method that helps to develop *controlled* drinking behaviors by teaching the individual to recognize when the alcohol in his blood reaches a certain level—at which point he stops drinking.[2]

In another method, the drinker is trained out of alcoholic behaviors and into patterns of *moderate* social drinking. Instead of imbibing large amounts of hard liquor over short periods of time, behavioral techniques are used to encourage the drinker to prefer small quantities of mixed drinks to be sipped over longer periods of time.[3]

There are several other methods for controlling drinking behaviors under professional consideration now, and hopefully, drinker and therapist will explore together the possibilities inherent in all of them.

Abstinence Program

Though, as mentioned previously, I urge anyone with a drinking problem to consult a specially trained therapist, there may be instances (I can't imagine too many of them, however) when working with a therapist is not feasible. Where this is the case, the following program, which assumes that it is very difficult or impossible for the individual to stop drinking once he/she has begun, is suggested:

1. *Join Alcoholics Anonymous.*

2. *Attend A.A. meetings regularly:* Many new members can find any number of "pressing" reasons for skipping this or that meeting. Don't. It is extremely important to show up regularly.

3. *Rely on your sponsor:* When the urge to drink is felt, channel your energy into calling your A.A. sponsor for support and encouragement. Make the call when you first begin to think about that drink; don't wait until you've got the glass in your hand.

4. *Make your decision known:* Tell three people whom you would hate to disappoint—and whom you have not told before—that you have decided to control your drinking. Your minister (or priest, or rabbi), employer and children are usually most effective choices.

5. *Enlist your mate's cooperation:* Your husband or wife should take an active part in the program. He/she must reinforce your decision with supportive words and behaviors ("You can do it." "I have faith in your ability to see this thing through," etc.). Your mate should make a point of *daily* encouragement so long as you avoid drinking. It's been demonstrated that frequent encouragement to "stay straight," or "on the wagon," increases the probability that one will do so.

The Social Drinker

While many husbands and wives who drink in a "social" context—i.e., with clients at business lunches, at cocktail and dinner parties, at weekend and evening gatherings in their own homes, or in a bar or tavern as a routine part of the unwinding process after a hard day's work—exhibit none of the danger signals of real alcoholism, liquor may still be a disruptive element in their lives—and thus, in their marriages.

We've all known or heard of husbands and/or wives who

regularly make asses of themselves at parties and other social gatherings because of one, two, or three drinks too many. This kind of behavior usually is not only the source of much morning-after embarrassment to both partners but also makes the prospect of any get-together where liquor will be served an anxiety-producing one indeed for the more sober of the two.

And then there's the partner who gets downright mean and nasty after a few drinks. I'm thinking specifically now of a young husband we'll call Jerry. He liked to drink because he said he considered himself "an uptight person, and liquor loosens me up." However, though Jerry was nowhere near being an alcoholic (he drank on the average of only once or twice a month), when he *did* drink, he inevitably consumed far more than enough to produce the desired "loosening up" effect. In fact, while drinking, his emotional gears shifted rapidly from conviviality to querulousness to hostility, and it was his wife, Maureen, who suffered most on these occasions.

"I remember one party," she told me, "where Jerry had been standing around arguing with a bunch of guys for about half an hour, and I was getting tired and wanted to go home. I went up to him and he wouldn't pay attention to me and then I pulled on his sleeve and he turned around and *glared* at me with this look of . . . *hate*. And then he bellowed at me to 'get the hell out of here and leave me alone.' I drove home myself and Jerry came stumbling in an hour later. I was in bed, and he stomped into the room, pulled the blanket off me and slapped me twice across the face. He'd *never* do that sober. Never. Ever. But when he drinks he's a different person. Thank God he doesn't drink very often."

People who have difficulty managing their drinking behaviors may want to consider behavioral techniques that will help them achieve greater self-control. For some, "self-control" may be equated with reducing the *amount* of alcohol consumed; for others, reducing the number of *occasions* on which it is consumed; and for still others, it may mean no more drinking whatsoever. The following suggestions can help establish "controlled" drinking behaviors more in line with whatever one's own version of "self-control" happens to be. (I suggest not drinking at all for two or three days before beginning this program.)

1. *Decide to limit your drinking:* Consume only what you feel is a "reasonable" amount. This may vary from individual to individual, depending on one's definition of what's reasonable. For many, however, two ounces or less of hard liquor during any twenty-four-hour period is "reasonable." (This sounds pretty reasonable to me, too.)

2. *Establish contingencies:* If you use alcohol daily and wish to continue to do so, make an agreement with yourself that each day's drinking is contingent upon not exceeding your limit on the previous day. In other words, the positive consequence of drinking a "reasonable" amount one day, is the privilege of doing the same the following day. The negative consequences of not staying within your pre-established limit is *no* drinking the following day, and in addition, the forfeiting of some enjoyable daily activity (such as watching TV, or reading the newspaper, etc.).

If you drink only occasionally—say, only at parties or other social gatherings—but tend to go overboard when you do, you can establish a two-drink limit and develop a contingency whereby the positive consequence of drinking no more than your quota are the privileges of staying at the party, attending the next party, and enjoying some other infrequently engaged in behavior that is particularly rewarding (going to the opera or the theater, if this is something you'd like to do more often; or perhaps getting tickets to some big upcoming sporting event, etc.). The negative consequences of exceeding the two-drink limit would be leaving the party immediately, forfeiting the privilege of attending the next party, and giving up some other pleasurable activity (such as not going to the movies for a month, or not playing cards for two weeks, etc.).

3. *Make your decision known:* Tell three people whom you would hate to disappoint (and whom you have not told before) that you have decided to limit your drinking. As previously suggested, your minister (or priest, or rabbi), your employer and your children are good choices.

4. *Plan your behavior:* When you order your second drink, tell the bartender that under no circumstances should he serve you a third. (You might want to reinforce the bartender's behavior here by telling him that you will continue to frequent his tavern if he does in fact refuse you that third drink.) When you've finished the second drink, stand up, leave the bar, and keep on going until you reach home.

If you are drinking at a party, *you* must be responsible for refusing the third drink. A simple "No, thank you," will do.

5. *Enlist your mate's cooperation:* Your husband or wife should take an active part by noticing and rewarding the desired behaviors ("you're great . . . when you make a decision, you really stick to it," etc.), while ignoring any slip-ups.

When Drinker Marries Nondrinker

Most often, like marries like, but I know of several relationships where one partner drinks moderately and the other not at all. This is all well and good except in those instances where the nondrinker finds it difficult to tolerate his/her partner's drinking behaviors, temperate though they may be. What the nondrinker may not be aware of is that fussing about the matter and attempting to deny the partner the freedom to drink in moderation may only encourage the partner to drink *more*.

There are three rather simple ways to help the nondrinking spouse develop a more tolerant and flexible attitude toward his/her mate's drinking:

In the first, the nondrinker is encouraged to drink all liquids out of a glass or container similar to the one from which the partner sips alcoholic beverages. The wife of a beer drinker can take an empty beer can, remove the top, and use it for drinking her own water, soda, tea, etc. The husband of a martini drinker should use a martini glass for all his nonalcoholic beverages. This in an effort to change the "stimulus value" of beer can or martini glass by associating it with pleasurable reinforcers.[4] (It is often argued that the negative association with alcohol is avoided when the stimulus value of beer can or martini glass is changed.)

Next, since one is more inclined to tolerate certain behaviors if one's friends and associates tolerate those same behaviors, the nondrinking partner should discuss with people he/she likes and respects the positive feelings they have about their own mates' moderate drinking. (It can also be pointed out to the nondrinker that a number of responsible, respectable people do drink once in a while—as evidenced by the occasional newspaper or magazine photograph of statesmen, educators, philanthropists, etc., holding what is obviously a drink in one hand.)

Finally, it helps to establish a contingency whereby some of the enjoyable behaviors of the nondrinking partner depend upon his/her mate's moderate drinking. For example, only if Barton has a beer can Estoy, his wife, go shopping.

Drinking and Driving

The National Safety Council estimates that alcohol is a contributing factor in 50 percent of all fatal accidents. Someone else said it first, but I'll say it again here: If you drink, don't drive.

According to the Uniform Vehicle Code, alcohol concentration in the bloodstream of .10 percent is *prima facie* evidence of drunkenness. Usually, this level is reached with the consumption of between five and six ounces of liquor—at which point coordination is seriously impaired, along with the ability to operate a moving vehicle with any degree of skill and accuracy.

Married people can develop their own individual "safety devices," in the form of a contingency agreement specifying that should the partner ingest more than five ounces of liquor, he/she forfeits the privilege of driving home and must either (1) call a taxi, (2) call a sober friend, or (3) call the spouse for transportation. Subsequent stops at taverns or bars would be contingent on (1) having had no more than four ounces of liquor or (2) being driven home by someone sober. The negative consequences of not abiding by this agreement may be death.

Soft Drugs

In some circles, marijuana has replaced alcohol as the preferred refreshment. The legal issue aside (one of the negative consequences of using grass, of course, is the possibility of getting caught), the available research suggests that moderate pot smoking is probably harmless. But excessive indulgence by either partner can interfere with the good interaction necessary for a happy marriage.

Frank, a thirty-five-year-old bank executive who says he "works his tail off every day and hates every minute of it," and Yvonne, his thirty-two-year-old wife, had been party pot-smokers for a number of years. Within a period of several months, however, Yvonne began to notice that Frank's smoking was increasing, along with his job dissatisfaction. While Yvonne continued to turn on only at parties, Frank began to keep fairly large supplies of the stuff at home and would light up the minute he walked in the door each evening.

Though Frank insisted he enjoyed their quiet, relaxed evenings at home, Yvonne was disturbed because, when high, Frank was "off in a world of his own. He would go for hours, this dumb half smile on his face listening to music, and as for me, well, I might as well have been off somewhere by myself for all the attention I got. I mean, I don't mind smoking once in a while—it's a nice feeling. But *all* the time the way Frank does is dumb. I want to be with him, talk to him, find out how he's feeling and what he's thinking about. But it's like talking to a zombie. No response. Or else he just mumbles. It's no fun staying home with a zombie."

Her suggestions that Frank "lay off the grass," were repeated more and more frequently—and with ever-increasing vehemence. But they went unheeded and, in fact, Frank's reaction was to increase his smoking.

Yvonne was advised, since Frank seemed unwilling or unable to control his pot-smoking behavior but was very concerned about her unhappiness over the situation, to decide how much of his at-home smoking would be acceptable to her. She was to communicate this information to Frank, and then ask him to name his price so that they could go ahead and negotiate exchange contracts to encourage new pot-smoking behaviors.

She did. One joint per day seemed reasonable to her, and Frank's "price" was that Yvonne stop nagging him about what she called his "permissiveness" with the children, and also that she initiate intercourse more often. (Twice a week was what he wanted.)

In addition, it was suggested that because Frank's work made him so unhappy, and because this unhappiness undoubtedly constituted a large part of his need to escape into pot, he probably ought to consult a vocational specialist to investigate other avenues of employment.

Frank and Yvonne's contracts for new pot-smoking behaviors are reproduced here:

INDIVIDUAL CONTRACT: FRANK
PART I

To show my willingness to do my part in making our marriage happier, I agree to engage in the specified behavior(s) below. It is clear that engaging in the desirable behaivor(s) below results in a positive consequence just as failure to engage in the behavior(s) has a negative consequence. The terms of this contract are fixed for one week only. After one week, this contract may be extended or another contract developed.

Desirable behavior	Positive consequence Daily / Weekend		Negative consequence Daily / Weekend	
1. Smoke only one joint per day.	Listen to stereo tapes	Go to a rock concert or have friends over	No listening to stereo tapes	No concert, no friends
2. Smoke this joint after 10:00 P.M. and before 12:00 P.M.				

PART II

To demonstrate how often the above desirable behaviors occur, I agree to keep a daily record of my behaviors for the next seven days.

Behaviors to occur (1 and 2)								
2	Y	N	Y	Y	Y	N	Y	Y = Yes
1	Y	N	Y	Y	Y	N	Y	N = No
	1st	2nd	3rd	4th	5th	6th	7th	
			Days of Week					

A "Y" (Yes) was marked to indicate that the new behaviors (1 and 2) occurred. A "N" (No) was marked to indicate that the behaviors (1 and 2) did not occur. It is clear that Frank failed to engage in the desirable behavior on the second and sixth day. Hence, he forfeited the right to listen to stereo tapes on those days and to go to a concert or be with friends on the weekend.

PART III

To practice observing good behavior in my mate, I agree to keep a daily record of my mate's behavior for the next seven days.

   a) The behavior my mate has agreed to do more often is:

      1. No comments about my interaction with the kids, and

      2. Initiate intercourse twice weekly.

   b) The daily record of this behavior is as follows:

Behaviors to occur (1 and 2)								
2	Y	N	Y	Y	Y	N	Y	Y = Yes
1	Y	N	Y	Y	Y	N	Y	N = No
	1st	2nd	3rd	4th	5th	6th	7th	

Days of Week

A "Y" (Yes) was to indicate that the behaviors (1 and 2) occurred. A "N" (No) was marked to indicate that the behaviors (1 and 2) did not occur. It is clear that Yvonne did not do as she agreed to do on the second and sixth day.

INDIVIDUAL CONTRACT: YVONNE
PART I

To show my willingness to do my part in making our marriage happier, I agree to engage in the specified behaviors below. It is clear that engaging in the desirable behaviors below results in a positive consequence just as failure to engage in the behaviors has a negative consequence. The terms of this contract are fixed for one week only. After one week, this contract may be extended or another contract developed.

Desirable behaviors	Positive consequence Daily / Weekend		Negative consequence Daily / Weekend	
1. No comments about Frank's interaction with the kids	Reading	Free Saturday afternoons (a baby-sitter for the kids)	No reading	No free Saturdays Scrub and wax kitchen floor
2. Initiate intercourse twice per week.				

Part II

To demonstrate how often the above desirable behaviors occur, I agree to keep a daily record of my behaviors for the next seven days.

Behaviors to occur (1 and 2)								
2	Y	N	Y	Y	Y	N	Y	Y = Yes
1	Y	N	Y	Y	Y	N	Y	N = No
	1st	2nd	3rd	4th	5th	6th	7th	

Days of Week

A "Y" (Yes) was marked to indicate that the behaviors (1 and 2) occurred. A "N" (No) was marked to indicate that the behaviors (1 and 2) did not occur. It is clear that the desirable behaviors did not occur on days two and six. Hence, Yvonne forfeits the right to read on those days, and free Saturday afternoons, and she must scrub and wax the kitchen floor during the weekend.

Part III

To practice observing good behavior in my mate, I agree to keep a daily record of my mate's behavior for the next seven days.

a) The behavior my mate has agreed to do more often is:
   1. *Smoke only one joint per day, and*
   2. *Smoke this joint after 10:00* P.M. *and before 12:00* P.M.

Behaviors to occur (1 and 2)								
2	Y	N	Y	Y	Y	N	Y	Y = Yes
1	Y	N	Y	Y	Y	N	Y	N = No
	1st	2nd	3rd	4th	5th	6th	7th	

Days of Week

I will not discuss "hard," addictive drugs, such as heroin or cocaine, except to say that the problems imposed upon their users are very often of such magnitude that the addicted individual is unable to deal *alone* with them according to the behavioral procedures we've been concerned with here—which is not to say that behavioral techniques may not be called upon, but only to urge anyone who is on hard drugs to seek immediate, professional help.

———◦⟨∞⟩◦———

CHAPTER 7

When Parents
and In-laws
Are a Problem

IN-LAWS, AND ESPECIALLY mothers-in-law, have been good joke material for a long, long time. But when relationships with one's parents and in-laws pose a real threat to marital happiness—as they often do (hence, the jokes, I suppose) —there's no cause for laughter. Tears, in fact, are more appropriate.

I know several fortunate couples with no in-law problems to speak of. On the contrary, the positive interaction between the parents of both husband and wife and the couple themselves is a source of great delight and joy to all. There is a lovely clarity in these relationships. In each, the young partners consistently "choose" each other over their parents, while the parents, far from feeling hurt or rejected by the subsidiary roles they play in their childrens' lives, are happy with the situation, probably because they all have rich, full lives of their own.

This consistent choosing of spouse over parent seems to

me to be the key element in maintaining harmonious inter-action all around. It is unusual, indeed, almost impossible, for an in-law problem to get out of hand when husband and wife value each other's happiness over that of their parents. On the other hand, I've seen some whopping big problems develop in those marriages where either one or both partners find it difficult to cut loose from their respective mothers and fathers, or where there is ambivalence about the "right-ness" of shifting one's primary allegiance and loyalty from parents to mate.

I've known many young married people who are torn between respect and regard for their parents' wishes and the desire to please their partners—and in a situation where the parents want one thing while the partner wants another, these husbands and wives are literally at a loss as to how to proceed. One case comes to mind here as a particularly vivid example of this kind of conflict: The husband wanted to move to a new city; his wife's parents wanted the couple to stay where they were, and the wife got caught in the middle. Clearly, she had to make a choice. But which choice? If she went along with her husband, she'd alienate her parents. If she sided with her parents, she'd hurt her husband.

The situation, or some variation of it, is not uncommon. Whenever husbands or wives are faced with circumstances that make a decision between parents and spouse inevitable, *they must* make an effort to predict and evaluate the con-sequences of deciding either way. It sometimes helps to ask the following questions:

1. Do you presently spend more time with your spouse or parents?
2. In the next year, will you spend more time with your spouse or parents?
3. If you decide in favor of your spouse, will happiness with your spouse be changed or increased?
4. If you decide in favor of your spouse, will happiness

with your parents be decreased, unchanged, or increased?

5. If you decide in favor of your parents, will happiness with your parents be unchanged or increased?
6. If you decide in favor of your parents, will happiness with your spouse be decreased, unchanged, or increased?

If your answers to the above six questions are: spouse, spouse, increased, decreased, increased and decreased, the consequence of deciding in favor of your spouse will produce more happiness with your spouse more of the time. If your answers are: spouse, spouse, unchanged, decreased, increased, and unchanged, the consequences of deciding in favor of your parents will be greater parental happiness with little sacrifice of happiness with your spouse.

As mentioned before, the difference between a marriage that is relatively free of in-law problems and the one that suffers because of them often is due to the ambivalent attitude of the partner(s). When there are good, loving feelings between husband and wife, it is "right" for them to do what makes each other happy—even if it makes the parents unhappy.

If the parents are disturbed by a decision made in favor of the partner, then it is, perhaps unfortunately, the *parents'* problem. I know that people who love and respect their mothers and fathers can take little comfort from this statement, but let's remember that the point of this book is to suggest ways to enhance the *marital* relationship and not how to smooth the ruffled feathers of those mothers and fathers who cannot quite accept the fact that their darling fledglings have left the nest and have lives of their own to live.

I remember a dark, slender twenty-three-year-old wife who was dreadfully upset because of her parents' attitude toward her husband, Bud. She told me her mother and father did not like Bud because he was, in their words, "just a no-good mechanic." The parents had denied themselves much in the way of material goods in order to send Martha to college. They wanted a good education for their only child, but perhaps even more than that, they'd wanted to see her "well-married." As an auto mechanic, Bud did not live up to their own hopes and expectations, and even after the marriage (which they'd done everything in their power to stop), they openly scorned their son-in-law.

Martha said she loved her parents but couldn't bear their overt rejection of the man she "so admired and adored." When asked whether she felt her parents feelings about Bud were justified, her answer was a tearful but emphatic "NO." It was suggested to Martha that since she felt her parents' attitude was unwarranted, their unhappiness over Martha's marriage was, after all, their problem and not hers. On this basis, Martha decided to tell her mother and father that if they could not learn to accept Bud—if they did not at least try to demonstrate courteous, civil behaviors when the couple came to visit—she would simply stop seeing them. (This, incidentally, is a good example of contingency management with those other than oneself or one's spouse.)

Martha's story had a happy ending. When she had defined her own values for herself and then communicated them to her parents, her mother and father did make the effort to warm up to Bud and the relationship between the four of them has improved considerably.

Mother Never Did It That Way

No husband or wife likes to be unfavorably compared to his/her partner's parents. Yet, young wives continue to remind their husbands that "Daddy always knew how to fix things for himself. He never had to call a carpenter (plumber, plasterer, etc.) like you do." Or some such. And young husbands frequently comment that "Mom's meat loaf was great. Why can't you make it like she did?" etc. Negative verbal comparisons to one's parents are *always* disturbing to one's mate, and any husband or wife who engages in this behavior on anything like a frequent basis is in for trouble. And so is the marriage.

If this is a problem in your house, I suggest you try the procedure outlined below, designed to decrease the frequency of making negative verbal comparisons:

First, since it's a fairly common one, let's assume a situation where the husband is in the habit of making negative comparisons between his wife's cooking and "Mom's," though of course the procedure can be adapted by either partner to any similar situation.

1. *Develop contingency contracts:* The wife should communicate to her husband the specific behaviors that cause her displeasure. For example, Carol said, "Jerry, one of the

INDIVIDUAL CONTRACT: HUSBAND

PART I

To show my willingness to do my part in making our marriage happier, I agree to engage in the behaviors specified below. It is clear that engaging in these behaviors results in positive consequences, just as failure to engage in them has a negative consequence. The terms of this contract are fixed for one week only. After one week, this contract may be extended or another contract developed.

Desirable behavior	Positive consequence Daily / Weekend		Negative consequence Daily / Weekend	
Compliment wife twice daily on her cooking.	Reading *Wall Street Journal*	Golf	No reading *Wall Street Journal*	No golf

things you can do to make me happier is to notice when I cook something you like and tell me that it pleases you. It hurts me to hear about your mother's cooking all the time." The couple can then go on to develop appropriate contingency contracts that will help to extinguish the husband's undesirable behavior. An example may be helpful.

PART II

In addition to the above, I agree to keep a daily record of my behavior for the next seven days.

One behavior is to occur*	1	Y	Y	N	N	Y	Y	Y	Y=Yes N=No
		1st	2nd	3rd	4th	5th	6th	7th	

Days of Week

---

* The chart clearly indicates that Jerry did not compliment Carol twice per day on two out of seven days. Hence, he forefeited the right to read the *Wall Street Journal* on the days following his oversight, and gave up his golf game on the weekend.

PART III

To practice observing good behavior in my mate, I agree to keep a daily record of her behavior for the next seven days.
 a) The behavior my mate has agreed to do more often is: *Thank me for complimenting her about her cooking.*
 b) The daily record of this behavior is as follows:

One behavior is to occur*	1	Y	Y	N	N	Y	Y	Y	Y=Yes N=No
		1st	2nd	3rd	4th	5th	6th	7th	

Days of Week

---

* It is clear that Carol did not thank Jerry on the third and fourth day of the contract since he gave her nothing to thank him for.

2. *Reward desirable behavior:* In accordance with the contingency contracts developed by the couple, when the husband makes a positive comment about his wife's cooking ("Terrific dinner, Carol," or, "Wow, let's have more of that dessert.") she should smile, perhaps hug and kiss him, and of course say "Thank you; I'm glad you liked it so much." By rewarding his verbal appreciation of her cooking, he will be more inclined to repeat the compliments.

3. *Ignore undesirable behavior:* When the husband slips up and compares his wife's cooking to his mother's, the wife should avoid making any overt negative response. To launch a verbal counterattack would be at least as unproductive as crying, though changing the subject or quietly withdrawing from the room are often effective ignoring techniques. By not responding in a negative way to her husband's "comparing" behavior, the wife discourages the frequency with which he engages in it.

4. *Control unwanted thoughts:* When the wife experiences angry feelings as a result of thinking about her husband's past (or occasional present) negative comments about her cooking, she should apply the stop-think technique. I've mentioned it before, but it's worth running through again: Positive thoughts about their relationship ("I am happy with my husband." "We're going to have fun on our vacation this summer." "I enjoy being with him.") should be jotted down on 3 x 5 file cards. As she feels hostile thoughts surfacing, she should yell "Stop!," and focus her attention to the positive aspects of their relationship, as noted on the file cards.

5. *Modeling:* Ideally, the husband should be able to identify from among his friends, business associates, and neighbors, those men who pay frequent compliments to their own wives—and whose wives in turn reinforce them for doing so. In this way, the husband has the opportunity to observe someone he likes engaging in behavior he would like to cultivate in himself. (Here's a thought: Wangle an

invitation to dinner with some notoriously happy couple.)

I cannot stress too much the importance of learning to choose partner over parent, and this concept includes complimenting one's partner for desirable behavior rather than making negative comparisons to one's mother or father. Husbands and wives are happiest and continue to engage in pleasing, positive behaviors when they feel they are primarily responsible for their mate's happiness.

"But I just don't like my in-laws"

Some husbands and wives simply do not like their partners' parents. But wait a minute. Maybe these negative feelings are not so simple after all. Maybe they occur as a result of the in-laws' behavior—things they've done (or not done) and said (or not said).

I remember talking with a husband who told me that his mother-in-law had taken him aside one day and told him she was wise to what he was doing. Puzzled, he asked what she meant. She went on to say that she knew about his affair with X and that he certainly wasn't pulling the wool over *her* eyes. This man insisted that he'd never had an affair with X, or anyone else for that matter, and their little tête à tête resulted in their not speaking for five years, even though they continued to live next door to each other. Incredible? Sure. But stranger things do happen.

Although partner and in-laws may harbor very bad feelings about one another, I think it's better for all concerned when outright expressions of these bad feelings are avoided. It may afford some momentary sense of relief to come out with it—to call one's wife's mother a "witch," or a "bitch," or one's husband's father a "lazy, no-good bastard," but consider the very real possibility that in doing so, one not only widens the gap between self and in-law but also very probably gives pain to one's partner.

Many husbands and wives can understand and accept a

situation where their partners do not like their parents, but unless they, too, have come to share in their partners' estimation of the parents' worth as people ("You're absolutely right, Sue; my Dad is as no-good as they come"), open expressions of hostility put them on the spot: It is one thing to decide in favor of one's partner when the outcome of some issue is at stake (such as choosing where the couple will live, which financial decisions they will make, how they will raise their children, etc.), but quite another to be expected to stand by and hear one's parents derided as "lazy bums," "lower-class slobs," "bourgeois pigs," "witches," "bitches," "bastards," and the like.

The procedure outlined below may be helpful when the goal is to cultivate better interaction (and this, in some cases, may mean little more than a live-and-let-live attitude) between married people and their in-laws.

1. *Apply behavioral principles to in-laws:* This is not always easy to do, but an attempt to modify the in-laws' upsetting behavior may be the quickest way to improve relations all around.

Let's imagine a situation where the wife has negative feelings about her husband's mother because she (the mother-in-law) phones every day to find out how her son is feeling, whether he's eating well, smoking too much, moving his bowels, whatever. In a case like this, the wife is going to feel better immediately if the mother-in-law can be persuaded to stop the daily phone calls. The goal may be accomplished if both partners communicate to the in-law their new expectations, and at the same time establish contingencies based upon them.

The wife and her husband should phrase their desires tactfully but firmly. A sample conversation might go something like this: "Mother, we enjoy talking to you and being with you, but there's no need for you to call every day. If something goes wrong, we'll be sure to let you know.

We'd like you to develop other relationships and not be so wrapped up in us. You have a standing invitation to dinner here on Wednesday and Sunday evenings. However, you may visit us on those days only if you do not call or visit on other days. Of course, you know you can always get in touch with us if there's an emergency."

This kind of communication indicates (a) concern and affection for the parent, (b) a desire to see her form other close relationships, (c) a contingency (time spent with her son is contingent on not making daily phone calls), and (d) a promise of aid and support in case of an emergency.

2. *Establish contingencies with partner:* When it doesn't seem possible to modify the behavior of the in-law (or in those cases where it is the *partner* who is overreacting to the in-laws relatively inoffensive behaviors), the couple can arrange a contingency to decrease the frequency of disturbing negative remarks.

If, for example, Bill—justifiably or not—has something vicious to say about Mary's mother at the rate of about twice a day (or approximately fourteen times a week), he can, if he is sufficiently concerned with Mary's pained reaction to those remarks, establish a contract with himself whereby he agrees to read the newspaper and watch TV (or engage in some other enjoyable daily behavior) only as long as he makes fewer nasty references to his mother-in-law.

After he is successful in decreasing the number of negative statements to one a day for seven days, he can agree to a new contingency whereby enjoyable behaviors are dependent on making fewer than seven critical remarks during the next week. And so on. He could continue to reduce the frequency of vicious remarks about his mother-in-law until, finally, he would engage in enjoyable behaviors only if he does not criticize her at all.

Mary, of course, can help Bill along by noticing those times when he has said nothing—or better still, made some *positive* comment—about her mother, telling him how good it makes her feel, and complimenting him on the success of his efforts to change. Conversely, she should ignore his failure to curb critical remarks.

Civility

Sometimes tactful, courteous behavior will have to suffice for genuine feelings of warmth and affections for one's in-laws. Civility can be encouraged by establishing an exchange contract, with each partner rewarding the appropriate behaviors of the other.

Let's assume that Marilyn is habitually rude and impolite to Nash's parents. (Maybe because they, in turn, were critical of her decision to return to work soon after the children were born. Or maybe because she simply finds them rather boring and difficult people to deal with. In this case, the reason for her rudeness doesn't matter.) Let's also assume that attempts to change Nash's parents' behavior were unsuccessful.

Nash and Marilyn must first specify what constitutes "tactful, courteous behavior." For our purposes here, let's say it has been defined as "making positive statements." Their exchange contract, then, is based on the idea of encouraging Marilyn to make more frequent positive statements to her in-laws.

EXCHANGE CONTRACT

PART I

Since I am aware that if our marriage is to be a happy one, we must do things for each other, I agree to make positive statements to Nash's parents if, in return, he will agree to thank me for making positive statements to them.

PART II

To demonstrate how often the desirable behavior occurs, I agree to keep a record of my behavior on those days when his parents visit.

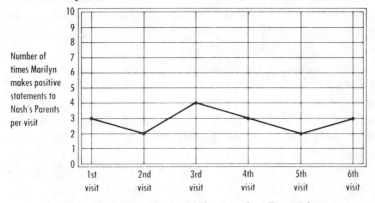

The chart indicates that Marilyn made 17 positive statements to Nash's parents on 6 occasions.

PART III

To practice observing good behavior in my mate, I agree to keep a record of my mate's behavior for the next 6 occasions when Nash's parents visit.

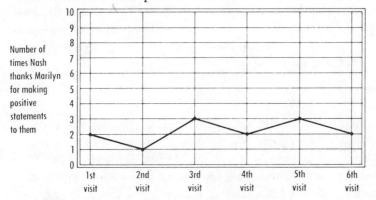

Nash thanked Marilyn for making positive statements 13 times on 6 occasions.

Visitation Rights

When one partner is bored, irritated, or inevitably comes away disturbed after a long visit with his/her in-laws, the couple may decide that it is in everyone's best interest for the other partner to visit his/her parents *alone*, and for a specified period of time, while the mate engages in some other, more enjoyable activity.

For example, if Carol, a city girl at heart, dreads visiting John's parents, who live in the country several hundred miles away, John probably ought to go and see them by himself (or perhaps with the children) over two or three long weekends during the year. During the time John is away, Carol is free to visit with friends, or her own parents, or to otherwise enjoy herself as she sees fit. With this kind of contingency, both partners can develop more positive attitudes about John visiting his parents.

Where there are great differences of opinion in regard to the amount of time each partner wants to spend with his/her parents, a compromise—backed up by a contingency agreement—should be made. Let's say John really would enjoy spending a month with his parents down on the farm, while Carol feels uncomfortable at the prospect of being apart from John for much more than a week. A fair settlement would lie somewhere in between—two weeks or so—and both could agree to make certain pleasurable activities contingent on the compromise.

When In-laws Live In

I've known some happily married couples who've avoided in-law problems simply by making the decision not to see them at all. Most of these people live far away from both sets of parents, though a few manage to maintain their distance even though they live within just a few miles of their respective mothers and fathers.

Way over at the opposite end of the spectrum are those husbands and wives whose parents live with them. Or would like to. When both partners are in favor of having a parent (or parents) sharing their home, the situation can be a good one for all involved. At one time, long before anyone ever talked about such things as "nuclear families," these arrangements were common; it was taken for granted that elderly or widowed parents would be supported by their children and in turn would take on some of the responsibilities of running the household. Everyone—including the grandchildren, who were thus given the opportunity to form close ties with people other than their own parents—benefited.

Obviously, though, when one partner likes the idea of living with a parent, while the other views the prospect with distaste, there are going to be problems.

The decision to welcome a parent permanently into one's home becomes an especially delicate one when the parent is widowed, ill, or very lonely. The son or daughter of such a parent feels caught in a bind: either abandon the parent, or bring unhappiness to the partner.

In order to make a decision, the couple must identify issues and clarify their values, both to themselves and to each other. Two primary questions arise: Who has what problem? And whose problem is more important?

An example may help: Stan and Barbara, two very verbal and articulate young people, both of whom teach at a local college, were married for nine relatively happy years. When Barbara's father died of a stroke, her fifty-year-old mother (let's call her Greta) went into an immediate and understandable depression. However, after two years of living alone and mourning, Greta had established patterns of dependency on Stan and Barbara and had made no effort to begin a new life of her own. She complained of loneliness, but said she knew no one—aside from Stan and Barbara—with whom she wanted to live. Rejecting the idea of living with an older, unmarried sister because they did not get along, and repelled by the idea of placing an ad in a newspaper to explore the possibility of living with another older woman, she began to plead with Barbara to take her in.

Stan, though, is a man who places a high value on privacy. This, coupled with the fact that he did not particularly like Greta—had never liked her, since she had objected to his marrying Barbara in the first place—resulted in his threatening to move out if Greta moved in. Although he told me he loved Barbara, he could envision no happiness in their staying together under one roof with Greta.

There are two issues here: Greta's loneliness and Stan's unhappiness. It was up to Barbara to decide which was more important—alleviating her mother's feeling of being alone, or maintaining a loving relationship with her husband. The consequence of taking responsibility for Greta's problem was the ruination of her own marriage. The consequence of saving her marriage was that Greta would continue to feel lonely.

Barbara decided in favor of keeping her husband, reasoning that Greta's unwillingness to seek other companionship and her inability to develop new relationships were problems that Greta would have to deal with for herself.

I'm aware that, compared to some, Barbara's decision was a relatively easy one. Her mother was neither very old nor very ill, and Barbara sincerely believed that Greta was capable of making a new life for herself—on her own. I know of other instances where the partners had to choose between living with an aged or ill parent or sending him/her to a nursing home, and in these cases the decision was always much harder to make. Though each couple must choose the course of action that best suits them, the elements that must be considered on the way to coming to a decision are always the same: issues must be identified and values clarified. Then two questions must be asked: Who had what problem? Whose problem is more important to the couple?

When In-laws Dislike In-laws

This can almost always be considered as the respective parents' problem. The married couple themselves probably ought to stay safely out of the way. In other words, if Harold rather likes Jan's parents and she his, they needn't worry too much if their in-laws don't see eye to eye. I wouldn't suggest inviting trouble by planning get-togethers that include both sets of parents, but otherwise the whole situation can be ignored.

The Partner Who Needs Weaning

Unlike the love relationship between partners, the usual ties of mutual affection and interdependency between parent and child are strongest in the early stages. As the child grows toward maturity, he/she also tends to separate from the parents. One might almost say that the most "successful" parents are the ones whose sons and daughters are able to leave them—to marry, to establish homes of their own, and to feel comfortable about making independent decisions.

Dependent behavior, expressed by the need to rely on some other person for information, advice, and assistance, like all other behavior, is learned. Parents often, and sometimes without meaning to, encourage dependent behavior in their children. Mothers and fathers may delight in daily phone calls or visits from their married children and welcome the opportunity to continue to act as protectors and counselors to their offspring. They may even send gifts of cash, etc., in direct proportion to the amount of support (emotional as well as financial) solicited by their "kids."

Depending on one's parents is neither "good" nor "bad" in itself. The rightness or wrongness of dependency can only be judged in terms of its degree and, more importantly, the consequences. In other words, if the husband's habit of consulting with his father before making any move of his own, if the wife's habit of calling her mother for moral support every single day of the week, interferes with personal growth —i.e., the ability to function independently when necessary —(as such extreme behaviors probably do); or, if these behaviors are a source of marital conflict (as they often are), then the consequences are negative and the behaviors should be modified.

Bill, a thirty-two-year-old salesman, and June, his thirty-year-old wife of eight years, had difficulties in this area. When Bill had a problem, he took it straight to his parents. Even during those periods when his life was relatively problem-free, he either phoned or visited his mother daily. June felt very much left out of things. She told me she had always been "an 'observer,' looking on while the three of them—Bill, his mother, and his dad—worked through Bill's life together. Just as disturbing to her as the feeling of being an outsider was the idea that at thirty-two her husband still had the *need* to "run home to Mommy and Daddy" for guidance, consolation, support, etc. "Emotionally, he's still a baby, and . . . well . . . I'm not sure I want to spend the rest of my life with a grown-up baby."

Bill himself was disturbed by his "grown-up baby" status; and his desire to be able to function more independently was a sincere one, but he didn't quite know how to go about "weaning" himself from his parents.

Thus, the following procedure was suggested as a way for Bill to decrease the frequency of dependent behaviors:

1. *Record baseline data:* Bill defined "dependency" in terms of his need to call and/or visit his parents. He was instructed to collect baseline data by charting the frequency

of calls and visits to his parents during a typical seven-day period.

2. *Develop contracts:* It was suggested that Bill make some of his enjoyable activities contingent on calling or visiting his parents less frequently than he did during the seven-day period when baseline data was collected.

His contract (actually, a *series* of contracts) went something like this:

BILL'S CONTRACT

Desirable behavior: functioning without contacting parents
Present frequency: 12 visits or calls per week
Desired frequency of behavior: 3 visits or calls per week

Reinforcers:	Behaviors	Frequency of behavior
	Reading	50 pages daily
	Tennis	once each week

CONTRACT I: First week

I agree to call or visit my parents a maximum of 9 times during the next week. I also agree that I will only read and play tennis the following week if I have limited contact with my parents to 9 times. I further agree to keep a chart near the phone to remind me of how many calls and/or visits I have made.
Goal of first week: reduce number of contacts with parents to 9
Signed _____
Date _____   Goal accomplished? Yes _____

CONTRACT II: Second week

Execute the second contract only after accomplishing the goals of the first contract. The terms of Contract II require an additional reduction in number of contacts with parents by 3. Hence, reading and tennis for next week are contingent on calling and/or visiting parents on 6 occasions.

Goal of second week: reduce number of contacts with parents to 6

Signed _____

Date _____   Goal accomplished? Yes _____

CONTRACT III: Third week

Reduce the number of contacts with the parents by 3 after fulfilling the terms of Contract II.

Goal of third week: reduce number of contacts with parents to 3

Signed _____

Date _____   Goal accomplished? Yes _____

(Notice that this contract involves a gradual reduction in the undesirable behavior and, illustrates the principle of shaping.)

3. *Reward desirable behavior.* June was encouraged to keep an eye on Bill's chart. When it indicated a decrease in the frequency of phone calls and visits to his parents, she was to reward him with smiles, hugs, kisses, and comments about how much better she felt about him and their relationship.

This is another story with a relatively happy ending. Bill phones or visits his mother and father at the rate of about twice a week now, and June reports that since the frequency of contact with his parents is so drastically reduced, Bill is undertaking to make more and more decisions on his own, or cooperatively with her.

The relationship between parents and their married children can be a rich and rewarding one, and like all other relationships must be cultivated, nurtured, and managed to survive. But where partner and parent are bound together in such close association that personal and marital happiness are affected, the ties must be loosened so that each has room to grow and function independently.

CHAPTER 8

When Friends Are a Problem

No MAN IS an island. And neither is any married couple. No matter how remote or removed we may be from the urban centers of our world, there are very few among us who do not have friends, neighbors, and business associates with whom to deal—if not daily, than at least often enough that relations with these others have a substantial impact on our lives, and often on our marriages.

Good mutual friends add significantly to the happiness of any marriage. But what about other friends? *His* friends? *Her* friends? As opposed to *our* friends? There are any number of variations on the theme of *why* one partner dislikes the friend(s) of the other.

The Discourteous Friend

At its very simplest, an initial personal contact with the friend of one's spouse may have been unpleasant. When Sylvia was introduced to Harold (her husband's friend) at a party, he mumbled "hello" and immediately excused himself. The consequence of Harold's behavior is predictable:

Sylvia dislikes Harold because he was discourteous. She has no basis on which to like him.

The "Bad-influence" Friend

One partner may dislike a particular friend of the other's because the friend appears to be a (perhaps potentially) bad influence. Shakespeare's Falstaff says "My friends have been the spoil of me," meaning that the wastrels with whom he associated encouraged him to engage in similar riotous behavior. "Modeling" is implied here, and our friend Sylvia may fear, and rightly so, that if her husband, Charles, consorts with the likes of Jay over there, who not only drinks too much but makes no secret of his many extramarital affairs, Charles may come to view these behaviors with greater tolerance. In fact, the probability that Charles will drink and consider having an affair may increase in proportion to the time he spends with Jay, since Jay spends his leisure hours drinking and chasing after women.

But wait a minute. Charles is—as we all are—responsible for his own behavior. If Charles notices a tendency within himself to drink more and think more about other women as a result of his friendship with Jay, he should reexamine their relationship. Assuming he is happy with Sylvia, he owes it to her, to himself, and to Jay to terminate the friendship. ("It's easier for me to go straight, Jay, when you and I spend less time together. See you around.")

Marie, a pale, blonde woman in her early thirties, dislikes Ben's friend George because George has a tendency to live above his means. She noticed that when they went out with George and his wife, they invariably dined in more expensive restaurants than she and Ben would have chosen on their own, that Ben overtipped, and in general spent more freely.

She discussed the situation with Ben, who, after sorting out his thoughts on the matter agreed that, like Marie, he valued paying bills on time and saving for the future over and above living up to George's impression of him as a big spender. As a result of their discussion, he explained to George that while he, Ben, did not necessarily disapprove of George's life-style, for *George*, it was distinctly not his own, nor was it Marie's.

The Monopolizing Friend

Sometimes one partner dislikes the other's friend because the friend takes up too much of the mate's time and attention. "Dislike" is perhaps the wrong word to use here; "jealousy" is probably more to the point.

Consider the case of Bill and Elaine and Elaine's friend Rachel. Bill has negative feelings about Rachel because Elaine and Rachel are, as he put it, "thick as thieves." The two women had gotten into the habit of spending Saturday afternoons in town together, going to museums and galleries, visiting boutiques, and antique shops. Bill was at first delighted, because it took some of the pressure off him (he personally had no interest in doing any of these things, and Elaine no longer nagged him to do so). But as months passed and the friends spent more and more time together and stayed out later and later, his feelings of delight turned to anger. Once, Elaine and Rachel dragged in, tired but happy, at 8:00 P.M., and then—insult on injury!—Rachel stayed on to dinner. Bill could hardly bring himself to say a civil word to either of them.

Elaine is too fond of Rachel to consider terminating their friendship, and even Bill would be reluctant to suggest that she do so. He does however resent having to be away from his wife all day every Saturday. After explaining his feelings to Elaine, she agreed that she would spend no more than four hours with Rachel on any given Saturday afternoon.

In order to make sure the desired change did occur, they drew up the following contract.

ELAINE'S CONTRACT

Desirable behavior	Positive consequence	Negative consequences
Spend no more than four hours in town with Rachel on Saturday afternoons	Four hours in town with Rachel the following Saturday afternoon	Forfeit Saturday afternoon in town with Rachel; wash the car; clean out the garage

I, Elaine, agree to spend no more than four hours in town with my friend Rachel on any given Saturday afternoon. The positive consequence of abiding by the terms of this agreement are four hours in town with Rachel the following Saturday. The negative consequences of not abiding by this agreement are forfeiting the following Saturday in town with Rachel and spending the time instead on washing the car and cleaning out the garage.

Another way to approach this particular kind of problem would be for Elaine and Bill to agree that she would spend no more than three hours in town with Rachel on one Saturday, and no more than five hours in town with Rachel the following Saturday.

A variation of this second approach would be for Elaine to spend only alternate Saturdays in town with Rachel and the other Saturdays with Bill. A contingency contract specifying the terms of such an agreement might read something like this:

I, Elaine, agree to spend every other Saturday in town with Rachel and to spend alternate Saturdays with Bill, fulfilling whatever plans he has made for these days. Furthermore, I agree to spend time with Rachel only if I have spent time with Bill the previous week, and that I will spend time with Bill only if he has not nagged me about spending time with Rachel the previous week.

Still another way to handle the same situation would be for Bill to enter into a contingency agreement with himself whereby he would decide to make some of his own pleasurable activities dependent upon Elaine's spending time with Rachel. Bill, for example, might go sailing, watch football on TV, or otherwise enjoy himself on Saturday afternoons only when, if, and as long as Rachel and Elaine are out of the house together. In this way, rather than sit and brood over Elaine's absence, he is encouraged to make good use of the time they spend apart.

Learning to Like Your Partner's Friends

Some husbands and wives are deeply troubled by the fact that their spouses display negative behaviors toward their friends.

"Vivian and I grew up together," Liz says. "She understands me and I understand her. We confide in each other and there's nothing we wouldn't do for one another. But Van doesn't like her and I'm miserable about it."

Liz would feel better if Van could develop a more positive attitude toward her friend. Liz and Van enjoy a good, loving relationship, and in order to make Liz happier, he agreed—though somewhat reluctantly—to try to like Vivian better.

Which is all very well and good, but how can Liz know that Van is making the effort unless he says and does things that indicate new positive feelings about her friend?

It was suggested that Liz make a list of the behaviors Van could engage in that would indicate to her that he likes Vivian. Here's an approximation of her list:

Van can:

1. Greet Vivian with a smile every time she visits their home.
2. Ask "How are you?" (and stick around to hear the answer) when he sees her or when she phones.
3. Suggest that Liz and Vivian go out to a movie together.

When Liz's list was completed, Van identified several behaviors that Liz could engage in to make him happy. His list went like this:

1. Golf with me on alternate Sundays.
2. Initiate intercourse twice a week.

With this information in hand, they drew up the following exchange contract:

VAN AND LIZ' EXCHANGE CONTRACT

Van: I agree to show my positive feelings about Vivian by engaging in the three behaviors specified on Liz' list if, in return, she will engage in the two behaviors specified on my list.

Liz: I agree to golf with Van on alternate Sundays and initiate intercourse twice a week if, in return, he will engage in the three behaviors specified on my list.

(It must be noted that this contract assumes that Vivian does not talk negatively to Van (i.e., she is reasonably polite to him most of the time), nor to Liz about Van.

Sometimes there's not much point in trying to reconcile one partner's feelings about the other partner's friend. I'm thinking now of those cases where a husband or wife doesn't simply *dislike* a particular friend of his/her mate's, but actually *hates* that person outright. For our purposes here, the reasons for such hate—though they may be intriguing in the extreme—are irrelevant. But where the situation exists, the partner is faced with choosing from among three alternatives: he/she must give up the friend, give up the mate, or manage both relationships in such a way that never the twain shall meet.

Debbie, a nurse and mother of three, and her insurance-salesman husband, Herman, rarely disagree except where Florence, Debbie's friend, is concerned. To Herman, Florence is "a crass, loud-mouth boor and a phony to boot," and the very sight of her is enough to upset him to the point where he feels he has to leave the room "to keep from socking that bitch in the mouth." To Debbie, Florence is "warm, spontaneous, earthy . . . really fun to be with. She knows how to bring me up when I'm down." (One gets the feeling they're referring to two very different people, but this is often the case in such a situation.)

Debbie arranged to see Florence during the day when Herman was at work, and occasionally they would get together on Wednesday nights when Herman attended classes at a nearby college. In other words, she continued to see Florence, but only at times when it was highly unlikely that the two of them would meet.

Needless to say, Debbie rarely mentioned Florence in conversation with Herman; but neither did she lead him to believe that they were no longer friends. As a matter of fact, Debbie and Herman established a contingency contract whereby Debbie would give Herman a massage—which he greatly enjoyed—only after she had spent time with Florence.

The situation was managed admirably. Herman never has to pretend to like Florence because he never sees her, but nice things happen to him (those massages) as a consequence of the continuing relationship between the two women.

Security Leaks: When the Ummentionable Gets Mentioned

In many marriages it is simply assumed that certain topics are not to be discussed with outsiders—that the things husband and wife do in bed, for example, or the amount of money they earn, or the problems they may be having with the children—are private. "Our" business. Not "theirs."

In other marriages there is no clear understanding of what each partner considers to be "confidential information." A young wife learned to her great dismay that her husband regarded discussion of their finances as taboo—only after she had gleefully informed half the neighborhood of his recent promotion and subsequent raise in pay, right down to the last dollar and cent.

I don't think it's a good idea to *assume* that one knows what one's mate considers "private and confidential." Rather, I suggest that each partner make clear to the other what information he/she regards as "mentionable" (i.e., okay to discuss with friends), and "unmentionable" (not fit for public consumption).

Even when these agreements have been made, however, some husbands and wives have a tendency to blurt out confidences—perhaps in an effort to impress; possibly as a bid for sympathy—often to their partners' great embarrassment or chagrin. When past experience indicates that one or both spouses are inclined to mention the unmentionable in their unguarded moments, they can draw up an exchange contract to discourage future security leaks. Here's an example of a contract drawn up by Doris and Bill:

OUR CONFIDENCE CONTRACT

Bill: I agree not to discuss our sex life with others if, in return, Doris will not discuss our finances. I also agree that I will use the stereo earphones during the week only if I have not discussed our sex life during the previous week.

Doris: I agree not to discuss our finances with others if, in return, Bill will not discuss our sex life. I also agree that I will watch TV during the week only if I have not discussed our finances during the previous week.

Bill and Doris can also make an effort to reinforce each others' new confidence-keeping behaviors. For example, in a social situation where the conversation seemed to be leading in that direction, Bill might praise Doris for *not* mentioning their debts ("I really appreciate the way you avoided talking about our finances when the Smiths started griping about their money problems"). Under similar circumstances, Doris, of course, would also reward Bill. And both of them in turn should express their pleasure at being praised for keeping up their end of the bargain.

No Friends?

Ours is a mobile society. We move often, leaving good friends behind, or when good friends move, we are left behind.

It is easy for some naturally outgoing, gregarious people to make friends in a new neighborhood, or to make new friends when old ones have moved away. Others do not fare so well.

Husbands and wives who need help in cultivating friendships with other couples should consider implementing a program similar to the one suggested to Nancy and Mel, who, after ten happy years of residence in midtown Manhattan, found themselves cast adrift—friendless and wretched because of it—on the shores of Long Island suburbia.

They were encouraged first to identify from among

their new neighbors those couples with whom they felt they might be compatible. Obviously, this was a hit-or-miss proposition, since they had no way of knowing beforehand whether these couples would indeed prove to be people they would ultimately enjoy. Still, it was necessary to make a start, so Mel chose the Browns (because Ted Brown has long hair—like Mel), and Nancy chose the Harringtons (because the Harrington kids were approximately the same ages as her own children).

To develop a friendship, it's necessary to engage in certain behaviors. Ordinarily, these behaviors occur spontaneously; hardly anyone thinks them through, and then implements them, in a methodical, step-by-step fashion. But under special circumstances, when couples are anxious to cultivate close relationships with others—as Nancy and Mel were— it is probably a good idea to do just that.

Among the behaviors that encourage the development of new friendships are (1) invitational behaviors, (2) engaging in other-oriented conversation, and (3) arranging frequent encounters.

(1) Invitational Behaviors: To get things moving, a couple must reach out to others. Usually, this means issuing invitations. Nancy walked two doors down to the Harringtons' split-level, introduced herself to Carol Harrington and invited Carol and her husband over for coffee the following evening. Similarly, Mel ambled over to Ted Brown, who was lovingly applying a coat of wax to his very obviously new Oldsmobile, made a few appropriately admiring comments about the car, and then suggested that Ted and his wife come over for a barbecue on Saturday afternoon.

It wasn't easy for either of them to initiate these contacts. Both were hampered by feelings of shyness and the fear of being rejected. So, to make it easier for themselves to make the first move, they drew up a "friendship contingency contract."

MEL AND NANCY'S FRIENDSHIP CONTRACT

We agree to hire a baby-sitter and go out together to dinner and a movie on Saturday night, only if we have invited the Browns and the Harringtons to our home during the previous week. We further agree that if either the Harringtons or the Browns refuse our invitation, we will invite some other couple in the neighborhood to our home.

(2) Engaging in "Other-oriented" Conversation: Relationships thrive when ideas as well as experiences are shared. Two-way (or in the case of couples, *four*-way) exchanges are implied. No matter how fascinating one's own life (ideas, interests, etc.) may be to oneself, it is rarely anywhere near as intriguing to anyone else. People who ramble on and on about themselves are turn-offs—and usually not very good candidates for potential friendship. So, whenever possible (and it almost always is), an effort should be made to encourage others to talk about themselves.[1]

(3) Arranging Frequent Encounters: Regardless of how promising or pleasurable an initial contact may be, incipient friendships wither away and die when there is no appropriate follow-up. Friends are acquaintances we've grown to know and love. Except in those few fortunate instances of immediate rapport, if we're going to know people better, we're going to have to see them with some degree of frequency.

Soon after Nancy and Mel's get-together with the Harringtons, the Harringtons responded by inviting them to dinner at their home. Nancy and Mel reciprocated. And so on. And on. The friendship was established.

The Browns didn't accept Mel's barbecue invitation, nor did they follow up with an invitation of their own. Mel and Ted Brown nod when they see each other and occasionally exchange pleasantries, but they did not become friends. "The

Browns didn't work out," Mel says, "but I heard that the Wingates down the block are ski nuts, like Nancy and me, so we asked them over for brunch next Sunday."

The Good Host/Hostess

Judy enjoys entertaining. Bob would rather be entertained. He grudgingly admits, however, that if they as a couple are to have ongoing relationships with people they like, they must from time to time have friends in for dinner or cocktails or brunch or an occasional more formally planned party.

Bob admits he's a lousy host and attributes his lack of concern, as well as his lack of expertise, to his own family background. Neither of his parents drink, and get-togethers in his boyhood home were confined to once-a-year family reunions, usually taking place on Thanksgiving Day. "Mom cooked, Dad carved, the rest of us ate, and that was about it."

Judy was disturbed by what she called Bob's "really rather gruesome manners" when guests came into their home, and at her request, he decided to learn to be a more gracious host—or, more precisely, to try to live up to her idea of what the gracious host should be.

She made up a list of "good-host" behaviors. (Your conception of what the gracious host or hostess says and does— and mine, too, for that matter—may be very different from hers. But the point, of course, is that if this is an issue in your house, *you* should draw up a similar list, incorporating your own ideas of what constitutes appropriately hospitable behaviors.)

1. Issue invitations.
2. Help people off and on with their coats.
3. Mix and serve drinks. (This was something Bob had

to learn, since at the time of their marriage, he didn't know vodka from vermouth.)

4. Offer to refill empty glasses.

Then, using Judy's list as a guide, they drew up the following contract:

BOB AND JUDY'S GOOD HOST CONTRACT

Bob: I agree to invite Gail and Herb to dinner at our house next Saturday and to engage in all the other "good-host" behaviors on Judy's list; furthermore, I agree that on Tuesday I will buy a book explaining how to mix drinks and experiment with two easy drinks before Saturday if, in return, Judy will wear the sexy dress I bought for her on our trip to San Francisco and allow me to sleep late on Sunday morning.

Judy: I agree to wear the sexy dress Bob bought for me on our trip to San Francisco and allow him to sleep late on Saturday morning if, in return, he will invite Gail and Herb to dinner at our house next Saturday and to engage in all the other "good-host" behaviors on my list.

Bob, to his great delight, has become an expert bartender, though he still feels ill at ease in the role of host. And perhaps hosting just isn't his thing after all. But Judy makes sure to reinforce his hospitable behaviors with hugs and kisses and significant smiles that more than make up for his temporary discomfort, and this particular issue has ceased to be a problem for them.

Incidentally, my own feelings about who should do what in so far as entertaining friends—or almost anything else— is concerned, is that the partner who demonstrates the greatest competence ought to take over the job. I know some women who mix a meaner Martini than any male bartender in town. I know some men who are far better at "hostessing" (planning, preparing, and serving the food) than their wives will ever be. What's important, I think, is not *who* invites the guests, or *who* cooks the food, or *who* empties the ashtrays, or *who* serves the drinks, but that the partners define for themselves what behaviors each considers appropriate in a given set of circumstances and that they work together to achieve these behavioral goals.

Friends and Money

"Neither a borrower nor a lender be, for a loan oft' loses both itself and friend, and borrowing dulls the edge of husbandry."

—Shakespeare.

I know. I know. It's not easy to refuse a friend in need of a loan. You want to help. You have the feeling that maybe your relationship will be an even closer one if you come through with the money. You may also have the feeling that if you don't make the loan, your friend will doubt your friendship.

You may be right on both counts.

But unless the loan is repaid within a reasonable amount of time—and especially if the sum in question is a large one—subsequent interaction with the borrower will be colored by your own feelings of anxiety ("Of course I'll get the money back . . . won't I?") and by his/her feelings of guilt and resentment (debtors always harbor negative feelings toward their creditors). Shakespeare was right.

Whenever the issue comes up, I think of J. Wright, Jr.'s way of handling a friend's request for a loan: "We have been friends for a long time. Because I believe that money between friends has the potential to destroy the friendship and because I value our friendship more than the five hundred dollars (you want to borrow from me), I will not lend it to you. However, I will give you fifty dollars which I never want to see again. If you find ten other people who love you as much as I, your money problems are over."[2]

Gossiping

Gossiping, as almost all of us have learned—either through personal experience or by viewing its effect on others—can ruin even the oldest, closest relationships.

Quite simply, it's a negative behavior with negative consequences: The person who is the subject of the gossip is compromised. The person who hears the gossip may have trouble handling the information (How does Stephanie interact with Linda now that she knows about Linda's affair?). And the person who spreads the gossip also unwittingly gets the message across that he/she is not to be trusted.

Almost everyone gossips from time to time and almost everyone would rather not. Inveterate gossipers who want to kick the habit can begin by making sure that whatever they say about their friends is both true and repeatable. In other words, unless you're sure that Joe lost his job, don't let on that he did. And unless you have no hesitation about telling Helen herself that you think her husband drinks too much, don't tell anyone else.

Consider this, too: Even when you're quite sure that what you're about to say *is* both true and repeatable, if the consequences of passing along a juicy bit of information are apt to be negative (i.e., if the statement can be easily misinterpreted, or could in any way be used against your friend), better let it go unsaid.

(Here's a little trick: Pretend there's a tiny transmitter pinned to your lapel, or attached to your wedding ring, and that each of your friends has a receiver tuned to your broadcast frequency. With this in mind, say anything you wish.[3])

Gossiping cost Marge a very dear friend, and she was

deeply shaken by the experience. So was Gary, her husband. In order to discourage further gossiping, they drew up the following contract:

Desirable behavior	Positive consequence	Negative consequence
Say only what is true and repeatable about our friends	Sailing together on the weekend	No sailing on weekend; doing six hours of yard work each on Saturday

They keep tabs on one another and, of course, praise one another for saying only what is "true and repeatable" about their friends. They are both hoping that they will never again lose a friend through gossiping.

Good mutual friends are embellishments to a marriage. Other friends, not so "good," and not so "mutual," may be quite another thing indeed. But as we have seen, when "his" friends are not "her" friends, the marriage need not always suffer.

It is said that happiness dies when it is not shared.[4] Mainly, we share our happinesses—and our doubts and disappointments, too—with our spouses, but we share these things also with our friends. And no matter how rich and fulfilling the marriage, how much richer and more fulfilling are our *lives* when we count good friends among our blessings? A minister I know, Dr. E. M. Arendall, includes as part of the marriage ceremony the phrase, "And they shall double each other's joys and halve each other's sorrows." I think the same may be said of good friends.

CHAPTER 9

When Religion Is a Problem

RELIGION ITSELF—FAITH in the existence of some sublime transcendent entity—appeals to our hearts rather than to our heads. It is intuitive. It is an embodiment of our feelings about the mystical and the divine. It is nonrational almost by definition. And yet religious *behaviors* are subject to the same principles that govern our behaviors in all the more mundane spheres.

Religious behaviors, like all other behaviors that operate within a marriage, are "positive" when they are pleasing, or at least acceptable, to both partners. Problems begin when one partner's religious behaviors are disturbing to the other.

Mixed Marriages

Different faiths place different demands on their followers. Good Catholics are expected to attend Mass, avoid the use of artificial contraceptives, and rear their children in the ways of the Catholic Church. Loyal Protestants hold to the particular set of beliefs espoused by their denomination and will act accordingly. Pious Jews may obey dietary laws, worship on the Sabbath, and observe holy days as prescribed by Jewish tradition. Even atheists and agnostics can be said to engage in "religious" behavior in that they, too, say and do things that are reflective of their attitudes toward God, man, and the nature of the universe.

Husbands and wives who love and respect each other may have very little regard for their partners' religious beliefs—or lack of them—and these differences can be a source of great conflict.

Let's consider those marriages in which each partner has an intense personal commitment to a different religion.

Occasionally, these couples can agree to disagree and leave it at that. They are the fortunate ones. More often, religious differences are translated into hostile behaviors that may in time undermine the very structure of a marriage.

If these marriages are to survive at all, husbands and wives must learn to demonstrate behaviors that indicate respect for—though not necessarily agreement with—their partner's religious practices.

Anne and Doug are the same age. They're both teachers. They share a love of nature, a desire for a large family, and a passion for Italian opera. They like the same people and even their political views are similar, though Doug tends to be slightly more liberal. They would seem to have everything going for them. But Anne is a devout Catholic and Doug a fervent believer in the doctrines of Christian Science.

Each entered the marriage with the belief that the other would eventually modify his/her religious convictions. But it didn't work out that way. Both were at first sadly disappointed and then deeply resentful. After five years of marriage the situation was such that any reference to religion became a clash of conflicting opinions, with each partner ridiculing and maligning the faith of the other.

Neither could nor would make compromises in so far as

their actual religious beliefs and pratices were concerned, but they both recognized that in order to save their marriage they would have to "teach" each other tolerant behavior. They set up the following contingency contract:

> *Anne*: I, Anne, agree to either praise or make no comment concerning Doug's devotion (reading the *Christian Science Monitor*) to his church if, in return, he will agree to either praise or make no comment concerning my devotion (attending Mass) to my church. I also agree that I will attend Mass on Sunday only if I have abided by the terms of this agreement during the preceding week.

> *Doug*: I, Doug, agree to either praise or make no comment concerning Anne's devotion (going to Mass) to her church if, in return, she will agree to either praise or make no comment concerning my devotion (reading the *Christian Science Monitor*) to my church. I also agree that I will attend services at my church on Sunday only if I have abided by the terms of this agreement during the preceding week.

In other mixed marriages, husbands and wives may place a higher value on the actual experience of worshiping *together* than they do on their respective faiths. Which is not to say that religion is not a problem in these households. It often happens that Baptist wife and Episcopalian husband live in relatively peaceful co-existence from Sunday afternoon all the way through to Saturday evening. But when Sunday morning rolls around again, there is the inevitable tug-of-war over which house of worship to attend: his or hers.

When neither partner has a very strong personal commitment to a particular faith or denomination, it may be a good idea to consider joining a "compromise" church or synagogue. Thus, the Baptist wife and Episcopalian husband could go to a Presbyterian Church. Or, Catholic wife and Presbyterian husband may decide to join the Episcopal Church. (And so on.)

Aside from resolving an immediate problem, there is another advantage inherent in this kind of arrangement: By the very act of settling on a compromise church, the couple also have decided the question of how and in which faith to raise their children.

Another possibility would be to attend alternate houses of worship on alternate weeks. Barry, a Jew, may agree to go to church with Suzanne, a Methodist, one week if she, in turn, will go to Temple with him the following Friday evening.

In a marriage where one partner is decidedly more religious than the other, a compromise may be reached whereby the less religious partner agrees to worship with the more devout.

Ben and Sally are a case in point. Ben is a reform Jew, and Sally, the product of a mixed marriage (Catholic/Protestant), describes herself as "not being very concerned with God one way or the other." Although she admits she'd rather curl up with a good book than go to Temple with Ben, she was anxious for Ben to take an a greater share of the responsibility for running their home, so they agreed upon the following contract:

SALLY

Desirable behavior	Positive consequence	Negative consequence
Attending Temple with Ben on Friday nights	Wednesday swimming class at the Y	No Wednesday swimming class

BEN

Desirable behavior	Positive consequence	Negative consequence
Vacuum the house and clean down- stairs bath- room on	Watch evening news through- out week	Forfeit watch- ing evening news through- out week

Sunday before 6:00 P.M.

What About the Children?

In many mixed-faith marriages religion presents no very great problems until the children are old enough to start asking questions, at which point the parents may disagree (sometimes violently) over what kind of religious orientation they want for their young ones.

There are three options open to couples who find themselves faced with this dilemma: They may decide to teach their children the religions of both parents. They may agree that the children be reared in the faith of the more devout parent. Or, finally, they may resolve to give their children no religious instruction.

When husbands and wives choose the first alternative, they are not only teaching two religions, they are also teaching tolerance. The children learn that no one faith has cornered the market on goodness, and that happy, kind, honest people spring from any number of different backgrounds.

In this kind of arrangement, the child would spend equal time in the house of worship of each parent and would be equally involved in both religious atmospheres. (The atheist or agnostic parent presumably would also observe the equal-time dictum in explaining his/her beliefs to the child.) Yet, this alternative runs the risk of confusing the child.

Obviously, when parents agree to rear their children in the faith of the more devout spouse, they must first decide which of them in fact has the strongest religious commitment. Often, one partner will simply concede. But when there are any doubts in the matter, a couple can rate their commitment to their respective faiths on a scale of 1 to 10. The high rating wins. (Although one spouse almost always emerges as the more devout, a tie score is a possibility, and when it occurs, the couple should probably resort to the first alternative: that of teaching the child both religions.)

A contingency agreement might be established to encourage the low-scoring spouse toward a more positive attitude about having the child reared in the faith of the other. For example, Ray, a luke-warm Methodist, did not dispute the fairness of sending little Alicia off to church with her mother, a devout Presbyterian. But he was not altogether happy about the arrangement, either. To help reconcile his feelings, he made an agreement with himself that he would smoke cigars during the week only if their daughter attended the Presbyterian Sunday school on the weekend.

A child reared in the faith of the more devout parent is exposed to a single set of values. This can be a positive thing from a sociological point of view. There are indications that children who identify and accept a core of values achieve greater intellectual, social, and psychological stability, and, having assimilated those values, is in a better position to make his own appraisals of alternative systems as he matures.

But there is also the possibility that children reared in one religion may close their minds to alternative perceptions of God.[1] Perhaps the ideal approach would be to provide the child with a core system of values while at the same time reinforcing open, friendly communication with people of different religious, ethnic, and racial backgrounds.

As for the third alternative—giving the children no religious instruction—let me say that children always learn *something* about religion, though they may not assimilate the values of any *particular* faith. In their efforts to maintain neutrality, parents may make the mistake of demonstrating behavior that indicates a lack of commitment to any standards, and this can be a source of great confusion to a child.

When husband and wife make the decision not to send their children to church or Sunday school, it is important that they themselves take on the responsibility of providing their children with some code of ethical conduct.

Contraception

The Catholic Church expects its followers to avoid the use of artificial means of contraception. In a mixed marriage where one partner is a practicing Catholic, husband and wife may find themselves in a state of continual disagreement over the issue of contraception.

A couple who have intercourse regularly without using contraceptives have in effect decided to have a baby. The rhythm method should not be depended upon to prevent pregnancy since it is not possible to determine with the means ordinarily available to most couples the precise time of ovulation, and also because sperm cells may continue to live in the uterus for several days after intercourse has taken place. The so-called safe days are safe only if they can be predicted with accuracy. Usually, they can't.

The question of whether or not to use contraceptives cannot even begin to be resolved without first considering the intensity of each partner's values and moral beliefs.

Elise, for example, felt that using artificial means of contraception was a crime against nature and God. For her, the issue was linked to the concept of the absolute sanctity of life itself. Furthermore, she believed that her immortal soul would be lost as a consequence of using contraceptives.

Bill's desire to delay starting a family because he felt he was not yet ready to take on the responsibilities of fatherhood may seem insignificant by comparison—but it did not seem so to Bill.

Elise may be successful in reassuring Bill that he is indeed a mature, responsible human being who is entirely capable of being a good father (she might use positive reinforcement techniques in order to do so), and thus Bill may feel less reluctant to enter into parenthood.

Or Bill may be able to modify Elise's behavior (her refusal to use contraceptives) by pointing out to her that the prohibition against artificial contraception is widely debated in Catholic circles, even among the ranks of the priesthood.

But what if neither is willing to compromise?

Behavioral techniques are viable when both partners agree on the desirability of certain behavioral goals, and when each is willing to give something in order to get something in return. But when compromise is impossible because intensely held values and moral beliefs are at stake,[1] it is desirable to seek the help of a professional therapist. A highly trained specialist will be able to separate the genuinely felt values expressed by each of the partners from other, possibly irrelevant emotional elements that may be operating within a relationship (unrealistic fears, for example, or the urge one partner may have to dominate the other, etc.) and, hopefully, help the couple to a solution that is tolerable to them both.

Church Attendance

In some marriages, problems arise not so much because the partners are of different faiths but because they differ in the amount of time (or sometimes money) that they are willing to invest in their religion. It's not at all unusual for a husband to sleep late, or stay home with the Sunday papers, while the wife goes off to church by herself. (It often works the other way around, of course.) This is all fine and dandy *unless* the churchgoing partner resents always having to go it alone. Here is another situation that is best resolved by some kind of compromise agreement.

Dan, a thirty-five-year-old dentist, who has always considered Sunday morning the ideal time for tennis, and Kathy, a tennis player herself, who nevertheless preferred Sunday sermons to mixed doubles, agreed on the following compromise.

OUR COMPROMISE CONTRACT
FOR CHURCH AND TENNIS

Dan: I agree to go to church with Kathy on alternate Sundays if, in return, she will play tennis with me on alternate Sundays. I also hereby make an agreement with myself that I will read the Sunday papers and smoke my pipe only if I abide by this agreement.

Kathy: I agree to play tennis with Dan if, in return, he will go to church with me on alternate Sundays. I also hereby make an agreement with myself that I will have my hair done on Fridays and eat desserts only if I abide by this agreement.

An alternative way to resolve a similar conflict—i.e., where one partner simply doesn't want to go to church or synagogue—is for the couple to decide that the reluctant partner will *not* go *ever*, as Bruce and Margaret did. In this marriage Bruce was the churchgoing spouse. They agreed to make some of Bruce's enjoyable behaviors contingent on his not requesting Margaret to go along with him. Thus, Bruce may bowl and play cards with his friends only if he does not badger Margaret about going to church. In return for not being nagged, Margaret agreed to walk the dog every day and to prepare Bruce's favorite dish (eggplant Parmigiana, it was) once a week.

This alternative did not get Margaret into church, but it did put a stop to the back-and-forth bickering that was their usual Sunday morning conversational fare.

Church Activities Vs. Family Life

Sam, a thirty-two-year-old salesman, calls his plump smiling wife, Ruth, a "religious fanatic." Ruth is not so much a religious fanatic as she is eager to participate in each and every activity sponsored by her church. As it happens, her church offers two services on Sunday and one on Wednesday evening. The Women's Home Mission meets on Monday. Visitation night falls on Thursday, followed by Family Night Supper on Friday. Tuesdays and Saturdays are free.

Husbands and wives who are devoted to their churches often expect to participate in several church-related activities each week, leaving lonely disgruntled mates at home to cope single-handedly with supper and the children's baths and bedtime.

When this is a problem the couple should discuss some kind of compromise agreement. Ruth wants to attend six church-related events each week, while Sam would prefer that she not go to any of them, since their household routine is disrupted when she does. However, they were able to agree on the following compromise contract:

OUR COMPROMISE CONTRACT
FOR CHURCH ACTIVITIES

Sam: I agree to go to one Sunday service and Friday Night Supper with Ruth, if, in return, she will attend only one additional church-related event during the week and will prepare supper (or make sure that there is easy-to-cook food in the refrigerator) before she leaves. I also agree that I will play cards on Saturday only if I have gone to church with Ruth two times during the preceding week.

Ruth: I agree to attend only three church-related activities each week and that if one of them occurs during the evening hours I will prepare supper (or have some easy-to-cook food in the refrigerator) before I leave if, in return, Sam will go with me to one Sunday service and Family Night Supper on Friday. I also agree that I will visit my sister on Saturday afternoon only if I have fulfilled the terms of this agreement during the previous week.

Notice that this agreement is reciprocal—as are all good compromise agreements. Ruth has not been forced to abstain from all church-related activities, nor does Sam have to put up with staying home alone with the children several nights each week. Instead, Ruth agrees to modify her churchgoing behavior because Sam, in turn, agrees to modify his. Each gives in order to get.

Financial Contributions to Church or Synagogue

Churches and synagogues are dependent on contributions from their members. Cash, not prayer, buys the organ, pays the mortgage on the building, and assures that pastor, priest, or rabbi has food on the table, clothes in the closet, and perhaps a car in the garage. Funds are raised in a number of different and often ingenious ways, but much of the money must come directly from the congregation. (The church rarely hesitates to remind us that it is more blessed to give than to receive.)

In some marriages, a problem arises when only one partner is loyal to a particular house of worship and feels an obligation to support it through financial contributions.

So it was with Diana and Curt, a very young couple, who,

because of Curt's modest salary (he is an unskilled laborer by day, a college student in the evening), were involved in a constant struggle to make ends meet.

Diana, however, believed that regardless of their financial problems, 10 percent of their gross income should be given to their church. Curt, for his part, considered some contributions appropriate, but certainly nowhere near 10 percent.

They arrived at a compromise, whereby Curt agreed to give 5 percent of their income in exchange for Diana's typing and proofreading his term papers and reports and locating, and when necessary Xeroxing, any articles or other research material he might require from the library.

In a marriage where there is no comparable financial hardship, the wife might tithe any money available to her; she could, for example, contribute her weekly spending money or funds set aside for replenishing her wardrobe or visits to the beauty parlor. Or, if the husband were the religious partner, he might decide to tithe in a similar way, by contributing money he would ordinarily spend on tickets to sports events, golf fees, or club membership dues.

A third possibility would be for either partner to take on an additional job and tithe the money earned therefrom.

Cursing

Words and phrases pertaining to sex and sexual acts—the same words and phrases that were once considered "filthy," or "dirty"—have lost much of their power to shock, and in some cases their use has definite therapeutic value. (See Chapter 4, p. 66.)

Husbands and wives who take their religion seriously may be altogether accepting of these sexual words and phrases, but gravely offended when their partners "take the name of the Lord in vain." Spouses who want to stop cursing—or, expressed in more positive behavioral terms, want to increase the number of non-curse words they use—may, like Frank, enter into a non-cursing contingency contract.

· FRANK'S NON-CURSING CONTRACT

Desirable behavior	Positive consequences	Negative consequences
Say "damn it," or "damn it all" instead of taking the Lord's name in vain	Watch TV and read newspapers daily	No TV, no newspaper, and no Wednesday night bowling.

I, Frank, agree to say "damn it" or "damn it all" instead of taking the name of the Lord in vain. Watching television and reading the paper daily are the positive consequences for doing so. The negative consequences of failing to do so are forfeiting TV, newspapers, and Wednesday night bowling.

Frank's wife encourages his non-cursing behavior by noticing his use of the phrases "damn it all" and "damn it" and by telling him how much she appreciates his new way of expressing anger.

"The family that prays together stays together"—a catchy phrase fostered by the religious community in an attempt to encourage churchgoing behavior in the population at large, and anyone over thirty will no doubt remember how it kept popping up in magazines and newspapers and in mile-high letters (or so it seemed) on billboards coast to coast.

Certainly, religion can be a source of rich and significant shared experience. But as we have seen, it is sometimes better for one's marriage to pray alone. Couples whose religious *convictions* are not perfectly matched need not allow religious *behaviors* to compromise their chances for marital happiness.

CHAPTER 10

*When Money
Is a Problem*

"MONEY MAKES THE WORLD go 'round, the world go
'round, the world go 'round. . . ." Or so they sing in the
musical *Cabaret*. True? I would have to say, unfortunately,
yes. For better or worse, money is one of the most powerful
influences on human behavior, and in my experience ranks
with bad communication and bad sex in its potential to cast
a dismal pall on the happiness of even the most loving of
couples.

Usually there's not enough of it. But sometimes it's too
hard to get (i.e., one or both partners invest so much of
themselves in the pursuit of cold, hard cash that there's
nothing left over for anything else). And other times the
issue is how to spend it. Or invest it. Or *who* shall spend it,
or invest it. And so on. And on.

But the behavioral approach may be effectively applied to
money problems, too, as we shall see. Money makes the
world go 'round, but it needn't end a marriage.

Too Little?

Betsey, a robust blue-eyed blonde, and Dick, her lanky, sandy-haired husband, are both in their middle twenties. They live in a small farming community, where Dick teaches school and Betsey runs the house (actually, a tiny three-room apartment) and cares for their two-year-old son. According to Betsey, their marriage was "just great . . . just the way I always knew it would be"—until she discovered she was pregnant again. Then she began to worry about money.

Dick's salary is about $8,000 a year and they had been "getting by," Betsey said. But the new baby was going to cost plenty, they had no savings, they'd need to move to a bigger apartment, and with food prices on the rise she was becoming more and more concerned with feeding their growing family—on top of which, with two babies, she didn't see how she was going to manage without a washing machine, and in her pregnant state she couldn't face the prospect of another summer without an air conditioner. "And"—by this time she was crying—"I look like hell. Maybe I shouldn't even care about it, but I never have anything nice to wear anymore.

"He could make more money if he wanted to—if he worked in the summer like all the other teachers we know, or if he switched jobs. His uncle wanted to take him on as a partner in the laundry business, but, oh, no, not Dick. He refused. He just doesn't give a damn."

Dick, for his part, thought they were managing just fine and would continue to do so. "Sure, I don't make much money, but I *like* my job, and after all, how much do we need. Lots of people don't have air conditioners and washers and dryers and fancy new clothes. I never wanted to be a money-making machine and I never will be, but I'm beginning to think that's all Betsey wants." Dick went on to express his feeling that Betsey had stopped loving him for himself and was more concerned with the material goods and services he could—but would not—provide than with his own sense of well-being.

Betsey began to refuse to have intercourse with Dick. She resented what she interpreted as indifference; she felt he didn't care enough to want to provide the material necessities for their growing family. Dick responded by shouting at Betsey that he "damn well wouldn't support any woman who wouldn't sleep with him." This once-happy couple fell into a self-perpetuating, mutually negative response cycle. The two behaviors—Dick's threatened withdrawal of financial support and Betsey's actual refusal to have sex—aggravated each other, and after one particularly violent scene, Betsey took the child and went to live with her mother.

This is perhaps an extreme example of the devastating effect money, or, more precisely in this case, the lack of it, can have on a marriage.

How much money is "enough" is a matter open to interpretation, but when both partners experience feelings of anxiety because their income doesn't provide for their present needs, they may want to consider one or more of several alternatives, which will not only ease their financial worries, but relieve some of the strain those worries impose on their relationship.

Moonlighting (the sound of which, for me, always conjures up visions of lovers meeting in meadows lit with softest silver—but which, as we all know, means the taking on of a second job, usually nightwork of some kind) is one alternative.

Moonlighting may be the answer when the problem is paying off a long-overdue debt, "financing" the birth of a child, or making some major purchase without resorting to applying for a loan or some other kind of credit. Most of us, however, don't have the physical stamina for moonlighting as a way of life. Holding down a second job on a long-term basis keeps husband and/or wife away from home and each other and practically eliminates a couple's social life and any regular participation in leisure-time activities—not to mention the fact that moonlighters invariably walk around bleary-eyed from lack of sleep. Thus, I think moonlighting should be considered as a short term solution to an immediate and pressing financial problem; otherwise, the monetary advantages are eventually canceled out by the very real physical and social hardships it imposes.

Liquidating one's assets may be another way out of an immediate financial bind—assuming, of course, that one has assets to liquidate. Some lucky couples start out their married lives with gifts of stocks, bonds, silver, jewelry, antiques, works of art, etc., and these can all be sold. I know of one couple who put the husband's stamp collection on the market in order to finance the wife's second year of medical school, and another who sold off all their wedding silver— which had been collecting dust in a closet during their five years of marriage, anyway—to help pay for the second car they desperately needed. (As for second cars, many husbands and wives decide they need them less than they thought they did—or at least less than they need the money for some other, more urgent purpose.) A third couple, heavily in debt, had a garage sale. They ransacked their own house as well as the homes of both their parents for any and all salable items, put a sign out on the lawn ("Bargains Galore") and ended up several hundred dollars less in debt.

The problem with liquidating assets, of course, is that once they're gone, they're gone for good, and unless the couple strike it rich or find some real means permanently of increasing their income, the problems are only temporarily solved.

Making a conscious and consistent effort to reduce expenses is a longer-term solution. Often, even those couples who at first feel they've already pared their expenses down to the dry, bare bone, find ways to further reduce their weekly cash outlay. I know one woman who gave up smoking; in her state, cigarets were 60¢ a pack and she ordinarily went through two packs a day, so the savings, calculated on a monthly basis, were significant. Another couple decided they were overinsured and canceled all but their car and medical insurance policies.

Revising the budget, which is actually what cutting expenditures is all about, must be done jointly. Husband and wife should sit down together for a brainstorming session to explore any and all dollar-stretching possibilities. After figuring out how the money really gets spent, each should make a list of what he/she considers "absolutely necessary" as well as "nice but not essential" expenditures and start the paring-down process from there. One couple, for example, whose passion was movies, could not bring themselves to give up their once-a-week treat, but by starting a neighborhood baby-sitting co-op (whereby several families agreed to swap evenings sitting with each others' kids) and having their post-movie coffee and cake at home in their own kitchen instead of in a restaurant, as was their past habit, they whittled the cost of their nights down to the price of admission to the theater and the 50¢ or so worth of gas it took to get them there and back.

And then there's the do-it-yourself method of reducing cash outlay. Converting part of a backyard into a garden means fresh vegetables in the summer—and for only the price of a few packets of seeds. (And with the time and cooperative energy spent in planting and tending a garden *together*, married people often find they are harvesting a lot of good, positive feelings about each other along with the carrots, tomatoes, beans, etc.) If one has the space, and zoning laws permit it, raising chickens would not only cut down on the family food bills but the sale of eggs and poultry might bring in some extra cash as well. Women who sew with a modicum of skill can dress themselves and their children for approximately half what it would cost for ready-made clothing. And a basic understanding of elementary carpentry, along with a working knowledge of the principles of plumbing and what makes such gadgets as television sets, automobile engines, power motors, toasters, washing machines, and, of course, clocks, tick, can stretch a meager budget a long long way.

The Two-income Family

At any given time, over 40 percent of all married women work outside the home—and 75 percent of all wives hold down a job at some point during their marriages. Most of them work to supplement the family income (though, of course, many others are committed to careers of their own, and some suffer feelings of boredom and frustration spending all their time and energies within the confines of their homes). In any case, the working wife may be the ultimate answer to the problems arising from too little money.

There is no consistent evidence pointing to a relationship between marital happiness and an employed wife.[1] In other words, while *some* research indicates that *some* couples describe their marriage as being good, or better, when the wife works, others indicate the opposite. Apparently, then, like almost everything else in marriage, whether happiness increases or decreases as a result of the wife's working depends on the individual feelings and attitudes of each partner.

Obviously there will be very few difficulties if both partners have a positive attitude about the wife's working (the problems that arise usually center on her getting the right job for the right money and then, when necessary, making adequate child-care arrangements). The same is true when husband and wife are in agreement about the wife's *not* working.

But where the wife wants to work and her husband disapproves, or where the husband wants his wife to work, while she would prefer to stay at home, the couple runs into difficulty.

Let's assume the more common of the two situations: that in which the wife would like to have a job but her husband objects. Once or twice before in this book, I've suggested rating individual desires on a scale of 1 to 10 as a way of deciding an issue over which partners are in conflict. In this imaginary instance, let's say the wife rates her desire to work at 9, while her husband disapproves at a level of 4. In all fairness, the question should be settled in favor of the wife's working.

A few behavioral techniques can ease some of the husband's dissatisfaction over the settlement:

1. *Compromise:* The wife, especially if she has no immediate full-time job prospects, might initially seek part-time employment. Thus, both husband and wife are given the opportunity to adjust gradually to some of the inevitable changes resulting from her new outside responsibilities.

2. *Reinforce desirable behavior:* The wife should watch for those instances when the husband seems least dissatisfied about her employment and make a point of telling him how much she appreciates his support and understanding.

3. *Ignore undesirable behavior:* The wife must act as though she does not hear any critical remarks her husband might make about her job. (Sometimes it's easiest to simply leave the room when he begins to express his dissatisfaction with the new arrangement.) Most important, under no circumstances should she respond with counterattacks, sulking, or crying.

4. *Establish a contingency:* This may be difficult if the

husband is vehemently opposed to the idea of his wife's working, but in the long run it's a good idea if the couple can decide together to make some of the husband's enjoyable activities (golf, fishing, basketball, TV, etc.) contingent on his wife's staying on the job. Thus, he is encouraged to think more positively about his wife's employment because it is associated with pleasurable behaviors of his own. (In one marriage that came to my attention, when the wife went back to work the husband joined a chess club. His Tuesdays out at the club were contingent on her continued employment.)

5. *Define responsibilities:* Partners should come to some agreement about the division of household labor. Many husbands decide (or are encouraged by their wives) to take over more of the responsibilities of running the home when their partners go out to work. And then again, many other husbands do not. (I can't resist expressing my own opinion about the unfairness of the latter arrangement; the working wife and mother whose husband does not help with the housework is, in effect, holding down not one but two-and-a-half or three jobs.) In any case, when the wife takes on outside employment, it's important for both partners to have a clear understanding of who is to do what and when. If their original system proves unsatisfactory, they may have to renegotiate, but the main point is that each always knows his/her responsibilities.

6. *Modeling:* The husband who has an especially hard time accommodating himself to the idea of his wife's holding down a job—who *wants* to be accepting, but can't get over his own negative feelings about it—can seek out from among his male acquaintances those who have good feelings about their wives' employment. By spending time with these men, by talking with them about their own experiences as husbands of working wives, he's more apt to begin to see some of the advantages of being part of a two-income family.

How Much Is Enough?

Emerson said: "I would have every man rich that he might know the worthlessness of riches," while Thoreau argued in the same vein that "A man is rich in proportion to the number of things he can afford to live without." The gist of what each was trying to get across, of course, is that great wealth does not happiness make.

Couples whose major money problem is simply to "get by" somehow may scoff, but our philosopher friends are right: When accumulating vast sums is an obsession, the relationship between husband and wife becomes just as tenuous as that between partners burdened by the strain of making ends meet. Let me cite an example:

Tom and Marion, both in their early forties (though Tom looks fifty-five, while Marion looks a good ten years younger than her age) are the parents of two grown sons. At the time of their marriage, twenty-two years ago, Tom was a bricklayer. But through luck, shrewdness, and hard work, he is now the owner of a small but thriving construction company. Though not "rich" they have *lots* of money. They own a ten-room Tudor-style house with swimming pool and tennis court, a $50,000 vacation home in the mountains and their sleek fifty-foot cabin cruiser is docked at the local yacht basin. But though Marion uses the pool occasionally, Tom neither swims nor plays tennis; the vacation house hasn't been summered in for five years now, and the yacht stays bobbing at its mooring.

Tom's too busy for any of it. He is one of those men whose self-esteem rises in proportion to this capacity for making more, and more, and *more* money. And the more he makes, the more he wants.

He arrives at his office before 7:00 in the morning, and rarely returns home before 8 P.M. When he does manage to get home by 6:30 or so, he spends most of the evening on the telephone, or juggling long columns of figures at his desk in the den, has a glass of milk, watches the evening news, and then collapses into bed at 10 or 11.

Marion loves Tom, but she's desperately lonely. She told me she'd trade in the swimming pool, the tennis court, the country house, the cabin cruiser—"the whole bit, if only we could have more time together. I've just about had it. Sometimes I think the only thing we have left to share are the boys—and heaven knows, *they're* off on their own now and we hardly ever see them anymore—and the joint checking account. Sure, sure, some of my friends from the old days, from before Tom started doing well, are green with envy. They don't understand. 'You've got *everything*,' they tell me. 'What's to complain about?' Well, try having a nice, cozy, intimate evening at home with a checkbook . . . just try it."

I've talked with many women—most of them not quite so well off as Marion—in similar situations. I've talked with their husbands, too. Usually these men justify their obsession with making money in terms of the necessity of "maintaining financial security" for their families. What they don't realize is that the wife who loves her husband suffers terribly when his behavior indicates that accumulating money is more important than she is. And that eventually many of these women decide to leave or get involved in an affair.

Tom, as it turned out, did indeed care a great deal about Marion's happiness. He had, he said, been trying to give her all the "things" he thought she wanted. When he was made to realize that the one "thing" that Marion wanted more than all those other "things" put together, was a *husband*, he expressed a desire to modify his behaviors.

It isn't easy for men like Tom to rid themselves of the feelings and attitudes that add up to the compulsion to make more money than they need, or even really want. Money, of course, is a symbol to them—an abstract index of their own value as people—and usually not the means to any concrete end. The following program, however, was suggested to decrease Tom's obsessive thoughts about money:

1. Tom was instructed to establish stricter and more regular business hours. He was to allocate a specific amount of time each day (in his case, a "normal" nine-to-five work schedule was decided upon) during which *all* activities related to the pursuit of money were to occur. Instead of spending his evenings phoning clients, making lists of what had to be done at the office the following day, reviewing accounts, and reading trade papers, he would watch TV, listen to music, read for pleasure (fiction and nonfiction unrelated to the construction business), visit friends with Marion—in short, to engage in any pleasurable behaviors that were not business-oriented.

2. He established a contingency contract with himself whereby he would not go into his office on one day if he had spent more than eight hours there the preceding day.

3. Marion was told to notice and reinforce Tom's efforts to confine money-making activities to the hours he spent in his office. ("Tom, you're really doing a marvelous job. You can't know how much I appreciate you're not bringing the business home." Kiss, hugs, etc.)

4. The "stop-think" technique was explained to Tom so that he would be better able to control his thoughts. (It often happens that even though a husband is successful in not *talking* about work and in not engaging in work-related *behaviors*, his mind remains cluttered with the details of his business. This state of affairs obviously is not conducive to reestablishing a close, warm relationship with one's partner.) Thus, Tom was told that when off-duty work thoughts began, he should yell "stop," pull an index card from his pocket and read whatever was written on it. He had several cards: One said: "Ask Marion if she wants to go out to dinner tonight." Another read: "Tell Marion I enjoy being

with her and that she makes me happy," while a third had jotted on it: "Go talk to Marion about how nice it's going to be next month when we go to the mountains."

5. Since Tom—like many ambitious men who are pre-occupied with the next day's business activities—tends to have trouble getting to sleep, it was suggested that he engage in some recreative behaviors just prior to bedtime. This tends to "soften" the tension that's been built up during the day. Sex, of course, when it's good sex unaccompanied by anxiety about performing, is one way to enjoy oneself at bedtime. Tom had floodlights installed on the tennis court and occasionally late at night he and Marion would lob a ball back and forth for half an hour or so. Other times they went for moonlight swims in the pool. (Most of us do not have tennis courts and pools, but so what? Another couple in a similar situation might play two or three hands of rummy before bed, or read to each other, or listen to music, or go out for a stroll around the neighborhood.)

In addition, Tom was to establish a regular bedtime, and if he was not sound asleep after thirty minutes, he was in-structed to get up and practice the relaxation techniques outlined in the Appendix (see p. 275).

Spending It

It will come as no great shock to most married people when I say that money problems are not confined to how to get enough of it, on the one hand, and how to stop want-ing too much of it, on the other. To the contrary, the vast majority of Americans *do* have enough money to meet their basic needs, and then some—most of us take a trip now and then, go to the theater on occasion, belong to a club, etc. Nor are there very many among us who are so success-oriented that accumulating money motivates the whole of our lives.

In fact, in my experience, a far more common problem

between husbands and wives is disagreement over what to do with the money they have. Or, in other words, who shall decide how much to spend on what.

Some couples function best if either husband or wife is solely responsible for handling family finances, and this is especially apt to be the case when one has a real knack for managing, while the other goes glassy-eyed at the mere sight of a column of figures. As I've mentioned before, my personal feeling has always been that the partner displaying the greatest competence in any given area should probably take charge in that area, and although some financial decisions must be jointly made, this is just as true in regard to money matters as it is in, say, meal preparation, or seeing to household repairs—the person who does it best and enjoys doing it, should be the one who actually *does* it.

However, in many "traditional" marriages—though by no means all—it is assumed that since it is the husband who earns the money, it is also the husband's privilege to decide how to spend it. Fine. If both partners feel this is fair and are happy with the arrangement, then why not?

Another arrangement is for each partner to make financial decisions within his/her rather roughly defined spheres of jurisdiction. It is common for the wife to decide what food to buy and how much to pay for it and also to be in charge of money allocated for the purposes of dressing the family and decorating the home, while the husband defines the amount to be spent on rent, or home repairs and improvements, automobile maintenance, and whether or not they can afford a new car, or a trip, etc.

(I would like to stress that I am not suggesting that the examples just cited are representative of the "way things should be." Far from it. "The way things should be" is a matter for each couple to decide between themselves. I know a couple of men, both of whom work in the art field, who make most or all of the decisions concerning the decor of their homes. I also know several women who are uncommonly canny about such matters as when and how and where to get the car fixed, etc.)

This last arrangement can be an okay one if each partner knows what areas he/she is responsible for, and then assumes total decision-making power in those areas. Which is not to say that neither need ever consult the other. Jane, for example, might ask Bob if he likes the idea of green wallpaper in the bedroom, and his answer may influence her final choice, but if she's responsible for decorating their home, she retains the authority to decide whether to buy it, and where and at what price. In the same way, Bob may choose to consult Jane about the advisability of using flagstone for the terrace, or building a raised wooden deck instead, but reserve the ultimate decision for himself.

In other words, when an agreement is made that each will make financial decisions in his/her own clearly specified areas, an additional agreement should be made that control over money allocated to those areas is complete, and not contingent upon the partner's approval. Many, many spending arguments begin, innocently enough, when the husband gives his wife cash to buy something she wants, or needs, but expects her to spend only *some* of it. ("She wanted a new dress for a party we were going to, so I gave her seventy bucks, and by God, she spent every last cent of it!") When something like this happens, the two partners apparently have not clarified the issue of who is to spend how much on what.

I've seen a lot of hostility and resentment generated in disagreements over how to spend discretionary income (whatever's left over after the basic necessities have been provided for). One partner may yearn for a piano, while the other wants an expensive new camera. Assuming there's not enough money for both, what's the fairest way to decide the issue?

One can always resort to rating desires on a scale of 1 to

10, the partner with the lowest rating deferring to his/her mate. But this is a tricky method under the circumstances— what if both piano and camera are wanted at a level of 10?

A better way to resolve this kind of problem would be for both husband and wife to identify their respective desires in regard to spending and make an agreement. It might work this way: After budgeting a specific monthly amount for food, housing, clothing, automobile maintenance, insurances, savings, etc., the partners equally divide any money left over. Each may spend (or save) his/her portion in any way, and on any thing only so long as the partner has the right to do the same. Neither is accountable to the other, and in this way both are given the opportunity to gratify their desires.

Bills

In some respects a marriage functions like a small business: There is income and outgo and continuous and wide-ranging financial transactions with other entities. Goods (food, clothing, shelter) and services (electricity, babysitting, visits to doctors and dentists) are used and must be paid for. And this, of course, brings up the matter of bills.

There is a rather fine line of distinction between the issue of deciding who is to be responsible for what financial decisions within a marriage and the question of whether both— or which?—partner is to be in charge of paying the bills. Each needs to be settled in a way that is mutually satisfactory. But while in the first instance, a good working arrangement may allow for a certain amount of flexibility ("you do your thing; I'll do mine") bill paying should probably be an either/or proposition. In other words, either the husband or the wife must assume complete and total responsibility for making sure that bills are paid. Otherwise, chaos, accusations of irresponsibility when one assumes the other has taken care of a certain account ("You never do anything right"), counterattacks ("Well, if you're so terrific, why didn't *you* do it?") accompanied by guilt, and, in all probability, a drawerful of past-due notices.

Most of the really bitter disagreements arising over the issue of bills occur because the partners have no "system," and never have assigned responsibility in this area. "Systems" are not very fashionable these days. From all sides and many sources we are exhorted to be "freer, more spontaneous," to do what we want to do when we want to do it. This can be very good, healthy advice, but I don't think it applies to bill paying.

I remember a terribly confused young couple who had decided that it made sense to share all the responsibilities of running their home—including the job of paying bills. One night, several months after they'd moved into their new apartment, they came home from work to a dark apartment because their electrical service had been discontinued. The reason: Though each had taken time out on occasion to look through and pay a few of the bills that were accumulating in their dresser drawer, neither took the chore very seriously, and the utility bill (along with its past-due notices) was somehow overlooked.

I know many young couples like these two, to whom the idea of "organization," "systems," and "schedules" are anathema, but most of them do finally come around to the realization that to run a home smoothly and efficiently requires a few "business-like" behaviors, and a system for bill paying is one of them.

As previously mentioned, the system that seems to work best for most couples is to assign to either husband or wife (hopefully the one who has demonstrated the greater skill at managing money, though if neither has much talent in this regard, the job might go to the partner for whom getting to and from the bank is most convenient—or the decision

might be made by flipping a coin) the responsibility for
overseeing all financial transactions: including allocating
pocket money for each, paying bills on time, keeping an
up-to-date checkbook, and making deposits in savings and
checking accounts.

There is a second alternative—less desirable, I think,
because any division of labor where bill paying is concerned
increases the possibility of costly and possibly embarrassing
slipups as well as disagreements between partners.

In this second arrangement, each partner opens a separate
checking account. Then financial responsibilities are divided
and assigned so that there is no overlap in function. When
this plan is adopted, it's important to establish a schedule,
specifying which partner is responsible for paying what bills
and when. An example may be helpful:

Spouse	Responsibility	When
Sam	Make loans from bank	At our discretion
Sam	Make mortgage pay-ments	By the tenth of the month
Sam	Give Gail all re-ceipts of expenditures made on credit cards	Within five days after bill received
Gail	Pay all bills other than mortgage payments	By the tenth of the month
Gail	Keep twenty-five dollars in the house at all times	Every day
Gail	Deposit income in bank	Within two days after pay checks received

When the couple decide to divide their financial responsibilities in a way similar to the one just outlined, it's always
a good idea to follow up the agreement with certain behavioral techniques:

1. *Reward "remembering behaviors":* Sam might, for example, praise Gail for paying the electric bill on time, while

Gail in turn may express thanks to Sam for not forgetting to give her any receipts he may have acquired. Praise and thanks, accompanied by smiles, hugs, and kisses, will insure that remembering behaviors will occur with greater frequency.

2. *Establish contingencies:* Sam and Gail could agree to engage in enjoyable activities (movies, tennis, whatever) contingent on satisfactory performance of their respective "assignments."

Fairy Godmothers, The Stock Market, Gambling, Cheating The IRS and Other Money Problems

Fairy godmothers . . . ? Well, except for a few of the less sophisticated four-year-olds of my acquaintance, hardly anyone believes in them anymore. And yet again, one hopes . . . one dreams. The hot stock tip *may* pay off. Big. A lucky gambling streak might solve a lot of problems. And if you can get away with it, why not claim a few hundred bucks worth of illegitimate tax deductions. Doesn't everybody?

Many otherwise happy relationships are flawed because one partner does not approve of—or is perhaps morally outraged by—some of the financial behaviors of the other.

I spoke with one husband who thought his wife was "crazy" for continuing to speculate in the stock market. "It's her money," he told me. "She works for it and keeps only one-third of her salary for herself, to do with as she pleases, so I guess I shouldn't complain. But she *always* ends up losing and it gripes me to see so much money going down the drain."

However, it was important to this woman—let's call her Amy, and her husband Ted—to buy stocks. She told me she really believed she was going to "strike it rich" one day, but even if she didn't, she *enjoyed* the behavior. "It's kind of like a hobby. I get a big kick out of reading the *Wall*

Street Journal, keeping track of my stocks, seeing how they're doing."

On the other hand, since her "hobby" was so upsetting to Ted, and because, where once she reacted to his nagging with good-natured smiles and shrugs of the shoulders, she was now beginning to respond with counterattacks and expressions of resentment, she wanted to modify the behavior in order to keep their marriage on good, solid footing.

The following guidelines were suggested, and both Amy and Ted agreed to try to live up to them:

1. *Compromise:* Since Amy so enjoyed speculating, it was decided that she would continue to engage in this behavior, but it was also suggested that the two of them sit down together and work out a compromise as to the *amount* of money she would invest. Amy previously had spent a full third of her weekly paycheck on stocks, and it was this, along with what he considered her poor judgment that had been so disturbing to Ted. After much discussion it was decided that Amy would invest one-sixth of her money in the market (in other words, half as much as she had been used to) and to deposit the remainder in a savings account.

2. *Reward desirable behavior:* Amy was advised to notice when Ted went for relatively long periods of time without criticizing her investment decisions, and to tell him how much she appreciated his trust in her judgment. When Ted says, "I really hope that Chrysler stock you bought today shoots up," or something like it, Amy smiles, thanks him, and tells him they'll go off for a couple of weeks to the beach if the stock hits a certain price. Thus, by indicating that they will spend some of her profits (if there are any) on something they'd both like to do, Amy can help Ted develop a new and more positive attitude toward investing.

3. *Ignore undesirable behavior:* Amy was instructed not to react to any critical statements Ted might make about her investment decisions. "I see Xerox is down again . . . you

sure know how to pick the losers," or "Everything you buy goes under like lead" should be met with absolutely no response from Amy. If she were to express resentment, Ted's critical behavior might only increase.

4. *Draw up an exchange contract:* To encourage positive attitudes in both partners, Amy promised to go bowling with Ted once a week and to cook his favorite meals more often (he would tell her what he wanted and when) if, in return, he would either ignore or say only positive things about her stock market speculation.

Gambling is an enormous disturber of the peace in many households. Some spouses express the opinion that gambling is "wrong," or "immoral" and one young woman told me she felt "terrible pangs of guilt" spending the money her husband brought home from Thursday night poker with his cronies. Even in those marriages where gambling per se is not considered "bad" in a moral sense there may be problems simply because the family budget cannot withstand the strain of possible losses.

A lot of people get hooked on gambling. Many would like to stop, but the behavior is a difficult one to extinguish. For those who cannot quit cold turkey, however, the following procedure is often helpful.

1. *Establish a gambling limit and contingency:* The gambler should stipulate to him/herself (before going) that after losing or winning a specified number of dollars, he/she will leave the gambling table (or race track, or whatever) and that the privilege of gambling on future occasions is contingent on abiding by this agreement. (The gambler might also make a personal decision that for every dollar lost, he/she will put an equivalent amount in a permanent savings account, opened in the partner's name.)

2. *Develop alternate behaviors:* It's possible to experience some of the thrill of gambling by playing poker, gin, or

monopoly with gambling or nongambling friends—and for false stakes. It is less painful to lose a game of Monopoly than one's house.

3. *Reward desirable behavior:* The nongambling partner should demonstrate both verbally and nonverbally his/her appreciation when the gambling spouse stays within specified limits, honors the self-imposed contingency agreement, and also when he/she plays for false stakes with friends.

4. *Ignore undesirable behavior:* It is important that the nongambling partner make no comment if and when the gambling spouse fails to live up to his/her agreement (i.e., does *not* leave the table after winning or losing the specified amount, etc.). To nag, to berate, or to otherwise express disappointment will only add to the gambling partner's feelings of failure and encourage a "Why bother?" attitude, since his/her attempts to kick the gambling habit are, apparently, futile.

Claiming false deductions on income tax returns is another financial behavior that may become a source of great discord between partners. Couples who are in agreement that cheating the government constitutes appropriate behavior probably will experience no problems in this regard. But it often happens that while one partner views falsifying income tax returns in a positive light, the other feels it is not only dishonest but also "downright unpatriotic" (as one woman put it) and loses respect for the mate who does so.

The guilty partner will often justify his/her actions by theorizing that "Everybody does it, so why not me?" In truth, of course, everybody *doesn't* do it, and many who do, get caught. (A young husband claimed $2,000 worth of dental expenses one year, even though neither he nor his wife had been to a dentist. As it happened, his return was reviewed, the truth came out, and the wife, who had been unaware of the false claim, was not only furious but told me that in her estimation, Greg [the husband] was no longer a person she could look up to with any feelings of respect and admiration.)

Though marital happiness might be increased if I did, I cannot in good conscience suggest ways to encourage both partners to develop positive feelings about falsifying their income tax return. But I will outline a procedure that discourages cheating behavior.

(Just one note here: The first step, as always, is for one partner to acknowledge dissatisfaction, and then for both to come to some kind of agreement that the undesirable behavior should be terminated. But unless an accord is reached here, there's not much point in trying to apply behavioral techniques to this particular problem. Falsifying one's income tax return, though it may be a tempting proposition, is not a compulsive habit, like gambling, and can more easily be engaged in or not at will. In this instance, then, the primary motivation for new honest behavior is the unhappiness expressed by the spouse over the old, dishonest behavior.)

1. *Establish a contingency:* The guilty partner should agree to a self-imposed arrangement whereby he/she will retain the privilege of continuing to enjoy some pleasurable activity only so long as truthful and accurate income tax returns are filed.

2. *Reward desirable behavior:* The partner who wants this undesirable behavior to be terminated should encourage the mate to brag about his/her honesty when completing the next income tax return—at the same time expressing feelings of pride and admiration for this new honesty.

When In-laws Enter the Picture

Here's a little riddle: When is a gift not a gift?

Give up? When it's tied up with conditions.

Money problems with in-laws begin when the young couple fail to distinguish between borrowing and receiving

—or, when in-laws fail to make it clear whether they are loaning or giving.

When one borrows money, there is an implied intent to repay. When one loans money, repayment is expected. There are no strings, financial or otherwise, attached to a gift.

One young wife who accepted money from her parents so that she could continue her education, confessed that she felt she had to do as they wished to keep them from terminating their "gifts." In effect, then, the money was not a gift, but a loan, which the daughter was expected to repay by acquiescing to her parents' desires.

If a marriage is going to stay happy and relatively free of problems, the partners must make an effort to identify issues and choose values. In the situation just described, the young woman was made to realize that she was borrowing and not simply receiving gifts of money from her parents, and was thus faced with the choice of maintaining her own (and by extension, her husband's) independence from her family and the conditions implied by her acceptance of the money.

This particular girl valued independence over financial assistance and refused further "gifts" from her parents. Another sort of person might have done otherwise, and the important point here is of course not *which* decision is made but to understand the circumstances and the possibility that there *is* a decision to be made.

Many husbands and wives feel obligated to engage in certain behaviors toward their in-laws—such as phoning often, visiting once a week, consulting them when there is a decision to be made, etc.—in return for money or gifts. These feelings of obligation are a natural result of the couple's unwillingness or inability to distinguish between "receiving" and "borrowing."

To encourage married people to make the distinction between the two is not to imply that mutual reinforcement and exchange should not exist between them and their respective parents. On the contrary, mutual reinforcement and exchange are good for all concerned. I do, however, feel it is important to know what issues are involved and what choices are being consciously (and sometimes perhaps not so consciously) made.

In other words, realize that the "gift" that must be paid for by deferring to the giver is in actuality a loan, and that sometimes it's easier to maintain good, positive feelings all around when it's repaid in cold, hard cash.

CHAPTER 11

---◆∞◆---

When Fun and Games
Are a Problem

RELAX. ENJOY. Let yourself go. "All work and no play . . ."
etc. These are high-pressure times for most of us, and it is
desirable—no, it is an absolute necessity—that some of
our time be spent on recreational activities. Recreating ourselves.

One of the reasons that men and women decide to get
married in the first place is that they enjoy each other.
Ordinarily, premarriage togetherness is characterized by an
emphasis on fun, on "playing" behaviors. No matter how
tight their schedules, young people who are "in love," or
"serious about" each other usually can manage to set aside
a certain amount of time for "play." They go to concerts, to
movies, to museums, to restaurants. If they're athletic, they
hike, swim, ski, play tennis. Or, they dance. They party.
They go for long walks or drive out into the country. (Sex
might also be considered a "playing" behavior, but it's not
our primary concern here.)

Marital togetherness may be quite another thing, indeed.
Certainly most married couples spend more time together

than most unmarried couples. They sleep together. They often eat breakfast and dinner and sometimes lunch together. And many of their evenings are spent together—at least in the sense that they occupy the same room, or different rooms, in the same house. But the emphasis has shifted over to what might be called "business-like" behaviors. Married couples are concerned with the business of earning money. The business of keeping house. The business of rearing children. The business of maintaining positive relationships with relatives and in-laws. The business of being married.

It may be unrealistic to expect that the fun and games of courtship will not in some way be modified by the responsibilities of running a home and raising children. But it is equally unrealistic to assume that the business of being married is "business." Happy, meaningful relationships—indeed, happy meaningful lives—depend on setting aside a certain amount of time for "play."

Although in some marriages, husbands and wives may choose to play separately part of the time (the "You go your way; I'll go mine" school of thought), a relationship *always* suffers if the partners do not spend at least *some* of their playtime together. Shared activities contribute to a continued enjoyment of, and a real involvement with, one's mate. When married people make consistent choices to spend *all* their time apart, in a very literal sense they lose contact with one another and feelings of closeness are inevitably diminished.

Thus, when a satisfying and fulfilling marriage is the goal, husbands and wives should cultivate recreational activities, and at least some, though not necessarily all, of these activities should be shared. Like all statements of a "thou shalt" nature, this is easier said than done, but let's go on from here to discover how the various problems that arise in this area can be handled.

Playing Together

You and your partner may agree that "playing together" is a good idea, yet your ideas about what activities can be lumped under the heading of "fun" may not match up at all.

Couples who find themselves in this kind of situation may consider one of two alternatives. The first is to develop an interest in an activity that is new to you both.

Abby is a vivacious thirty-one-year-old mother of two, whose primary interests are drawing and painting. Steve, her tall, soft-spoken husband, enjoys stamp collecting. They both felt it was important to develop an interest in something they could do *together*.

But quite frankly, to Abby, stamps are simply boring little snippets of paper (though she admits that some of them "really are quite pretty"). And Steve confesses that he can hardly draw a straight line, let alone a pictorial representation of anything. Neither felt they could manage to work up any enthusiasm about the other's existing interest, but during one of their discussions it was decided that since they both greatly enjoyed taking pictures of their children, it might be fun to take a course in photography. And so they did.

Several months later, they had converted part of their cellar into a darkroom; their talk was full of references to various lighting techniques and the relative merits of "posed" versus "unposed" pictures; they had invested in a Nikon, and were spending many long and happy hours (sometimes with and sometimes without the children) rambling their city's streets in search of interesting photographic possibilities.

They were lucky in that photography was something they both took to immediately. But I suspect that many other couples might discover a mutually enjoyable activity that would be just as absorbing and pleasurable to them as taking pictures is to Abby and Steve.

In other marriages where either husband or wife is already involved in a particular activity, the partner might decide to develop an interest in that same activity.

Charlie, for example, is an ardent tennis player, though admittedly "not an ace." (He has a weight problem, which slows him down considerably.) Maureen had never even held a tennis racquet until after she and Charlie were married, but she enjoyed physical activity and wanted to be able to share in some of Charlie's good times, so she decided to try to learn the game.

I would like to suggest a few guidelines for men and women in situations comparable to that of Maureen's—i.e., for the husband or wife who wants to achieve a degree of competency in an activity in which the partner has an existing interest. The activity in question might be tennis, or any other sport, but the guidelines apply more or less equally to other recreational pursuits—to bridge or chess or dancing, for example, or to learning a musical instrument.

1. *Take Lessons:* When basic skills are required—as in tennis or bridge or in learning to play an instrument—it is far better to enroll in a course for beginners than to try to learn from one's mate. Charlie, for example, may become impatient with Maureen if it seems to him that her skills are developing very slowly, and as a result he may say or do things (on and off the court) that not only discourage her newly developing interest but might lead to a lot of unnecessary negative interaction (fighting).

2. *Practice Together:* When the basic skills have been acquired—and not until then—the couple should allocate a specific amount of time each week to practicing together. Charlie's *real* enjoyment may come from the games he plays with more advanced players like himself, but only if he devotes a certain amount of time to playing with Maureen will she be able to improve her own game. (And let's not lose sight of the fact, either, that Maureen's primary reason

for learning tennis is so that she and Charlie can spend more fun time together.)

3. *Reward Desirable Behaviors:* Selective reinforcement from Charlie is a great help to Maureen in developing her skills. Frequent comments, such as "That was a good backhand," or "Terrific return" (or whatever), will increase the probability that Maureen's backhands and returns will keep getting better and better. (Charlie should also keep in mind the principles of "shaping," discussed in Chapter 3. In "shaping" Maureen's tennis-playing behavior, he would first reinforce *any* improvement in her game and later on make reinforcement contingent on the development of greater competency.)

4. *Establish a Contingency:* Maureen conceived her own desire to play tennis with Charlie, but in those marriages where one partner displays an initial hesitancy to become involved in the activity enjoyed by the spouse, interest can be encouraged by establishing a contingency. Each spouse can make pleasurable activities contingent on engaging in the desired behavior.

Herb, for example, might make visiting with his friends and shaving daily contingent on taking swimming lessons and going to the pool with Jill twice weekly.

It often happens that, with time, "natural" reinforcers take the place of those which have been artificially arranged. When Herb has mastered the breast stroke, his own enjoyment of the sport will probably maintain his interest in swimming with Jill.

I can think of only one condition under which a mutually enjoyable activity may have possible negative consequences, and that is when either or both partners equate "enjoyment" with "winning": If Abby's pictures must always be better than Steve's, or if Charlie must always beat Maureen at tennis, then they've all missed the point of sharing time together.

When one partner is particularly competitive, the couple

may consider working as a team. For example, Abby may arrange the composition and lighting of a picture, while Steve develops and enlarges it—or vice versa. Or Charlie and Maureen might challenge Scott and Joyce to a tennis match.

Of course, some activities just don't lend themselves to teamwork, and when this is the case, a couple might draw up a contract similar to that of Ginny and Richard's. They both enjoy chess and though their strategies are very different, they are about equally matched as to skill and technique. Ginny, however, places a very high value on winning and has been known to sulk for hours after losing a close match. They drew up the following contract:

Ginny: I, Ginny, agree to smile and thank Richard for a good game, even if I am the loser, if Richard, in turn, will agree to thank me for being a good sport whether I win or lose. The positive consequence of smiling and thanking Richard when I lose is the privilege of calling a baby-sitter and spending an afternoon in town. The negative consequence of not smiling and thanking Richard is scrubbing and waxing the kitchen floor (even though it may not be dirty.)

Richard: I, Richard, agree to thank Ginny for being a good sport whether she wins or loses, if Ginny, in turn will smile and thank me for a good game even if she loses. The positive consequence for complimenting Ginny on being a good sport is the privilege of going to the health club for a sauna and massage. The negative consequence of failing to make a favorable comment about her sportsmanship is cleaning out the basement.

Parties and Other Entertainments

People keep giving and going to parties for any number of reasons: to repay social obligations; to introduce (or to meet) a family new to the neighborhood, or to say good-bye to one who is leaving; to celebrate some special occasion (a holiday, a birthday, an anniversary, a promotion, etc.).

Whatever the reason for the get-together, a party is supposed to be fun. It is ostensibly an opportunity to relax and
enjoy ourselves, to spend time with good friends, and to get
to know other people better. It also often provides the circumstances under which we can say and do things we would
not ordinarily say and do—especially when a liberal supply
of alcohol or pot is being passed around.

As the situation stands today, it is assumed that a husband
and wife will accompany one another to parties and other
social gatherings. They are, after all, a "couple." But as we
already know, couples don't necessarily share the same feelings about parties, or indeed about anything else.

Lucky are the husband and wife whose feelings about
parties are roughly the same: who either both look forward
to "making the scene" (as one couple calls it), or who view
any social situation where two or more conversations occur
simultaneously with equal distaste—as events to be gotten
through as quickly as propriety allows.

But, as we also already know, opposites do sometimes
attract, and in many marriages one partner loves to live it up
while the other only wants to get the whole thing over with.
Bob and Rita are such a couple. Bob hates parties, and if it
were up to him he would turn down every single invitation
that comes their way. He does, however, enjoy having close
friends over for dinner. Rita, on the other hand, loves to
dress up, meet new people, dance, drink, smoke pot if there
is any, and is always the last to leave.

They were able to reconcile their differences by working
out an arrangement that satisfies them both: For every party
invitation Rita accepts, Bob may in turn invite friends to
their home for dinner. The following is an example of one
of their exchange contracts:

Bob: I agree to go to the Browns' party with Rita on
Friday night if, in return, she will prepare dinner for the
Stevensons in our home on Saturday night.

Rita: I agree to prepare dinner for the Stevensons in our home on Saturday night if, in return, Bob will go with me to the Browns' party on Friday night.

Janet and Pete had a different kind of party problem. They're both sociable and enjoy inviting people to their home for parties, for Sunday brunch, for dinner, for after-dinner coffee and conversation. Janet, however, though she liked being with her friends in her own home, began to resent the fact that *she* was the one who did all the planning and preparation for these get-togethers, while Pete did little or nothing to help. She wanted a more equitable distribution of the work involved in making their parties run smoothly. Together, she and Pete drew up the following contract:

Janet: I agree that when *I* invite people into our home for dinner or cocktails or Sunday brunch or any other kind of get-together, I will take sole responsibility for planning and cooking the food and cleaning up afterward. The positive consequence of abiding by this agreement is the privilege of buying a new book. The negative consequences of not abiding by this agreement are that the party will be a dud and that I will not go to the beauty parlor for two weeks afterward.

Pete: I agree that when *I* invite people into our home for dinner or cocktails or Sunday brunch or any other kind of get-together, I will take sole responsibility for planning and cooking the food and cleaning up afterward. The positive consequence of abiding by this agreement is the privilege of buying a new book. The negative consequences of not abiding by this agreement are that the party will be a dud and that I will not watch the news on TV for two weeks afterward.

(As a result of their contract, Janet and Pete found they were entertaining far less often than before but were spending more time alone together—which, they agreed, had positive consequences of its own.)

Jealousy

Some husbands and wives feel threatened when their mates look at, talk to, and dance with other people at parties.

Tom, off in a corner nursing a drink by himself, thinks: "Hedy dances with me as though I'm an old shoe, or something, but she certainly doesn't seem to mind cuddling up to Roger." He meets Hedy's glance with a glare.

Tom's jealous behavior—which by implication accuses Hedy of more interest in Roger than she should have—may actually increase the number of times Hedy dances with Roger. It has been demonstrated that people—including married people, of course—often do what they are expected to do. If a husband expects his wife to spend most of her time with other men at parties, she probably will.

The following guidelines may be helpful when you and your partner want to encourage behavior indicative of trust:

1. *Make Verbal Expressions of Commitment:* Husbands and wives want to hear their partners say, "I love you." Say it. But say it on the way to the party when he/she is *not* engaging in jealous behavior. To respond to jealous behavior with reassurances of your affection is, in fact, to reward and encourage the jealous behavior.

2. *Engage in Behaviors That Indicate Trust:* Partners who trust each other do not feel threatened when their mates pay attention to others. As a wife, you might indicate trust in your husband by calling his attention to some particularly beautiful woman, to her voluptuous figure, her flawless complexion, or her glamorous hair. As a husband, you might point out to your wife an especially attractive and well-dressed man. When you encourage your partner to enjoy looking at others, you are *acting* like a trusting mate, and by *acting* like one, you may come to feel like one.

Remember, it is sometimes easier to act yourself into a

new way of thinking than to think yourself into a new way of acting.

3. *Balance Time Together and Apart at Parties:* One way to avoid the feeling of "I didn't see my partner for the whole party" is to mutually agree that, minute for minute, you will spend as much time with your partner as you spend with others. If you dance three dances with your spouse, you would spend three dances "away," and vice versa. This agreement assures that your spouse gets "equal time."

And Shyness

Just as some married people dread parties because of the feelings of jealousy that arise when they see their mates paying attention to others, some are distressed by feelings of shyness. To these husbands and wives, the prospect of facing a roomful of strangers—or even a roomful of acquaintances (people who are "known," but with whom there are no strong ties of friendship or affection)—can be a terrifying one indeed.

Shyness can be a source of extreme personal discomfort. It is also often annoying and puzzling to one's mate.

"He doesn't mingle," one wife comments. "He stays glued to my side all evening. It embarrasses me."

A husband complains: "She sits in a corner with this strained and obviously phony smile plastered on her face, waiting for someone to come up and notice her. Or else she avoids people altogether by spending the whole time in the kitchen helping the hostess. It's no fun going to a party with her."

Shyness, like jealousy, is a feeling, and feelings may be difficult to control. But shy behaviors can become social behaviors, just as any other behaviors can that might be considered "negative."

The techniques outlined below can help husbands and

wives encourage behaviors that indicate a sense of self-assurance.

1. *Ignore Shy Behaviors*: Let me emphasize yet again that people often act as they are expected to act. When one partner indicates by word or deed the assumption that the other will simply sit in a corner and speak only when spoken to, the assumption will probably be proved correct.

2. *Reinforce Outgoing Behaviors:* Notice and reward any of your partner's behaviors that indicate a sense of self-assurance. (These may be few and far between, but it is very important to watch for them and to make appropriate comments when they occur.)

As the wife of a shy husband, for example, you might compliment him on the masterly way he handled the introductions between X and Y. As the husband of a shy wife, you could praise the way in which she expressed her opinions on suburban vs. city living, children vs. no children, and career vs. just having a job.

Contracts are also helpful when one or both partners want to modify shy behaviors. Linda (the shy partner) and Howard (less shy but not exactly hail-fellow-well-met himself) devised the following contract.

> *Linda*: I agree to introduce myself to two strangers and to talk for at least five minutes with each of them at the Carrys' party on Saturday night if, in return, Howard will put up new wallpaper in our bedroom next week.

> *Howard*: I agree to put up new wallpaper in our bedroom next week if, in return, Linda will introduce herself to two strangers and talk for at least five minutes with each of them at the Carrys' party on Saturday.

The point was made previously but it's worth repeating here: By acting like a self-assured person, you may come to *feel* like one; it is sometimes easier to act yourself into a new way of thinking than to think yourself into a new way of acting.

Getting Away from It All

Carl envisions fishing as the ideal way to spend his two weeks with pay. Patsy prefers surfing.

Louise looks forward to a trip to Paris. Len wants to ski in the Alps.

Jack is planning to camp in the Ozarks. Connie is anxious to visit her sister in Florida.

There are three options open to couples who disagree about where and how to spend their vacation. They can (1) compromise, (2) reinforce positive attitudes in one partner toward the vacation choice of the other, and (3) take separate vacations.

When interests overlap, as they seem to with Carl and Patsy, the compromise approach works best. They can decide to go to the beach and establish contingencies for his fishing and her surfing.

For example, Carl would agree to fish only while Patsy surfs and *after* they have spent two hours together. Likewise, Patsy's surfing would be contingent on Carl's fishing and the obligatory two hours spent with one another. Thus fishing, surfing, and togetherness are combined and everybody's happy. (This is a rather simplified and idealized example of what might actually be a somewhat more complicated situation, but such compromise arrangements are made often and to very good effect.)

When the respective interests of husband and wife do not overlap, this particular kind of compromise may not be feasible. In which case the couple might resort to another type of compromise—that of encouraging one partner's positive attitudes toward the vacation choice of the other.

Let's consider Len and Louise. It has always been their policy (and I believe it's a very good one) to take turns choosing how and where to spend their vacations. Len calls the shots one year, Louise the next.

It's Louise's turn this year and she wants to go to Paris.

Len agrees—because that's part of the bargain they've made with each other—but his feelings about the trip are decidedly negative. Paris is one of the few places he's never wanted to see.

Len's reluctance to visit the City of Light can be modified through modeling, thought control, and reinforcement techniques. Through use of these behavioral techniques he may actually begin to enjoy the trip. (At any rate, he'd better make the effort, because it's going to cost a bundle.)

1. *Modeling*: Len should identify from among his friends those who have visited Paris and discuss with them their positive impressions of the city. If no one he knows has ever been to Paris, he might go to a travel agency for information. He could also go to the library for books about Paris. (He should however avoid anything distinctly Francophobic.)

2. *Thought Control*: If Len continues to harbor negative feelings about vacationing in Paris, he can apply the stop-think technique. For example, when he begins to chafe at the high price of their hotel accommodations, or ruminate about the distance from home and their children, or regret the fact that he isn't schussing the virgin white slopes near St. Moritz instead of strolling along the Seine, he should yell "stop" (subvocally if he is not alone) and take from his pocket an index card on which he has jotted positive thoughts about Paris.

3. *Reinforcement Procedures*: Louise can reward Len for exhibiting any behaviors that indicate enjoyment of their trip. (When Len expresses astonishment at his first glimpse of the Louvre, Louise might put her arms around him and tell him, "It's fun being here with you.") She should not respond in any way to statements such as "The weather is lousy," or "I can hardly wait to get back home."

Hopefully, behavioral techniques will have been successful in reconciling Len's negative feelings about the Paris trip. It is even possible that years later he will remember it with great fondness. In any event, such procedures can prevent one partner's dream vacation from becoming a fourteen-day nightmare for both.

Jack and Connie decided to try separate vacations. Jack and two of his friends rented a camper and headed south to the Ozarks for two weeks' worth of roughing it, while Connie boarded a plane for Miami and spent many happy days basking in the Florida sun. Each missed the other but came home refreshed and eager to take up again where they'd left off.

Playing Apart

Up until now we've been concerned primarily with how to resolve the problems that come up when couples choose to spend most of their leisure time together. Now let's consider what happens when husbands and wives decide—either for reasons of conflicting interests or because of a simple desire for greater independence—to spend some of their fun time apart.

Men's/Women's Night Out

In many happy marriages—including some of the happiest ones I know—one or both partners enjoy spending an occasional evening "out" with friends. Husbands frequently set aside a night or possibly two each week for poker or bowling or basketball "with the guys." Less traditional perhaps, but becoming more and more an accepted part of the American way of marriage, is women's night out, when wives get together for a movie or cards or (increasingly common in recent years) to attend a weekly women's consciousness-raising group.

Men's night out, or women's night out, can be a welcome

and pleasurable break in the weekly routine of husband and wife. And then again, it may pose problems.

Mike, a twenty-eight-year-old accountant, enjoys playing poker with the fellows at his office. He enjoys it so much that he wants to play poker two or three times a week. Nancy feels one night of poker playing for Mike is fine—it gives her a chance to catch up on her reading. But she resents his being away two or three evenings a week since she, too, wants a night out and, as she puts it, "When he's out three nights and I'm out one, I begin to feel very unmarried—we see so little of each other."

Some couples can see even less of each other and still feel very married indeed, but this was not the case with Nancy, nor with Mike, after he'd given the matter some thought. So, in order to maintain some semblance of harmony, it was obvious that either Mike must achieve a positive attitude about playing poker only once a week, or that Nancy must give up her night out and in addition achieve a positive attitude about Mike's poker playing two or three times a week. They opted for the former.

Mike tried to help himself accept the idea of once-a-week poker by drawing up the following contingency contract:

Desirable behavior	Positive consequence	Negative consequence
Play poker on Wednesdays only	Play poker the following Wednesday	Forfeit Wednesday night poker the following week. Prepare dinner and clean up afterward during the following week

I, Mike, agree to play poker on Wednesday nights only. If I play poker on an additional night during any one week, I forfeit the right to play poker during the following week and agree to prepare dinner every night and clean up afterward during the week in which poker is forfeited.

Nancy, of course, reinforces Mike's new once-a-week poker behavior by praising him when he adheres to the contract.

Incidentally, Mike's experience resulted in an impressive example of the power of the concept we call "modeling": When he announced to his friends that in future he would be limiting his poker playing to once a week, they, too, decided to play poker on Wednesdays only. (Of course, it could have worked the other way around: If Mike's personal charisma hadn't lent much to the enjoyment of their game, his friends might just as well have decided to replace him and go on playing as per usual.)

Judy and Harvey had a different kind of problem. Harvey, a tall, thin, introspective twenty-six-year-old, and Judy, a quiet, dark-haired girl, who has recently made the decision to go back to school to earn a degree in library science, disagreed violently over Judy's joining a consciousness-raising group.

Harvey felt Judy belonged at home, with him, and that since he did not go out in the evening, neither should she. Judy, however, felt she needed friends, and that though she loved Harvey, their relationship didn't make up for the lack of close ties to other women.

Their problem began to be resolved when Harvey decided to try to develop more positive feelings about Judy's consciousness-raising group. They established a contingency contract whereby some of Harvey's pleasurable activities (jogging, drinking wine with dinner, reading) depended upon his making no critical remarks about Judy's night out. In addition, Judy notices and rewards any positive statements Harvey makes about the group. Finally, Harvey began to play poker with two men who had encouraged their wives to join the group. Talking with them further enhanced his positive feelings about Judy's evenings with her friends.

When the Problem Is Opposing Interests

"Larry would rather fish than make love," Diane says. She considers fishing a foolish waste of time ("He never catches anything, anyway") and resents the weekend after weekend she spends home alone while Larry is off "Chasing after some trout or whatever you call those things."

When one partner dislikes a leisure-time activity enjoyed by the other, the couple can decide to resolve the situation in one of two ways: the activity in question can be given up altogether, or the spouse who dislikes the activity can be encouraged to develop positive attitudes toward it.

To return to Diane and Larry, it was decided that Larry would continue to fish and that Diane would·make an effort to modify her negative feelings about his fishing. Here's how the behavioral principles of modeling, reinforcement, and contingency contracting were applied to this particular situation:

1. *Modeling:* Diane was able to identify among her friends two women who had positive attitudes about their husbands' fishing. One of them—a wife whose feelings had at first been negative, but who now enjoyed fishing with her husband—proved to be an ideal "model." Diane began to shop each week with these women and came to know them. She liked them and respected their opinions in general, and in time came to respect their opinions about fishing, too.

2. *Reinforcement Techniques*: Larry made a point of rewarding Diane for not criticizing his fishing behavior. One day when Diane made no comment about his plans to go fishing the following weekend, he expressed his pleasure at her response and immediately suggested that they go out for dinner. He was equally intent on ignoring any negative comments she made about fishing.

3. *Contingency Contracting*: As we have seen over and over again, contingency contracting can help reconcile one partner's negative feelings about something the other partner says or does. In the case of Diane and Larry, where the goal was to modify Diane's feelings about Larry's fishing, a contract was developed whereby some of Diane's enjoyable activities became contingent upon her making positive statements to Larry about fishing.

Diane is a crossword-puzzle addict and her hobby is sewing. The contingency contract she set up with herself went something like this:

> I, Diane, agree to work the crossword puzzle appearing in the daily paper only after I have made some positive comment about Larry's weekend fishing. If I should make a negative comment or fail to make a positive remark about Larry's fishing, I agree to forego the privilege of working crossword puzzles for one week.
>
> Furthermore, I agree that for every hour Larry spends fishing, I will spend an equal amount of time sewing (over and above the time I ordinarily spend on this hobby).

In all probability Diane's negative attitude toward Larry's fishing—and the difficulties it brought to their relationship —would go on unchanged unless the behavioral techniques of modeling, reinforcement, and contingency contracts were brought to bear on the issue; negative feelings and the divisiveness that go along with them do not just suddenly disappear all by themselves.

When Time Is of the Essence

It often happens that husbands and wives who are in vigorous opposition to their mates' independent recreational interests are not so much troubled by the nature of the interest itself as they are by the number of hours their mates devote to it.

Wilma, for example, is involved in a little theater group.

Tom was at first enthusiastic ("My wife, the actress," he would say with obvious pride). But as Wilma began to spend more and more time with members of the group and then later on enrolled in acting classes as well, Tom's attitude underwent a gradual change. He became critical of the group and its members ("A bunch of two-bit ham amateurs," he called them), and accused Wilma of neglecting him and her household responsibilities. Wilma's response was to spend even more time away from home. Both began to consider the possibility of divorce.

In discussing the matter, Wilma stated flatly that she was not willing to give up her involvement with the group. Nor, as it turned out, did Tom feel it was necessary that she do so; his primary objection was to the number of hours that she devoted to it.

When time is a problem, as it was with Tom and Wilma (and as it is in many, many marriages where one partner is absorbed in an activity in which the mate has little or no interest), disagreements can begin to be resolved when the two partners specify the number of hours per week each feels can be fairly devoted to the activity.

What with rehearsals, acting classes and getting together informally with other group members to discuss new plays and theater in general, Wilma estimated that she spent approximately fifteen hours a week on her outside interest, and said she considered fifteen hours a "fair" amount of time to devote to these activities. Tom, on the other hand, felt seven hours a week would be "fair."

Although they were in obvious disagreement here, it was equally apparent that unless they could reach some kind of compromise, their marriage would continue to be in jeopardy. So, both revised their estimation of what was "fair," and it was decided that Wilma would devote no more than eleven hours per week to the theater group.

In order to minimize each partner's natural reluctance to

go along with the compromise, they established contingency contracts whereby some of the pleasurable activities of each depended on Wilma's adherence to the agreed-upon eleven hours per week of theater group involvement.

Thus, Tom earns time for golf and basketball contingent upon Wilma's eleven-hours' worth of time with the group and automatically forfeits golf and basketball privileges when he makes critical remarks about her group activities. Similarly, if Wilma spends more than eleven hours with the group in any one week, she automatically forfeits acting classes and rehearsals for the following week.

Each partner also makes an effort to reward desirable behaviors exhibited by the other. When Tom makes positive comments about the theater group, Wilma immediately expresses her appreciation with hugs, kisses, and perhaps a suggestion that they make love later on in the evening. In the same way, Tom reinforces Wilma for her willingness to reduce the amount of time she spends with members of her group.

The Dependent Spouse

One partner's utter dependency on the other almost always leads to unhappiness for both. (For our purposes here, the overly dependent spouse may be defined as one who becomes depressed and unable to function when absent from his/her partner.) In regard to recreation, the overly dependent spouse has no very well-defined interests of his/her own and demands the constant time and attention of the partner.

"I feel more like his mother than his wife," says the mate of an overdependent husband. "He won't go anywhere or do anything without me. Last year I wanted to take a night school course, but he acted as though I were deserting him forever. So I didn't."

The husband of an overdependent wife says: "She's like a parasite. She expects me to be her constant companion, to keep her always entertained and happy, and heaven help me if I want to go to a football game or something."

Relationships such as these often can be improved—sometimes enormously so—when the dependent partner is encouraged to develop recreational interests of his/her own. The following behavioral techniques may be helpful:

1. *Identify a Possible New Interest*: Each and every one of us is endowed with the potential for enjoying a number of different activities. They only need to be identified and cultivated. The dependent partner should make up a list of possible new interests. Just for starters, it might be helpful to think back to the days before marriage and try to remember how one enjoyed spending one's time then. Such a list might include sports—either new ones or those in which a certain proficiency was established during high school or college—membership in a health club or gym or the local Y, learning (or perhaps relearning) a musical instrument, collecting (stamps, books, records, antiques, etc.), arts and crafts, community volunteer work, involvement with a little theater group, book discussion group or amateur choral society, classes in painting, photography, dance, yoga, etc.

2. *Make a Commitment*: Choose from the list of possible new interests the activity with the strongest immediate appeal and then make a commitment to explore that interest for a period of at least six months. Contingency contracting can be a big help with the follow-through of making the commitment. Jed, for example, might make an agreement with himself that he will read the Sunday papers (or eat desserts, or use the phone, or whatever) only if he actually does join the Y and use the pool once a week. Or Sally, who has decided to learn to play the piano, might make weekly visits to the hairdresser contingent on weekly piano lessons.

It is up to the partner of the dependent spouse to reinforce desirable behavior, to notice and to praise either verbally or by actions the spouse's attempts to achieve a degree of autonomy. Thus, Meg would be wise to have warm smiles, coffee and cake ready for Jed when he comes home from the Y, accompanied perhaps by a phrase such as, "It's nice when you go out for a while by yourself because when you come back I appreciate you all the more."

Once in a while, a spouse will ask whether it is "right" for husbands and wives to spend some of their leisure hours apart. I can only say that the "rightness" or "wrongness" of it all can be discovered in terms of the consequences. Do the partners feel better about themselves and each other when some of their free time is devoted to activities in which their mates cannot or do not wish to share an interest? Often they do. Sometimes they don't.

I do know that even some of those couples who make a virtue of their inseparability—who have always stressed the fact that everything they do, they do together—have found that an independent interest or two which may involve an *occasional* evening or weekend away from each other brings new vitality and richness to their relationship.

At any rate, it is not my purpose here or in any part of this book to induce couples to modify their life-styles—either by an attempt to keep up with the changing times, or by an effort to re-create the stable (and perhaps, somewhat rigid) traditions of the "good old days"—but rather to explain how certain behavioral procedures can be used to reconcile existing differences between husbands and wives and thus contribute to a happier and more satisfying relationship for both.

CHAPTER 12

---◄∞►---

When the Children Are a Problem

"Wendy's room looks like a pigsty. I've tried *everything* to get her to be neater, but nothing works. I guess she's just a natural-born slob."

"I'm worried about Kirk's low grades. He's a bright kid, but he simply won't study. When I tell him it's time for homework, he grunts and mumbles and then goes in to the TV."

"Rachel and Rebecca fight constantly. They drive me up the wall with their screaming and shouting, and there are times when I'm afraid one of them is really going to hurt the other. As a matter of fact, the other day Rebecca actually blackened Rachel's eye."

I've seen many despairing parents who were convinced that somehow or other their kids had gone "bad," because none of their efforts to restore and maintain discipline—from quiet, reasonable talks on the one hand, to spankings and threats on the other—had been successful.

But if you find yourself in this same situation, reconsider.

And take hope. From a behavioral point of view, we know that "bad" children are only kids who do "bad" things. And just as surely as there are ways to modify unpleasing adult behaviors, these same techniques, somewhat modified, will discourage manifestations of your kids' "bad" behaviors and encourage the development of new, more desirable ones.

Way back in the first section of this book, I suggested a procedure for clarifying and defining the real problems in one's marriage. Before going to work on a behavioral change program for your kids, it's necessary to follow through with these same preliminary steps.

To recapitulate, ask yourself the following questions:

1. *What's Wrong?* You should come up with answers that identify the *specific* behaviors your children engage in that upset you. Remember, it's not enough to define the problem in terms of saying to yourself, "He's lazy," or "She never does anything right." *How* is he lazy? (Or, in other words, does he refuse to do household chores assigned him? Is his room a mess [shoes on the floor, T-shirt on bedpost, bed unmade]? Has he failed to develop habits of personal cleanliness [brushing teeth, taking a bath regularly and the like]? And, what are those things that she "never" does right? Is she discourteous? Does she not share her toys? Is she always getting into fights?)

2. *What's Right?* Your answer to this must also be specific. Identifying what's wrong takes you only halfway. Here, you must decide what new behaviors you want your child to engage in more often—i.e., if your "lazy" boy doesn't help around the house, you must redefine in precise terms those jobs you want him to do (take out the garbage, wash the car, empty ashtrays).

3. *What's Happening?* Record-keeping is an important element in the behavioral approach to problem solving. So, when you have been able to specify new behaviors for your children, you should keep score of the number of times these

behaviors presently occur. Only by keeping accurate records of what your kids actually do (or say, as the case may be), will you know for sure whether the desired behaviors are on the increase.

Strategy

After you've identified those behaviors that will make "what's wrong" right again—or, in other words, the things you want your child to do and say more often—make up a list of treats and activities he/she enjoys. By observing what your child likes to do, you will be able to make up a list of reinforcing events or behaviors. Revise the inventory so that it's set up in order of descending importance, with the things your child likes *very* best up at the top of the list, followed by other things he/she is fond of, but perhaps only moderately so. One mother's list went something like this:

Marcy likes:
　Spending the night at Lori's house
　Watching TV
　Drawing
　Roller skating
　Cookies and ice cream
　Movies
　(etc.)

The treats and activities specified on this inventory—in case you haven't guessed by now—are the rewards or reinforcers that you will use to encourage new behavioral patterns.

Now, with list in hand, sit down with your child and explain as clearly, calmly, and succinctly as you know how that (1) you want him/her to do such and such, (2) that you will be watching to see that such and such gets done, (3) that if he/she does such and such the reward is (fill in the blank, according to your list), and (4) that the consequences of not doing such and such are the withdrawal of certain privileges (again, you will use your list to decide which privileges are to be denied).

When you've told your child what behaviors you expect of him/her and what consequences are attached—both the positive ones for engaging in the desired behaviors, and the negative ones for failing to do so—you, as parents, are responsible for the follow-through; distasteful as the term may be, you must become "watchdogs" (at least for the time being), continually enforcing the terms you have set forth and always making sure that the positive and negative consequences for engaging in certain behaviors really do come to pass. This obviously entails more record-keeping.

In this regard I cannot emphasize too strongly the importance not only of having *both* parents involved in a behavioral-change program like this one, but also their *consistent* backing up of one another. Kids are smart, as anybody who lives with one already knows, and in many families the child learns at an astonishingly tender age that when Mommy says "no," maybe—just maybe—Daddy will say "yes." It's suspected that a variety of behavioral problems arise in the very young because of just this kind of lack of parental consistency, and if it has not been your custom up till now to present a united front—at least insofar as the children are concerned—I suggest you and your partner immediately begin to do so. (As a matter of fact, it might not be such a bad idea to notice and praise each other for being consistent with the children in order to encourage this behavioral pattern in *each other*.)

It may be helpful here to present examples of how two actual behavioral-change programs were implemented by two different families.

Janice and Tom wanted their eight-year-old son, Johnny, to learn to be "less sloppy." More specifically, they wanted

him to be responsible for keeping his own room reasonably
neat and clean. They listed the following in answer to the
questions:

What's Wrong?

Johnny leaves his bed unmade, shirts, pants, and dirty
underwear are left on the floor, books, records, and other
possessions are always strewn about the room.

What's Right?

Johnny should (1) make his bed each morning, (2) hang
up his shirts in the closet, (3) hang up his pants, (4) put
dirty underwear in the laundry hamper, and (5) return
books, records, and other possessions to their proper places
in his room.

For one week they recorded how often Johnny engaged
in the desirable behaviors listed above. The results were
dismal: At no time during the seven-day period did Johnny
make his bed. He hung up his shirt on one occasion, but
never hung up his pants, and put dirty underwear in the
hamper only three times. Books, records and other possessions were put away twice.

The top three items on the list of treats and activities
Johnny particularly enjoyed were: watching television, rid-
ing his bicycle, and spending the night with his friend
Luke.

Janice and Tom decided to adopt a point system whereby
Johnny could earn a certain number of points for engaging
in specified desirable behaviors. Johnny could "trade in"
the points for the privilege of doing those things he liked
best.

On a daily basis, for example, he got 1 point for making
his bed, one for hanging up his shirt, one for hanging up
his pants, 1 for putting dirty laundry in the hamper, and 3
for keeping his possessions where they belonged. In addition,
Johnny could earn 2 bonus points if he did all of these
things before breakfast on any given day.

In their agreement, Johnny was allowed to trade in his points at the following rate:

1 point earned 30 minutes of TV
4 points earned an hour of TV
8 points earned unlimited TV watching
8 points also earned him the privilege of riding his bicycle that day

In order to spend the night with his friend, Johnny was required to earn a minimum of 32 points during any given week.

Johnny's parents check the number of points he has earned each morning before Johnny leaves for school. His score is then posted on a chart which hangs on the refrigerator door—thus, the whole family knows at a glance how many points and privileges Johnny has earned. One week's chart looked something like this:

	Points earned	TV	Bicycle	Night with friend
Monday	4	1 hr.	no	
Tuesday	8	all	yes	
Wednesday	8	all	yes	
Thursday	8	all	yes	
Friday	8	all	yes	yes

In another family, the parents were disturbed by the constant fighting that went on between their two children, Glynis, ten, and Bruce, eight and a half. The parents, Sally and Hugh, defined "what's wrong" as the kids' "yelling at and occasionally kicking and hitting at each other."

Sally and Hugh's behavioral goal for their children was that they play together in a way that would not disturb them (the parents). For one week, they recorded how often Glynis and Bruce played cooperatively, as defined above. The children's behavior was observed three times a day— from 4:00 to 4:15 P.M., from 7:00 to 7:15 P.M., and from 9:00 to 9:15 P.M.—for seven days. On only nine of those occasions were the children interacting cooperatively.

As suggested, Sally and Hugh, through observing their children's behavior, drew up a list of treats and activities each child especially enjoyed. It included playing in the tree house, spending the night with friends and listening to records for Glynis; watching TV, riding his bike and going to the movies for Bruce.

Since both children are old enough to read, the parents drew up a rather formal document. The agreement was first discussed with the children and then posted on the bulletin board in their family room.

TO   GLYNIS AND BRUCE

Mother and Dad want you to play cooperatively. We no longer want to be disturbed by your yelling, screaming, kicking, and hitting at one another. We have decided on a plan that will encourage the two of you to play together in a way that will make this house a more peaceful one in which to live:

In the kitchen, you will find two large glass jars, one marked "Glynis," and the other marked "Bruce." These are for poker chips.

On three occasions each day, Mother or Dad will blow a whistle. If you are playing cooperatively when the whistle sounds, each of you will receive two poker chips. Put the chips in the jar marked with your name.

You needn't be playing together when you hear the whistle. The only condition for being awarded the chips is that you are not disturbing us at the moment it is blown.

However, if you happen to be fighting when the whistle is blown, each of you will lose one poker chip and be separated for thirty minutes from the other, regardless of who started the fighting or what you are fighting about. Each of you will also lose one poker chip any time one of us has to intercede because of your yelling, screaming, kicking, or hitting one another.

In other words, by playing cooperatively, each of you has the opportunity of earning six poker chips each day (two chips on each of three occasions). Each of you loses a poker chip if you are fighting when the whistle is blown or at any time one of us has to break up a fight.

Poker chips may be traded in for the privileges specified below:

Glynis
    Playing in the tree house—3 chips
    Spending the night with a friend—3 chips
    Listening to records—1 chip per hour

Bruce
    Bike riding—3 chips
    Movies—3 chips
    Watching TV—1 chip per hour

By earning these chips for cooperative play you can cash these in for the privileges of your choice.
                  Lovingly,
                  Mother and Dad

School Behavior

I've spoken with many parents who felt their children could and should be doing better in school. The following program was suggested to Keith and Marlene as a way to encourage their fourteen-year-old son Billy to raise his grade average.

At the time I first talked with the parents, Billy's most recent report card showed a D+ average—with an F (for failure) in Math and an A in Physical Education. Both Marlene and Keith were certain that Billy was capable of at least a B average and that in no case should he bring home less than a C in any one subject.

Billy particularly enjoys playing baseball with his friends and driving his motor scooter. He's looking forward to having a car of his own when he is old enough to drive. (In their state, a sixteen-year-old is eligible for a driver's license).

During a family round-table discussion, Keith and Marlene presented Billy with the document outlined here.

CONTINGENCY CONTRACT
FOR BETTER GRADES

Billy: Because we know you are capable of maintaining a B average, and because we want to encourage you to do better in school, we have decided on the following plan, effective immediately:

Each afternoon after school, you must study from 4:00 to 5:00, and then hit the books again from 8:00 to 9:30 in the evening. *Positive consequence:* The privilege of driving your motor scooter the following day. *Negative consequence:* No motor scooter.

Each Friday afternoon you must bring a note from each of your various teachers indicating your weekly grade average in their respective classes for the preceding week. You must maintain an overall B average, with no grade below C in any subject.[1] *Positive consequence:* The privilege of playing baseball with friends on Saturday and Sunday. *Negative consequence:* No weekend baseball.

At the end of each grading period, we will deposit money into a special car-fund account at the rate of $25 for each A, $10 for each B, and $5 for each C on your report card; while for each mark of D (or below), $10 will be withdrawn from the account.

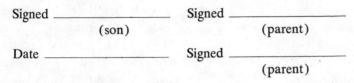

Signed _____   Signed _____
            (son)   (parent)

Date _____   Signed _____
                                      (parent)

There are any number of different kinds of contracts and agreements that can be made between parents and children. I've given just a few examples: one for encouraging neatness, another for discouraging negative interaction between siblings, and a third to promote the development of better study habits. Obviously, I have not touched on all the possible problems that may arise, but I hope the point has been made that behavioral principles can be applied equally as well—and in many cases better—to children as to adults.

However, I hope you will keep the following guidelines in mind no matter what kind of behavioral-change program you decide to implement with your own kids:

1. Make sure your child knows exactly what you want him/her to do. If your child is old enough to read, put it in writing. Explanations must be phrased clearly and explicitly to the younger child. It may be necessary to list the various steps involved for completion of complicated tasks. (For example, if you want your son to wash the dishes, you should probably indicate in step-by-step fashion how he ought to go about it—i.e., (1) fill the sink with hot water, (2) add soap, (3) wash and rinse each dish, etc.)

2. Establish specific positive consequences for specified desirable behaviors. Just as important, make sure your child understands what they are. The premise, of course, is similar to that of the exchange contracts that can be so helpful in establishing good interaction between mature adults—i.e., if you do X for me, I in turn will do Y for you.

In fact, since you are requesting behavior change in your son or daughter, you should ask them what new behaviors they want *you* to engage in (or old ones they want you to do more frequently—or what behaviors they want you to stop to please them). "Don't be so grumpy," "Stop finding fault with everything I do," and "Let me cut the lawn the way I want to" are examples of what youngsters ask their parents to do to please them. It's a fact that changing your own behavior to please your children has a tremendous impact on their willingness to change their behavior to please you.

3. Establish specific negative consequences for specified undesirable behaviors, and, as above, make it very clear to your child that when he/she fails to do what you want, "bad" things will happen (treats and privileges will be withheld).

4. Decide which parent will be primarily responsible for carrying out the behavioral-change plan. Several pages back, I stressed the importance of having *both* parents involved and in consistent agreement with one another as to how to implement whatever kind of program might be decided upon. But in order to avoid the possibility of parent's assuming that the other is (or has been) keeping tabs on the situation, it's best to elect an "administrator" whose job it is to make sure that privileges and treats are allowed or withheld according to the terms of the agreement.

There are two very valuable and easy-to-read books written to help parents understand how to be better managers of their children's behaviors. One is *Families*, by Gerald Patterson. The other is *Parents/Children/Discipline: A Positive Approach*, by Clifford H. Madsen and Charles H. Madsen, Jr. I suggest you get hold of either or both for more detailed information on the behavioral approach to child rearing.

Sex Education

Perhaps one of the deepest concerns of today's young parents is that their children grow up into healthy, happily married adults. The best marriages, though not necessarily predicated on good sex, always have as one of their main ingredients the partners' mutual physical enjoyment of one another, and so I believe it is one of your major responsibilities, as mothers and fathers, to make sure your children learn about sex in positive ways.

Keep in mind that your children *will* pick up ideas and attitudes about sex regardless of whether or not you say anything specific to them. Parents often "teach" their children how to think and feel about sex without meaning to.

They will learn an awful lot simply by observing the way you behave toward one another. Not too long ago, I spoke with a young woman who told me she never remembered seeing her mother and father kiss. "He never even put his arms around her, and I never saw her put her head down on his shoulder or even straighten his tie or muss his hair. In fact, I don't think they ever touched at all when I was around. I grew up thinking, 'Well, that's the way married people act,' and now my husband accuses me of being cold and undemonstrative. But how could I be any other way?"

When parents say nothing to their children about sex, express no physical affection for one another, switch off the TV when the love scenes come on, or otherwise respond in an embarrassed, self-conscious way when sex is mentioned in the children's presence, the kids, obviously—and especially the girls, who probably get the worst of it in our society—are going to get the idea that sex is "bad," or "dirty," and this attitude can only hinder their chances for happiness in their own marriages.

I would like to see *all* parents make a conscious effort to give their kids healthy, positive information about sex. I'm not alone here; most social scientists express the same wish and have been doing so for some time now. Yet, in a Purdue poll[2] of 1,000 teen-agers, only 32 percent of the girls and 15 percent of the boys said that they got sex information from their parents. Both boys and girls reported that most of what they learned came from books and friends. And while there are many good, worthwhile books about sex written for young people, unless the children were directed to them by parents or teachers, these are probably not the books those kids were referring to. As for learning from friends, it is the rare child who is well-enough informed to pass along the kind of information most of us would wish our children to receive.

In my experience, most reasonably well educated people are eager and anxious to provide some kind of sex education for their kids, but many are at a loss as to how to proceed. This, coupled with the really not too accurate assumption that all schools today offer sex information, probably accounts for the Purdue study's finding that only 47 percent of the teen-agers in the sample group learned about sex from their parents. Although many schools do make an attempt to integrate some kind of sex education into their curriculums, I feel the parents must assume the ultimate responsibility. You are not only your kids' *first* teachers, you are also their most influential ones.

When parents decide to take on the responsibility of teaching their children about sex, the most frequently asked question is "WHEN?"

The answer here is really a rather simple one: Tell your children about sex when they express an interest in the subject. The three-year-old girl who suddenly discovers that boys have penises will probably ask questions. "What is it?" Tell her it's called a penis. "What's it for?" Tell her he uses it for urinating and that later on, when he's a grown up man, he can help make babies with it. The five-year-old boy who asks where he came from should be told that he developed in a special place in his mother's body called the uterus. Probably he will be satisfied with this answer; but if he wants to know more—"But how did I get in there?" —you should tell him about intercourse in simple words that he can understand. In any case, he should never be put off, or given the old bit about the stork or the doctor's little black bag. (Parents who feed their kids on such stories are telling lies and sooner or later will be found out. Children, like adults, resent being lied to, and the liar—except in some very rare instances—is hardly a person one can easily respect.)

For those of you who are not quite sure how to phrase your explanations in a way that is honest but not over-whelmingly loaded down with clinical detail (usually younger children want the simplest answers to the most basic questions, while some parents feel it as their duty to tell *all*, immediately), I recommend an excellent book, *What to Tell Your Children About Sex*, which was put together by the Child Study Association of America.

It's important, I think, to understand that "sex education" —the really not too difficult task of answering your child's questions about reproduction—is only one part of the job parents must undertake when their goal is to encourage, good, healthy attitudes about sex in their kids. Children, for example, must also acquire some understanding of the way men and women relate to each other sexually within a moral and social context.

In this regard, Lester Kirkendall[3] believes that children ought to learn that each part of their bodies and each phase of their growth is good and has meaning and purpose—that a girl should feel proud about having a vagina and a boy happy about having a penis—and that kids must be pre-pared for the physical changes associated with approaching maturation. Every boy should know, for example, about "wet dreams" before they occur. Every girl should have menstruation explained to her before her first period. (One poor child whose first period came as a complete surprise wept for days, convinced that her "insides were rotting," until the mother, discovering the girl's hidden blood-stained underpants, finally sat down with her to reassure her about what was happening. Such things *do* happen.)

Later on, the budding young woman should be told that her boyfriend probably gets an erection when she puts her hand on his leg. And a young man should understand that quite possibly his girlfriend does not know that certain things she does are sexually exciting to him.

Most important, perhaps, is to get the idea across to young people that meaningful sex is always person-oriented, rather than body-oriented, and that sexual conduct should be based upon a sincere regard for the happiness and welfare of their partners.

Masturbation

Many parents, especially the mothers and fathers of boys, are aware, or suspect, that their children masturbate.

What, they wonder, should children be taught about self-stimulation? Is it good? Is it bad? Should it be discouraged? Tolerated? Encouraged?

It may help to keep in mind that it is normal and natural for human beings, young and old, to seek pleasure in sex— whether through self-stimulation or with a partner. Modern medical science has come up with no evidence indicating that physical or psychological damage results from masturbation. The real damage is done by parents who view it as a disgusting, filthy, or unnatural act, and who threaten their kids with dire consequences unless the habit is dropped. And when this is the case, the behavior usually is not extinguished, but is carried on instead under a tremendous burden of guilt and shame. It is the rare child who can survive such a situation and go on to develop good, positive sexual attitudes in later life.

In my personal best of all possible worlds, all parents would view masturbation as a healthy, normal behavior which occurs in the process of normal development, and all children would learn that self-stimulation is but one of many ways of enjoying their sexuality. The only prohibition would be that the behavior be indulged in privacy.

Parents always have worried about their children and I suppose they always will. And this is as it should be. But while concerned young mothers and fathers ruminate about this psychological theory or that, they may lose sight of the simplest fact of all: that children learn what they are taught and that when parents demonstrate kindness, consideration, and love through their own behaviors, their kids have a far better chance to grow up to be healthy, normal people, aware of the positive and negative consequences of their actions but at the same time joyous savorers of life.

CHAPTER 13

And What About
These Other Problems

I ALMOST DIDN'T write this chapter. If you've managed to come along with me this far, and I've managed to communicate the fundamentals of the behavioral approach to problem-solving in marriage, then you already know how certain specific techniques can be modified and applied to any number of different situations.

But I wrote it anyway, mainly to relieve my own nagging sense that several unrelated issues—relatively minor in the overall scheme of things, but of possible major import in some few marriages—had gone unacknowledged and deserved at least a brief mention in passing.

The matter of food, for example, and buying it and cooking it and eating it and how to handle disagreements over who does what with it and when. And the problems associated with housework. And driving the car. And late behaviors. And maintaining physical attractiveness.

Minor issues? Petty? Yes, in the sense that none of them rate up there in the big leagues along with Communication, Sex, and Money. But all potential sources of conflict. I've seen more than one couple teetering on the brink of divorce precisely because they let disagreements over just such "piddling" matters get the better of them and their marriages.

Who's Cooking?

In the "traditional" marriage, the question needn't even be asked. The wife cooks.

But more and more women, even those who had assumed on their wedding day that they, and they alone, would be solely responsible for planning and preparing all the family meals, are beginning to feel that it might not be such a bad idea if their husbands occasionally took over in the kitchen. And more and more husbands are coming around to the same conclusion. (President Ford fixes his own toast.)

I am not suggesting that wives cook less and husbands more. Or that wives do all the cooking and husbands none (or vice versa). I do feel it is important, though, that both partners verbalize their feelings about this issue and then take steps to arrive at an arrangement whereby each knows what is expected of whom, and when.

Millie, a young mother of two, working on a masters degree in physical therapy, and Jack, her lawyer-husband, had problems in this area. Their concept of a happy marriage was one in which household tasks—including shopping for groceries and meal planning and preparation—were divided "about equally." But both placed a high value on spontaneity, and neither liked the idea of being "locked into a schedule." Thus, their arrangement was totally haphazard. There were times when they both felt like cooking and other times when neither did. Mealtimes became occasions for chaos and worse, and since nobody was keeping score, each began to harbor a sneaking suspicion that the other might be "copping out."

They finally decided that, like it or not, they would have

to draw up a timetable specifying when each of them would be responsible for shopping, cooking, and cleaning up after meals. Here's an example of how they scheduled one week's duties:

	Shopping	Breakfast Cook/Cleanup		Lunch	Dinner Cook/Cleanup	
Mon.		Millie	Jack	Millie	Jack	Millie
Tues.		Millie	Jack	Millie	Jack	Millie
Wed.		Millie	Jack	Millie	Jack	Millie
Thur.		Millie	Jack	Millie	Jack	Millie
Fri.	Jack	Millie	Jack	Millie	Jack	Millie
Sat.		Jack	Millie	Jack	Millie	Jack
Sun.		Jack	Millie	Jack	Millie	Jack

Since Jack has lunch at work on the weekdays, Millie prepares this meal for herself (and for the children when they are not in school). Jack makes lunch on the weekends. Otherwise, all duties as scheduled above are alternated on a weekly basis.

As part of their agreement, they decided that though assistance may be freely offered (they often shop for groceries and cook together), once a chore has been assigned, neither will expect, nor ask for, help from the other.

Splitting the chores equally may not be everybody's idea of an ideal arrangement, but again, the point is not so much *who* is to do what, as it is *knowing* who is to do what.

What's cooking?

One young husband made the comment that "I don't care what's for dinner as long as there's plenty of it." Most of us are not so sanguine in our approach to what we put into our stomachs. We have our preferences and our definite dislikes and when these are not taken into consideration, food becomes a problem.

Randy and Molly (whose marriage can best be described as "ultratraditional" in that Molly does *all* the shopping, cooking and cleaning up after meals, while Randy confines his visits to the kitchen to those rare occasions when Molly is not around to bring him a beer) almost came to blows over a piece of broiled halibut.

Randy is a man of few words, but several weeks before the big blowup took place, he had expressed his great enjoyment of a special fish dish Molly had concocted. Understandably gratified by his appreciation of this particular meal, she served it again the following week. And again the week after that. When it appeared before him on the fourth consecutive Friday, Randy slammed his fist down on the table and bellowed that he never wanted to see another damned halibut in their house again, that he wasn't any too happy about meat loaf all the time, either, and why in heaven's name didn't she give him a lamb chop once in a while? Molly's response was to take the fish, dump it in the garbage, and run from the room in tears.

They laughed about it later on, but the incident made them both aware that after seven years of marriage, Molly *still* didn't know what Randy liked to eat—because Randy never *told* her—while Randy had always assumed that she did, and that the reason she rarely served his favorites was because she "simply didn't care enough to want to please me."

Randy realized that although Molly is a woman of many talents, mind reading is not one of them. It was suggested that they set aside half an hour or so every Thursday evening to plan the following week's dinner menus. Three of the meals would be of Randy's choosing, three would include dishes they were both fond of, and the seventh meal would be up to Molly: either her favorite food at home, or dinner in a restaurant.

As a result of their agreement, Randy feels "fussed over

and loved" because Molly cooks the food he likes, and Molly is relieved of the burden of having to guess what suits him and when he wants it.

Housework and Other Dirty Work

In many traditional marriages, earning money is "his job." It begins when he arrives at work and ends when he leaves. "Her job," though it is hardly ever called that, is to take care of the house and children. It begins when she awakes in the morning and ends when she goes to sleep at night.

Many couples go along with this division of labor—they take it for granted, it corresponds with their own images of themselves as men and women, and perhaps there is a certain logic to it: He spends eight hours a day at more or less intensive work, while her fifteen or sixteen hours on the job may be interrupted by occasional "breaks"—a few minutes here, a half hour or so there—when she has caught up with her work and is thus temporarily "off duty." Couples whose marriages operate along these lines and who are satisfied with this arrangement might just as well skip the rest of this discussion and go on to the section on Driving.

The fact is, however, that many married people—especially the wives, and particularly those who are also mothers of very young children, or who hold full or part-time jobs outside the home, or who are in school or job-training programs so that they will be prepared to go back to work when the children are older—feel that the traditional arrangement is unfair.

"I have three children under five," one woman says. "They demand *all* of my attention from the minute I wake up until they're all in bed at night. On top of which, I cook, shop, clean and do all the family's laundry.

"When my husband comes home at six o'clock each evening, he plunks himself down in front of the television set until dinnertime, then he eats and goes back to the TV while I wash dishes and give the kids their baths. And then he wonders why I'm too tired for sex."

Another woman tells pretty much the same story except that she is a working mother of two. "I work from nine to three five days a week and I'm not complaining about that: We need the money and I was lucky to get the job. But I do resent my husband's expecting that I should also *single-handedly* care for the children and our home."

Wives who for whatever reason want to encourage their husbands to take on more of the work involved in raising their children and running their homes must begin by specifying the desirable new behaviors they want their partners to engage in. (Many men, it seems, are not so much reluctant to help out as they are mystified by what it is they are supposed to do.)

Marion, for example, wanted Al to take charge of the children's baths and get them into bed every evening, fold and put away clean laundry twice a week and vacuum the entire house once a week. Al agreed, though he insisted that he didn't know how to do any of these things. (To which Marion replied that neither had she, seven years ago when they were first married.)

The very same techniques that we've been discussing all through this book—those that encourage positive attitudes toward desirable new behaviors—apply equally as well to this kind of situation:

Modeling: It was suggested that Al identify from among his friends those men who also shared housework and child care with their wives. As it turned out, a surprising number of them did. They bowled together and though they were in unanimous agreement that "housework is a drag," most of them expressed the feeling that the quality of their marriages had improved as a result of helping out around the house. ("She's more affectionate . . . I guess because she appreciates me more," one of them said of his wife. Another commented: "She nags a whole lot less, because she's got a whole lot less to nag about.")

Contingency Contracting: Al made an agreement with himself that (1) he would not play tennis on Saturdays unless he had vacuumed the house during the week, (2) that he would not watch evening TV unless he'd put the children to bed, and (3) he would not shower or shave on laundry days unless he'd folded the clean clothes and distributed them in their proper drawers.

Exchange Contracting: Al and Marion drew up the following exchange contracts to further encourage Al's positive attitude toward housework:

Al: I, Al, agree to bathe and get the children to bed every night, fold and put away clean laundry twice a week and vacuum the entire house once each week if, in return, Marion will initiate intercourse on two occasions each week and be solely responsible for managing our finances (i.e., make sure all bills are paid on time, balance the checkbook monthly, transfer funds from checking to savings account, keep all financial records in order and make out our annual income tax returns).

Marion: I, Marion, agree to initiate intercourse on two occasions each week and to be solely responsible for managing our finances according to the stipulations in Al's contract if, in return, Al will bathe and get the children to bed every night, fold and put away clean laundry twice a week and vacuum the entire house once each week.

Reinforce and Reward Desirable Behavior: Each of them, of course, makes a point of noticing and rewarding, by word or deed, the other's desirable new behavior.

In some marriages, one partner is far more concerned with "neatness" than the other, and (surprise!) the "neat" partner is very often the husband. In one of these marriages,

Corinne, the wife, simply decided that since her husband, Phil, valued a spotless home so very much more than she did, he could—if he wished—be responsible for maintaining the degree of cleanliness that he desired. She specified what household chores she felt it was reasonable for her to perform, and it was agreed that any additional cleaning would be done by Phil. In return for Phil's straightening the house to meet his own level of neatness and not nagging Corinne, she agreed to prepare pizza for Phil's Thursday-night poker friends.

In another marriage that came to my attention, members of the family functioned independently in the sense that each was assigned responsibility for maintaining his or her own room, clothing, and other possessions.

Husband and wife are both in their forties and hold full-time jobs, and their children, a boy and a girl, are in high school.

Saturday is cleaning day and everyone pitches in. Cooking and shopping are done on a rotating basis. Both children and parents are responsible for laundering their own clothing and picking up after themselves. "Anything left lying around where it doesn't belong gets 'confiscated,' " the wife explains. "Baseball mitts, school books, sneakers, things like that, all go into a locked trunk when they're not in their proper places, and the owner must pay a fine (usually a temporary loss of some privilege, sometimes a dime or a quarter) to get it back again. The kids get a big kick out of confiscating *my* things," she adds with a little laugh.

"We've been operating this way for a couple of years now and it works out pretty well. We don't have the neatest house in town, but at least I don't feel that I am personally to blame for it. Some of my son's friends think it's 'weird' that he cooks and does his own laundry, but *he* doesn't. I'm very proud of my kids and I think as a family we're closer than most."

Who's Driving?

I'm not aware of any compilation of statistics indicating the number of accidents per year that are directly attributable to the distracting influence of that loathsome creature, the backseat driver. I am aware, however, that many couples who get along famously in their own living rooms and bedrooms turn into raging, snarling beasts when they get into a car together.

"Watch out for that stop sign, you meathead."

"You're going too fast. Do you want to get us both killed?"

"Imbecile! You missed the turnoff."

Some of us are better drivers than others and, as I've noted before, I believe it's preferable for the partner who displays the greater degree of competence—whether it be in driving, or cooking, or bookkeeping, or hanging wallpaper, or reading bedtime stories—to take over the bulk of the responsibilities in the area in question. The better driver ought to do most of the driving.

In any case, husbands and wives should agree that there can be only *one* driver at any given time—the person behind the wheel—and that interference from one's partner is not only infuriating but distracting, and, thus, potentially dangerous as well.

I suggest that husbands and wives who value arriving at their destination safe, sound, and in a calm, unruffled state of mind, over and above gratifying their own impulses to direct the movement of the vehicle from any location other than the driver's seat, consider abiding by the following guidelines:

1. Have an understanding that the person driving is solely responsible for all movement of the vehicle and that he/she will decide not only what route to follow but also when to slow down and accelerate, when to switch lanes and make turns, and where to park.

2. Make a rule that the person *not* driving will comment upon movement of the vehicle only when asked to do so by the driver (or of course when and if it suddenly becomes apparent to the nondriving partner that the car is about to leave the road or make direct contact with some other object). The consequence of backseat driving is wearing a handkerchief tied over the mouth for the next ten miles.

Backseat driving is a behavior and subject to the same "extinguishing" techniques as any other negative behavior. Thus, the driver should ignore so far as is humanly possible any interference from the nondriving partner and reinforce by word and deed the desirable new behavior (in this case, silence about the movement of the car is what we're after).

Late Again?

Lateness (or, in behaviorese, "failure to engage in agreed-upon behaviors at the expected time") is not a problem in many, many marriages. Some men have regular schedules and arrive home at the same time every evening; you can set your watch by them ("If Dad's home, it must be six o'clock"). Others work more unpredictable hours, but it would never occur to them *not* to call their wives to tell them when they will be home. And some couples have reached an agreement whereby the husband forages for himself on week nights (this, usually after long experience with elaborate dinners left charred and forgotten in the oven because frequent business meetings or hospital emergencies make coming home on time and phoning equally impossible).

Still, for some few couples, lateness is a problem. And a big one at that. The waiting spouse often interprets unexplained late behavior as discourtesy, pure and simple (which it is), and goes on from there to infer that "If he/she really cares about me and my feelings, he/she wouldn't be discourteous and make me wait. He/she just doesn't love me" (which isn't necessarily the case). When the late partner finally puts in an appearance, there are recriminations and counter-recriminations and a good old-fashioned Donnybrook is under way.

Sharon is a chronic worrier and Ed was chronically late. It was suggested that in order to bring back some semblance of harmony to their relationship, they work out an agreement: When Ed leaves, he tells Sharon when he expects to return, but in naming the hour he allows himself some margin for error. (In other words, if he *thinks* he might be able to get home by 9 P.M., he tells Sharon to expect him by 9:30.)

Sharon in turn was instructed to allow Ed an hour's grace period (during which time he will either come home or call), so that she has no legitimate cause for worry unless she has not heard from him by 10:30.

In addition, Ed established a contingency contract whereby he allows himself the privilege of playing chess and listening to records only if he lives up to the terms of their agreement.

An exchange contract might be an alternative solution to the same kind of problem: Amy agrees not to expect George to adhere to any explicitly defined week-day schedule in return for unlimited time off for herself on Saturdays.

Supper time can be a far more relaxed and less anxiety-provoking occasion when husband and wife establish a definite hour for the meal—say, forty-five minutes or so after the husband's usual arrival home from work. Let's use 7 P. M. as an example:

In this arrangement, if the husband is not home at 7 P.M., wife and children will have their supper, and the husband will warm up his own meal when he does finally appear. There are some real advantages to this kind of agreement: Children and wife are not inconvenienced by the husband's lateness and thus not hungry and/or angry with him when he arrives. Furthermore, the natural negative consequences of lateness (the husband's having to see to his own dinner) discourages its frequency.

Up until now we've been concerned with late arrivals. Late departures may be just as big a problem.

I've heard it over and over again:

"We're supposed to be at the Carson's by eight-thirty, but at eight forty-five she's still fussing with her makeup." (or)

"He sits around reading the paper or playing with the kids until ten minutes before we have to leave. Then it takes him thirty minutes to get showered, shaved, and dressed."

One partner occasionally accuses the other of *"never* being ready on time." This is very rarely absolutely true, and to get a more accurate idea of the frequency of late-departure behavior, the couple should over a period of two weeks or so keep a record of how many times the late partner *is* ready to leave on time.

Assuming that both partners value on-time departure behaviors—even though one of them has trouble living up to the other's expectations—it may be helpful to establish a contract similar to the one drawn up by Peggy and Sam. In this case, Peggy was the "late" partner, but very often it works the other way around, and I personally would like to see the myth of the female's eternal propensity for lateness, eternally scotched.

PEGGY'S ON-TIME CONTRACT

I agree to be ready to leave the house within five minutes of our preestablished time of departure. I also agree that Sam is to leave without me if I cannot be ready on time, in which case I will either make my own arrangements for transportation (drive our son's Ford if it is available, take a bus, etc.) or stay home.

Maintaining Physical Attractiveness

Many physically less well endowed men and women suffer enormously because of our society's misplaced (or so it seems to me) emphasis on beauty. We all admire beauty, but we do not all marry it. We choose our partners and our partners choose us for any number of reasons and physical attraction is only one of them.

However, it can't be denied that when married people "let themselves go," when they give up making an effort to maintain a reasonably neat and attractive appearance, their partners suffer and so may the relationship.

The wife of a husband who has gained twenty, thirty pounds or more and has taken to slopping around the house in undershirt and shorts may not leave him because of it, but chances are she is more than a little bit disappointed that the presentable young man she married has turned into such a slob.

And the husband of a wife who showers at infrequent intervals, who rarely bothers to run a comb through her hair, and whose clothes always seem to be held together by safety pins is apt to be similarly disenchanted.

When one partner is troubled by the other's apparent lack of concern for maintaining physical attractiveness, he/she can attempt to encourage a more positive attitude by specifying desirable new behaviors.

After five years of marriage and three children, Felice had fallen into slovenly ways. For her, children and house came first and she spent all her time and energy on them. The two older children were scrubbed and shiny as they went off to nursery school each morning, the baby was kept as dirt-free as any baby who is continually poking about in sandy, muddy, and other interesting but messy places can be, and the house was spotless and surprisingly neat as well, considering that three small children spent most of their time there.

But Felice herself, so busy managing the circumstances of other people's lives, was a mess. She ironed her husband's shirts and some of the children's things, but her own clothes were wrinkled. Her hair went unwashed for weeks and was stringy and unkempt. Her hands were rough and reddened from dishwater, bath water, wash water, water from the garden hose, etc. She sometimes tumbled into bed too exhausted even to brush her teeth.

Conrad, her husband, loved her, sympathized with her busy schedule, and appreciated the time and effort she spent on their home and children. Still, he was dismayed that the vital, glowing young woman he had married had become, in his words, "a dowdy, slovenly housewife." He presented her with the following exchange contract:

> I, Conrad, agree to take charge of the children each Saturday from ten to five and to bathe and get the children into bed each evening if, in return, Felice will agree to spend part of her free time on Saturdays at the beauty parlor, having her hair washed and set and her nails manicured, and that when I am finished giving the children their baths, Felice will immediately get into the tub, herself.

Felice happily agreed. Conrad's taking her out to dinner by candlelight gave her additional incentive to look attractive.

Sometimes one partner's overweight is a source of unhappiness to the other. Lisa, for example, was not only repulsed by Howie's great bulk but feared for his health as well. Howie often talked about losing weight and Lisa always encouraged him to do so. But it was not until behavioral techniques were brought to bear on the situation that Howie, with Lisa's help, actually did begin to shed excess poundage.

After some discussion, Lisa and Howie drew up the following exchange contract:

LISA'S CONTRACT

I, Lisa, agree to initiate intercourse twice weekly and to golf or play tennis with Howie whenever he likes if, in return, Howie will agree to consult his doctor about a weight-reducing program and to do what he says.

HOWIE'S CONTRACT

I, Howie, agree to consult my doctor about a weight-reducing programs and to do what he says if, in return, Lisa will agree to initiate intercourse twice weekly and to golf or play tennis with me whenever I suggest it.

(In regard to dieting, the first step is *always* to see a doctor in order to check out the possibility of an abnormal thyroid condition and also to decide upon a realistic weight-loss goal, calculated in terms of one's age, height and frame.)

In accordance with their agreement, Howie made an appointment with his doctor, who advised him to lose forty pounds at the rate of approximately two pounds per week, and gave him a diet plan that would enable him to do so.

Since diet books are a glut on the market and have been for some time now (anyone who is interested can pick up five or six different ones at a local bookstore), and since no one weight-reducing regimen is "right" for everyone, there's not much point in reproducing Howie's diet in detail here.

I will, however, indicate how behavioral techniques were used to encourage Howie's new eating habits.

Eating, like all other behaviors, can be modified by manipulating the events that influence it—by arranging the environment, if you will, so that good things happen when one sticks to one's diet and bad things happen when one doesn't. Married people are very much a part of each other's environment, and I strongly urge the dieting partner to enlist the help of his/her mate.

It was suggested that Howie identify a number of pleasurable activities. He listed reading, watching TV, listening to records, playing chess, fishing, and going to the movies. These were to be the basis of daily and weekly contingency contracts made with himself.

It was also suggested that Lisa engage in certain reinforcing behaviors to encourage Howie to stay on his diet. Lisa understood that *under no circumstances was she to say anything negative to Howie about eating.*

Howie's diet was a 1,400 calorie per day plan. He made an agreement with himself that he would listen to records, read, play chess and watch TV on any one day only if he had consumed no more than 1,400 calories worth of food the previous day. Furthermore, he agreed to fish or see a movie on the weekend only if he had been successful in sticking to his diet during the preceding week.

At the end of each day, Howie indicated success, or lack of it, on a sheet of paper taped to the refrigerator door. Success was represented by an "X," failure by a "O." Thus, Lisa knew at a glance and without discussing the matter with Howie how well he had fared on any one day.

She was especially ingenious and creative in her manner of reinforcing Howie's dieting behaviors. In the beginning, she approached him for sex whenever he recorded an X on his chart. Later on, as the X's appeared with greater frequency, she initiated intercourse less often and instead planned small but nevertheless meaningful surprises: One night, after the X had gone up on the chart, she presented him with a record he'd been planning to buy for himself. On another night, she brought out a new pipe he had admired in a store window. On two occasions, she had flowers sent to his office; each time the enclosed card read, "You're great. I love you. L."

When Howie had lost seven pounds, she took a long, admiring look at him as he was undressing for bed and said she thought she'd better take all his old clothes in to be altered soon. When he'd passed the halfway mark, she planned a private little surprise party: there was a Jello-mold "cake" with candles and she toasted his health and their happy marriage with No-Cal soda.

In actuality, Howie's diet was a joint venture, and though he spent many TV-less evenings and more movie-less weekends, the experience was a positive one for both of them. Howie lost weight (though he never did quite achieve the desired forty-pound loss, he came very close and weighs only seven pounds more than he should) and Lisa honestly finds him more attractive than ever now.

Like Howie's diet, and like the countless other examples of working together toward behavioral goals, happiness in marriage is *always* a joint venture. It cannot be any other way.

Conclusion

I'M INCLINED to believe that if you've taken the trouble to buy and read this book you did so with the intention of finding a solution to some problem(s) in your marriage. I'm also inclined to believe that by studying the contents, you have already taken the most important step in finding that solution: You've indicated a willingness and a desire to *act* on the problem.

It would be tempting and logical to conclude with the obvious injunction: "Now that you know what needs to be done, go ahead and start doing it." But you've already started. You've already made the first step. So, my concluding remark is: "Keep it up. You're doing fine."

APPENDIX I

GOALS: Husband and Wife

THE FOLLOWING ARE examples of goals that spouses have established for themselves and each other using the diagnostic procedure outlined in Chapter 1. The goals are positive and are presented for both the husband and wife.

HUSBAND'S GOALS

COMMUNICATION

I want to:

spend at least 30 minutes alone with my wife daily

tell the truth

be able to talk about sex to my wife

learn to express my feelings

control my temper

I want my wife to:

compliment me rather than nag me

notice when I talk to her

speak softly to me

smile when I see her in the evening

SEX

I want to:

create and maintain an erection (I am impotent)

delay ejaculation during intercourse for 20 minutes

talk about things other than my previous sexual experiences
decide whether to leave my mistress or wife
I want my wife to:
    ask me to have intercourse with her three times a week
    have an orgasm
    tell me she enjoys making love with me

ALCOHOL
I want to:
    control my drinking (drink a maximum of 2 ounces of
        hard liquor per 24-hour period)
I want my wife to:
    control her drinking (drink a maximum of 2 ounces of
        hard liquor per 24-hour period)
    notice when I am sober

IN-LAWS
I want to:
    make decisions without consulting my father
I want my wife to:
    choose me over her parents
    visit her parents without me
    tell her mother she can't live with us
    call her mother a maximum of 3 times per week

FRIENDS
I want to:
    spend a maximum of 10 hours per week with my friends
    speak kindly to my wife's friends
I want my wife to:
    associate with women who are faithful to their husbands
    spend at least 30 minutes with me alone daily
    repeat about others only what is good, honest, and true
    talk with friends about things other than my business
    develop a positive attitude toward my friends

RELIGION
I want to:
    develop a positive attitude about my wife's religion
    develop control over my cursing
I want my wife to:
    be happy going to church alone

avoid asking me why I don't contribute to her church
take the pill
teach the children a more liberal outlook on life
reduce her church activities to two per week

MONEY

I want to:

reduce my gambling to once a week and control my limit
invest only 5 percent of our income in the stock market
be honest on my income tax

I want my wife to:

tell me she has faith in my ability to provide
change her working hours or work fewer hours
spend money carefully (buy only what is necessary for us
   to live relatively comfortably)
be responsible for paying bills

RECREATION

I want to:

develop a mutual recreational activity with my wife

I want my wife to:

show a positive interest in my hobbies
develop interests of her own
agree to go to the beach
trust me

CHILDREN

I want our son (daughter) to:

clean up his (her) room ("cleaned up room" is defined in
   Chapter 13)
make a "B" average in school
develop a positive attitude about sex

OTHER BEHAVIORS

I want to:

avoid an argument over being "late"

I want my wife to:

serve the food I like
cook when she is supposed to
be silent about my driving
be ready to leave on time
lose weight

WIFE'S GOALS

COMMUNICATION

I want to:

control my screaming

I want my husband to:

talk to me

tell me the truth

talk about sex

say something positive

control his temper

SEX

I want to:

achieve an orgasm

develop a positive attitude about sex

I want my husband to:

achieve and maintain an erection (he is impotent)

delay his ejaculation during intercourse for 20 minutes

hug and kiss me when he doesn't want intercourse

not mention his previous sexual experiences

terminate his relationship with "the other woman"

shower before we make love

kiss me and talk to me *after* his ejaculation

ALCOHOL

I want to:

control my drinking

I want my husband to:

admit he has a problem with alcohol

control his drinking

call me when he will be late

call a taxi when he is drunk

accept responsibility for his drinking

be a sober example for the children

IN-LAWS

I want to:

make decisions without consulting my parents

I want my husband to:

choose me over his parents

stay home when my parents visit

> visit my parents with me
> talk to me before he talks to his dad when he is trying to
>   make a decision about something
> make positive statements about and to my parents

FRIENDS
> I want to:
>> repeat only what is positive, honest, and true
> I want my husband to:
>> associate with friends who are faithful to their wives
>> spend at least 30 minutes alone with me each day
>> speak kindly to my friends
>> talk about things other than our sex life with others
>> ask our neighbors to visit
>> be a good host (e.g., fill empty glasses)
>> tell his friends he will not lend them money

RELIGION
> I want to:
>> reduce my church activities to two per week
> I want my husband to:
>> go to church with me
>> contribute to church and charity
>> take the children to Sunday School
>> refrain from using God's name in vain

MONEY
> I want to:
>> be punctual when I pay our bills
>> spend money more wisely (save $10.00 each week)
> I want my husband to:
>> try to increase our income
>> talk about things other than "money, money, money"
>> invest only 25 percent of our income in the stock market
>>   per year
>> gamble with only 5 percent of our income per year
>> give me $10 a week to spend as I choose
>> be honest on his income tax

RECREATION
> I want to:
>> develop an interest of my own
>> develop a good attitude about my husband's fishing

I want my husband to:
   spend at least 30 minutes daily with me
   take me to parties

CHILDREN
   I want our son (daughter) to:
      clean up his (her) room ("cleaned up room" is defined in
         Chapter 13)
      make a "B" average in school
      develop a positive attitude about sex

OTHER BEHAVIORS
   I want to:
      lose weight
   I want my husband to:
      tell me what he wants to eat
      help me to prepare meals when he is supposed to
      come home on time or call
      notice when I am on time
      help me to lose weight

APPENDIX II

---············⟨∞⟩············---

Individual Contract

PART I

To SHOW MY willingness to do my part in making our marriage happier, I agree to engage in the specified behavior(s) below. It is clear that engaging in the desirable behavior(s) below result in a positive consequence just as failure to engage in the behavior(s) has a negative consequence. The terms of this contract are fixed for week only. After one week, this contract may be extended or another contract developed.

Desirable behavior	Positive consequence Daily /Weekend	Negative consequence Daily / Weekend

PART II

To demonstrate how often the above desirable behavior(s) occur, I agree to keep a daily record of my behavior(s) for the next seven days.

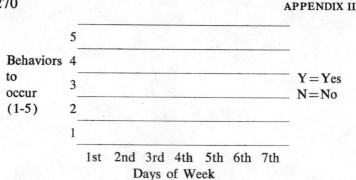

A "Y" (Yes) should be marked to indicate that the behavior(s) (1, 2, 3, 4, or 5) occurred on each of the seven days. A "N" (No) should be marked to indicate that the behavior(s) (1, 2, 3, 4, or 5) did not occur on each of the seven days.

PART III

To practice observing good behavior in my mate, I agree to keep a daily record of my mate's behavior for the next seven days.

a) The behavior my mate has agreed to do more often is

_____.

b) The daily record of this behavior is as follows:

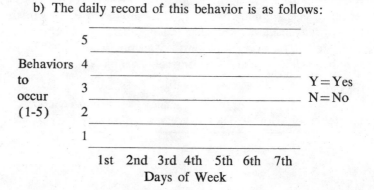

A "Y" (Yes) should be marked to indicate that the behavior(s) (1, 2, 3, 4, or 5) occurred on each of the seven days. A "N" (No) should be marked to indicate that the behavior(s) (1, 2, 3, 4, or 5) did not occur on each of the seven days.

APPENDIX III

Exchange Contract

PART I

SINCE KEEPING HAPPINESS in marriage involves doing things for each other, I agree to _____ for my mate if, in return, my mate agrees to _____ for me. The terms of this contract are fixed for one week only. After one week, this contract may be extended or another contract developed.

PART II

To demonstrate how often I do what I agreed to do, I will keep a daily record of my behavior(s) for the next seven days.

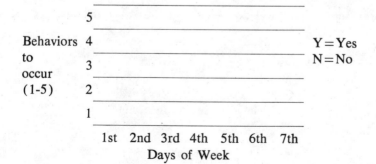

Behaviors to occur (1-5)   5 4 3 2 1

Y=Yes
N=No

1st 2nd 3rd 4th 5th 6th 7th
Days of Week

A "Y" (Yes) should be marked to indicate that the behavior(s)
(1, 2, 3, 4, or 5) occurred on each of the seven days. A "N"
(No) should be marked to indicate that the behavior(s) (1, 2,
3, 4, or 5) did not occur on each of the seven days.

PART III

To practice observing good behavior in my mate, I will keep
a daily record of my mate's behavior for the next seven days.

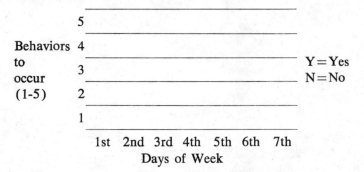

A "Y" (Yes) should be marked to indicate that the behavior(s)
(1, 2, 3, 4, or 5) occurred on each of the seven days. A "N"
(No) should be marked to indicate that the behavior(s) (1, 2,
3, 4, or 5) did not occur on each of the seven days.

MARRIAGE AGREEMENT

To show what I will do to make our marriage happier, I agree

to_____for my

spouse. If I do what I have agreed to do, I will_____

_____to reward myself.

If I don't do what I have agreed to do, I will_____

_____to punish myself.

To keep a record of how often I will do what I have agreed to do, I will mark the chart for the next seven days.

	1st Day	2nd Day	3rd Day	4th Day	5th Day	6th Day	7th Day
Yes							
No							

Another new behavior: _____

_____

Reward: _____

Punishment: _____

Chart

	1st Day	2nd Day	3rd Day	4th Day	5th Day	6th Day	7th Day
Yes							
No							

PART II

To practice observing what my partner will do in exchange, I agree to keep a daily record of my partner's behavior for the next week.

1. Behavior: _____

	1st Day	2nd Day	3rd Day	4th Day	5th Day	6th Day	7th Day
Yes							
No							

2. Behavior: _____

	1st Day	2nd Day	3rd Day	4th Day	5th Day	6th Day	7th Day
No							
Yes							

APPENDIX IV

———⟨❦⟩———

Relaxation Techniques

Relax Yourself

IN THE CHAPTER on sex I mentioned the importance of feeling relaxed as a prerequisite to experiencing an orgasm. A woman who is "up-tight" about sex needs to let loose and feel free to experience those wonderful pleasures her body is capable of. The impotent male may also need to relax since he is anxious about not getting an erection. The point is the same for both—anxiety interefers with your body's response to erotic stimuli. Becoming relaxed frees your body for sexual pleasure.

Relaxation, as pointed out in the chapter on money, will also help you to get your mind off business and other situations that tend to upset you—arguments with clients, parents, bills, climbing interest rates, etc. In short, the relaxation exercises presented here can help you to unwind whenever and for whatever reason necessary.

Deep Muscle Relaxation Training Exercises*

With this method you can learn to be more relaxed and comfortable than you have been since early childhood. You will be able to gain conscious control over the skeletal-muscle tension produced by anxiety. (Since the muscles in your body cannot be both tense and relaxed at the same time, your ability to relax through training can be used to counter anxiety or stress.)

When you are anxious, the feelings of tension you experience are based on the fact that antagonistic muscle systems of certain parts of your body—the flexor and the extensor muscles—are contracting simultaneously. The first step in learning to relax is to become conscious of these muscle systems.

Directions for Deep Muscle Relaxation

While considerable relaxation can be accomplished in any position, it is probably best to begin by sitting in a chair. First, hold your left arm, slightly bent, out in front of you. Place your right hand on top of your left wrist and hold it tightly. Try to bend your left arm back toward you while you push it away from you with your right arm. You will feel the inside muscle (biceps) contract. Hold this for a while (until it feels painful or uncomfortable). Now, reverse the pressure with your left arm. Try to extend it, at the same time holding it tightly with your right hand. As you do this you will feel that the muscles on the outside of the upper left are contracting (triceps). Now let go, This exercise demonstrates the working of opposing muscles of the upper left arm. The biceps is used to flex the arm, while the triceps is used to extend the arm. Should these two muscles contract at the same time you would feel extreme tension in your upper arm. The feeling of tension in the skeletal muscular system throughout the body is caused when both extensors and flexors contract simultaneously.

Now, let's repeat this procedure with the other arm. Hold the

---

* These exercises have been developed by Dr. Jack Turner and are available on cassette tape for $8.50 (record: $7.50) from Cybersystems, Inc., P. O. Box 3365, Huntsville, Alabama 35810.

right arm out in front of you. Grip your right wrist with your left hand. Try to flex your right arm while holding it steady with your left. Concentrate on the feeling in the upper part of your right arm. Now, reverse the procedure and try to extend your right arm, still holding it stationary with your left. You will now feel tenseness in the muscles on the outside of the right arm. Okay, let go and relax. Throughout these exercises, it is important for you to continue to concentrate on the feeling in the various muscle systems so that you become aware of how each system feels when it is tense.

Now, the step-by-step procedure for deep muscle relaxation:

1. Hold your left arm out in front of you again. Grip your left wrist with your right hand. Repeat the procedure in which you attempted to flex your left arm. That is, try to draw it back toward you while at the same time holding it away with your right hand. This time concentrate on the feeling in your upper left arm and in the forearm of your right arm. You will become aware of the tension in the right forearm as it opposes the force of the left arm. Concentrate on the tension in both arms. In a moment I will tell you to let go and when I do, let go with both arms *quite slowly* so that you become conscious of the muscles as they lose their tension. (Hold for a slow count of 10.) OK, gradually let loose with both arms. (Take about 10 seconds to let loose and let your arms return to your lap.) Let go with your left arm and let go with your right arm very slowly until they settle down in your lap. Let them rest there. It is possible to go much farther than this. Concentrate on letting your arms get looser and looser. (Do this for about 10 seconds.) Just keep getting looser. You may become aware of a kind of tingling feeling in your arms and hands as they relax more than they ever have before. OK, good. We are now ready for the next step.

2. Reverse the last procedure. Hold your right arm out in front of you and grip your right wrist with your left hand. (Repeat the above procedure.) Try to draw your right arm in toward you as you hold it stationary with your left hand. Concentrate on the tension in the upper part of your right arm and in the

lower part of your left arm. (Hold for about 5 seconds.) Now let loose again gradually (Take about 10 seconds.) Let them settle down again in your lap. Concentrate on the loose feeling in both your arms. (Take about 10 seconds more.) Let them relax farther and farther below your usual "resting baseline." If you feel some tingling feelings again in your arms or hands, it is a sign that you are concentrating well and relaxing better than you have ever done before.

You will find that *even* breathing contributes greatly to relaxation. Take several calm, medium breaths and notice how the muscles of your shoulders, chest, and arms seem to loosen during the exhalation half of the breathing cycle. Let me explain at this point how to use breathing to help you relax. You can use the exhalation half of a calm, relaxed breathing cycle to reduce the amount of tension a step further in each of the succeeding relaxation exercises. Some people find it helpful to establish a kind of steady breathing, counting for a few breaths —one, two—on the inhalation, and then taking a little longer— one, two, three, four—on the exhalation. You take about 2 seconds on inhalation and three or four for exhalation, or about five or six seconds for a complete breathing cycle. You needn't be particularly concerned about the number of seconds in your breathing as long as it is calm and relaxed. Some people will take 5 seconds for a cycle, some 6 seconds. As you are taking the deep breaths, I want you to imagine that your body is a balloon. That is, when you breathe in, the balloon becomes tight and tense; when you breathe out, the balloon becomes loose and limp. Your muscles are like the balloon and as you breathe out they become more loose and more limp with each exhalation.

3. Curl the toes of both feet as far under the sole of your foot as you can, squeezing down on your shoes. Feel the tension in the muscles of your foot and the fronts of your legs as you do this. Hold this position tightly for a few seconds (about 5 seconds) and then *gradually* let loose. Feel the muscles of your feet and legs getting looser and looser (about 10 seconds). Use the exhalation half of the breathing cycle to achieve more relaxation with each breath.

4. Fan your toes upward, as hard as you can, in your shoes so that they press against the tops of the shoes. Concentrate again on the feeling in your feet and legs (5 seconds). OK, let loose (about 10 seconds) and again, breathe to achieve a greater degree of relaxation.

5. Lift your feet slightly off the ground and point your toes forward and down as hard as you can. Feel the muscles tense in your lower legs. (Hold for about 5 seconds.) OK, relax (10 seconds) and let them settle back on the floor. In this, and in all the future exercises, be sure to breathe calmly, especially during the exhalation half of the breathing cycle. This facilitates relaxation.

6. Keep your heels on the floor and at the same time bend your feet upward as far as they will go, bringing the toes up toward your knees. Feel the muscles tense. OK, let go. (Take about 5 seconds to tense this and about 10 seconds to relax.) Breathe calmly.

7. Lean a little forward in your seat. Raise your right heel so that only the toes of the right foot touch the floor. Now, press the toes against the floor. Feel the muscles below and above your knees tense (5 seconds). OK, relax and let go (10 seconds).

8. Repeat Step 7 with your left leg.

9. Now, raise the toes of your right foot off the ground and press against the floor with your heel as hard as you can (5 seconds.) Feel the muscles of your calf and thigh tensing up. OK, now relax (10 seconds.)

10. Repeat this procedure with your left leg.

11. Place the palm of your left hand against your right knee. Support your left elbow against your left knee. Now, press as hard as you can against your left hand with your right knee. Feel the tension in the upper part of your right leg. (Hold this for about 5 seconds.) Now let go, lean back and relax those muscles. Feel them getting looser with each breath (10 seconds.)

12. Repeat this procedure with your left leg. Place your right palm against your left knee and support your right elbow with your right knee. Press as hard as you can against your right palm with your left knee, concentrating on the feeling in the upper part of your left leg. (Hold this for about 5 seconds.) OK, lean back and slowly relax these muscles.

13. This exercise is to make you aware of the muscles in your abdomen. Tense them up as though you were expecting someone to punch you in the belly. Hold tightly (about 5 seconds). OK, relax (10 seconds).

14. The next two exercises are to make you aware of the muscles in your chest and shoulders. Cross your arms in front of you and reach around with both hands as though you were trying to catch your spine, your right arm going around your left side up toward your shoulders and your left arm going around your right side up toward your shoulders. As you do this you will feel the muscles down the center of your chest and around your shoulders tighten up. Hold tightly (for about 5 seconds). OK, relax and let your arms come back to the arms of the chair (10 seconds).

15. Move forward again to the edge of your chair and swing your arms backward, trying to reach as far behind you as possible. You will again feel the muscles in your upper arms and shoulders and also those down around your shoulder blades and the center of your back. Hold tightly (5 seconds). OK, relax and let your arms come back to the arms of the chair.

In the next steps, we will concentrate on the facial muscles. With most of us, tension in the facial muscles is closely associated with anxiety. In the next few exercises, you will make a tight squinched-up funny face, squeezing all the muscles together as hard as you can.

16. Make a funny face, squeeizng all the muscles of your brow together as tightly as you can. Hold (about 5 seconds). OK, slowly relax (for 10 seconds). Remember to breathe calmly.

17. Make a tight squinched-up funny face again, this time clenching your teeth as tightly as you can. Concentrate on the tension in your jaw muscles. (Hold for about 5 seconds.) OK, relax (again for 10 seconds).

18. Make another squinched-up tight funny face. This time, concentrate on flaring your nostrils. Feel the tension around them and in your cheeks. (Hold for about 5 seconds.) OK, relax slowly (for 10 seconds).

19. The neck muscles are often affected in anxiety. Tense muscles under your lower jaw as tightly as you can, as though you were going to jut your jaw out forward. Concentrate on the muscles just underneath the jaw itself. Hold tightly. Feel the tension in the muscles of the upper front part of your neck and also in the muscles in the back part of your neck just behind your ears leading up to the top of your head. Hold tightly (for about 5 seconds). OK, relax (for 10 seconds).

20. The muscles in the back of the neck are frequently affected by anxiety and stress. Clasp both hands behind your head and try to force your head back while you resist with your hands and arms. Concentrate on the muscles in the back of the neck. Hold tightly until it feels uncomfortable (again about 5 seconds). OK, relax and concentrate on the pleasant experience of muscle relaxation.

21. You can also relax the muscles in the tongue. Place the tip of your tongue against the roof of your mouth and try to push it to full extension. Concentrate on the tension in the tongue muscles. Hold until it feels uncomfortable (about 5 seconds). OK, relax and again concentrate on the warm and pleasant experience of deep muscle relaxation.

These are the special exercises that promote deep muscle relaxation. Most people need to repeat them twice. You've been through them once. Pick the exercises for the parts of your body which have been most difficult to relax in the past and practice them at home. After you have practiced the above exercises once per day for five to ten days, you'll be ready to go to the next stage in learning relaxation. In this second stage, it will not be necessary to tense your muscles in any particular sequence and it will probably not be necessary to tense them at all before proceeding with relaxation. At home, try letting go without a prior tensing and work up from toes to head, either lying down or in a comfortable chair.

Notes

CHAPTER 1

1. Madsen, C. H. Jr. and Madsen, C. K. *Teaching Discipline: Behavioral Principles Toward a Positive Approach*. Boston: Allyn and Bacon, 1970–1971.
2. Rhea, B. Department of Sociology, East Carolina University. Personal communication, 1972.
3. D'Zurilla, T. Department of Psychology, State University of New York at Stony Brook. Personal communication, 1971.

CHAPTER 2

1. Watson, D. L. and Tharp, R. G. *Self-directed Behaviors: Self-modification for Personal Adjustment*. Monterey, California: Brooks/Cole Publishing Co., 1972.

CHAPTER 3

1. Madsen, C. H. Jr. Department of Psychology, Florida State University. Personal communication, 1968–1974.
2. I would like to thank Dr. Jack Turner, Research Psychologist of the Huntsville–Madison County Mental Health Center, Huntsville, Alabama, for his helpful suggestions in the development of this section.
3. Premack, D. Reinforcement theory. In D. Levine (Ed.), Nebraska Symposium on Motivation. Lincoln: University of Nebraska Press, 1965, 123–180.
4. Exchange contracts have received professional attention by Drs. Alan Rappaport, Jan Harrell, Ray Brannon, Robert Sammons, Gerald Patterson, Robert Weiss, Jack Turner, and Charles Madsen.

CHAPTER 4

1. I would like to thank Louise Haigwood, School of Nursing, East Carolina University, for her helpful suggestions in the development of this section.
2. Satir, V. *Conjoint Family Therapy.* Palo Alto, California: Science and Behavior Books, 1967.
3. Honest, dishonest, direct, and indirect questions were developed by Dr. Clifford K. Madsen, Department of Music, and Dr. Charles H. Madsen, Jr., Department of Psychology, Florida State University.
4. Caulkins, A. Roanoke–Chowan Mental Health Service, Ahoskie, North Carolina. Personal communication, 1973.
5. Knox, D. *The Science of Successful Family Living Series— Marriage Enrichment.* Human Behavior Institute. 3300 Northeast Expressway, Atlanta, Georgia 30341. Used by permission.

CHAPTER 5

1. Lindsley, O. "Lindsley's Law." First Annual Rocky Mountain Conference on Behavior Modification, Denver, Colorado, 1972.
2. Knox D. *The Science of Successful Family Living Series— Marriage Enrichment.* Human Behavior Institute. 3300 Northeast Expressway, Atlanta, Georgia 30341. Used by permission.
3. Goldberg B. Department of Psychology, State University of New York at Stony Brook. Personal communication, 1971.
4. Madsen, C. H. Jr. Department of Psychology, Florida State University. Personal communication, 1968–1974.
5. Developing the ability to experience sexual pleasure and/or a positive attitude toward sex can be an extremely complex task. Do not hesitate to consult a behavioral clinician if you are not achieving your goals.
6. This program is adapted from the work of Charles Lobitz and Joseph LoPiccolo. Their program includes the procedures used by Ellis, Lazarus, Madsen, D'Zurilla, and Knox.
7. Dearborn, L. W. Autoeroticism. In A. Ellis and A. Abarbanel (Eds.), *The Encyclopedia of Sexual Behavior.* New York: Hawthorne Books, 1967, pp. 209–215.
8. Kinsey, A. C., Pomeroy, W. B., and Martin, C. E. *Sexual Behavior in the Human Female.* Philadelphia: W. B. Saunders, 1953.
9. Dearborn, L. W. (See above.)
10. D'Zurilla, T. Department of Psychology, State University of New York at Stony Brook, personal communication, 1971.
11. The program is based on the work of Masters, W. H. and

Johnson, V. E., reported in *Human Sexual Inadequacy*. Boston: Little, Brown, 1970.

12. Rimmer, R. *Thursday, My Love*. New York: Norton–New American Library, 1972; Rimmer, R. *You and I . . . Searching for Tomorrow: The Second Book of Letters to Robert H. Rimmer*. New York: New American Library, 1971.

13. Wright, J. Director of Graduate Studies in Criminology, Loyola University, personal communication, 1974.

14. See Note 12 above.

CHAPTER 6

1. I would like to thank Dr. Barry Lubetkin for his help in preparing this chapter. Dr. Lubetkin is co-director with Dr. Steven Fishman of the Institute for Behavior Therapy in New York City.

2. Lovibond, S. H. and Caddy, G. Discriminated aversive control in the moderation of alcoholics' drinking behavior. *Behavior Therapy*, 1970, 1, 437–444.

3. Mills, K. C., Sobell, M. B., and Schaefer, H. H. Training social drinking as an alternative to abstinence for alcoholics. *Behavior Therapy*, 1971, 2, 18–27.

4. Madsen, C. H., Jr. Department of Psychology, Florida State University, personal communication, 1968–1974.

CHAPTER 7

1. Johnson, E. F. Jr. Norfolk, Virginia. Personal communication, 1971.

CHAPTER 8

1. Liebert, R. Department of Psychology, State University of New York at Stony Brook. Personal communication, 1971.

2. Wright, J. Jr. Director of Graduate Studies in Criminology, Loyola University, personal communication, 1974.

3. Jackson, T. Department of English, Wayne Community College, Goldsboro, North Carolina, 1973.

4. Wright, J. Jr. (See above.)

5. Arendall, E. M. Dawson Memorial Baptist Church, Birmingham, Alabama. Personal communication, 1971.

CHAPTER 9

1. D'Zurilla, T. Department of Psychology, State University of New York at Stony Brook, personal communication, 1971.

Chapter 10

1. King, K., McIntyre, J., and Axelson, L. J. Adolescent views of maternal employment as a threat to the marital relationship, *Journal of Marriage and the Family*. 1968, 30, 633–637.

Chapter 12

1. Dr. Ralph James has developed a behavioral system to encourage parent-teacher cooperation to improve the academic achievement of your child. Write to Dr. James, Behavior Management Systems Associates. P. O. Box 222A, Zebulon, North Carolina.
2. Family life and sex education. A course outline for Anaheim Union High School, Anaheim, California, 1966.
3. Kirkendall, L. A. Helping children understand sex. *Better Living Booklet*. New York: Science Research Associates, 1952.

References

AXELSON, L. J. Department of Sociology, Florida State University, personal communication, 1969.

BECKER, W. C. *Parents Are Teachers*. Champaign, Illinois: Research Press, 1971.

CARTHAM, R. *The Sensuous Couple*. New York: Penthouse–Ballantine, 1971.

Caulkins, A. Roanoke–Chowan Mental Health Service, Ahoskie, North Carolina. Personal communication, 1973.

CROAKE, J. Department of Housing, Management, and Family Relations, Virginia Polytechnic Institute. Personal communication, 1971.

DAVISON, G. Department of Psychology, State University of New York at Stony Brook. Personal communication, 1971.

DEARBORN, L. W. Autoeroticism. In A. Ellis and A. Abarbanel (eds.), *The Encyclopedia of Sexual Behavior*. New York: Hawthorn Books 1967, pp. 209–215.

D'ZURILLA, T. Department of Psychology, State University of New York at Stony Brook. Personal communication, 1971.

EASTMAN, W. Department of Psychiatry, University of North Carolina at Chapel Hill. Personal communication, 1971.

ELLIS, A. *The Art and Science of Love*. New York: Lyle Stuart, 1960.

FAMILY LIFE AND SEX EDUCATION. A course outline for Anaheim Union High School, Anaheim, California, 1966.

FRIEDAN, B. *The Feminine Mystique*. New York: Dell, 1963.

GOLDBERG, B. Department of Psychology, State University of New York at Stony Brook. Personal communication, 1971.

GOLDSTEIN, M. K. and FRANCIS, B. Behavior modification of husbands by wives. Paper, National Council on Family Relations, Washington, October, 1969.

GOODSON, W. H. Behavior therapy—a new tool. *The Alabama Journal of Medical Science*, 1971, 8, 279–282.

GREENE, J. Department of Sociology, Florida State University. Personal communication, 1966–1970.

GREER, GERMAINE. *The Female Eunuch*. New York: McGraw-Hill, 1972.

GUEST, E. A. Sermons we see. *The Light of Fate*. Chicago: Reilly, and Lee, 1926.

HAIGWOOD, L. School of Nursing, East Carolina University, Greenville, North Carolina, Personal communication, 1973.

HAGERTY, E. Department of Family Relations, University of British Columbia. Personal communication, 1971.

HARTZ, E. Department of Social Welfare, Florida State University. Personal communication, 1971.

"J" *The Sensuous Woman*. New York: Dell, 1969.

JACKSON, T. Department of English, Wayne Community College, Goldsboro, North Carolina, 1973.

JACOBSON, E. *Progressive Relaxation*. Chicago: University of Chicago Press, 1938.

JAMES, R. President, Behavior Management Systems Associates, Zebulon, North Carolina. Personal communication, 1972.

JAMES, R. *Student Achievement Record*. Behavior Management Systems Associates P. O. Box 222A, Zebulon, North Carolina.

JOHNSON, E. F. Jr. Norfolk, Virginia. Personal communication, 1971.

KING, K., McINTYRE, J., and AXELSON, L. J. Adolescent views of maternal employment as a threat to the marital relationship. *Journal of Marriage and the Family*. 1968, 30, 633–637.

KINSEY, A. C., POMEROY, W. B., and MARTIN, C. E. *Sexual Behavior in the Human Female*. Philadelphia: W. B. Saunders, 1953.

KINSEY, A. C., POMEROY, W. B., and MARTIN, C. E. *Sexual Behavior in the Human Male*. Philadelphia: W. B. Saunders, 1948.

KIRKENDALL, L. A. Helping children understand sex. *Better Living Booklet*. New York: Science Research Associates, 1952.

KNOX, D. *Marriage Happiness: A Behavioral Approach to Counseling*. Champaign, Illinois: Research Press, 1971.

KNOX, D. Behavior contracts in marriage counseling. *Journal of Family Counseling*, 1973, 1, 22–29.

KNOX, D. *The Science of Successful Family Living Series—Marriage Enrichment*. Human Behavior Institute. 3300 Northeast Expressway, Atlanta, Georgia 30341. Used by permission.

KNOX, D. *Marriage: Who? When? Why?* Englewood Cliffs, New Jersey: Prentice-Hall, 1975.

KNOX, T. Sacramento, California. Personal communication, 1972.

KRASNER, L. Department of Psychology, State University of New York at Stony Brook. Personal communication, 1970.

LAZARUS, A. Behavior therapy and marriage counseling. *Journal of the American Society of Psychosomatic Dentistry and Medicine*, 1968, 15, 49–56.

LIBERMAN, R. Behavioral approaches to family and couple therapy. *American Journal of Orthopsychiatry*, 1970, 40, 106–118.

LIEBERT, R. Department of Psychology, State University of New York at Stony Brook. Personal communication, 1971.

LINDSLEY, O. First Annual Rocky Mountain Conference on Behavior Modification, Denver, Colorado, 1972.

LOBITZ, C. W. and LOPICCOLO, J. New methods in the behavioral treatment of sexual dysfunction. *Journal of Behavior Therapy and Experimental Psychiatry*, 1972, 3, 265–272.

LOVIBOND, S. H. and CADDY, G. Discriminated aversive control in the moderation of alcoholics' drinking behavior. *Behavior Therapy*, 1970, 1, 437–444.

LUBETKIN, B. Co-director with Steven Fishman of The Institute For Behavior Therapy, New York City. Personal communication, 1971.

"M" *The Sensuous Man*. New York: Dell, 1971.

MACE, D. *Getting Ready for Marriage*. Nashville: Abingdon Press, 1972.

MACE, D. *We can have better marriages*. Nashville: Abingdon, 1974.

MADSEN, C. H. JR. Department of Psychology, Florida State University. Personal communication, 1968–1974.

MADSEN, C. K. and MADSEN, C. H. JR. *Parents/Children/Discipline: A Positive Way*. Boston: Allyn and Bacon, 1971.

MADSEN, C. H. JR. and MADSEN, C. K. *Teaching/Discipline: Behavior Principles Toward a Positive Approach*. Boston: Allyn and Bacon, 1970.

MASTERS, W. H. and JOHNSON, V. E. *Human Sexual Inadequacy*. Boston: Little, Brown, 1970.

MASTERS, W. H. and JOHNSON, V. E. *Human Sexual Response*. Boston: Little, Brown, 1966.

MCCARY, J. L. *Human Sexuality*, New York: Van Nostrand, 1967.

MILLS, K. C., SOBELL, M. B. and SCHAEFER, H. H. Training social drinking as an alternative to abstinence for alcoholics. *Behavior Therapy*, 1971, 2, 18–27.

OLSON, D. H. Behavior modification research with couples and families: A system analysis, review and critique. Paper, Association for Advancement of Behavior Therapy, New York, October, 1972.

PATTERSON, G. R. *Families*. Champaign, Illinois: Research Press, 1971.

PATTERSON, G. R. and WEISS, R. Behavioral treatment for marital discord. Paper, Association for Advancement of Behavior Therapy, New York, October, 1972.

PATTERSON, G. R. and HOPS, H. Coercion, a game for two: intervention techniques for marital conflict in R. E. Ulrich and P. Mountjoy (eds.) *The Experimental Analysis of Social Behavior.* New York: Appleton-Century-Crofts, 1972.

PREMACK, D. Reinforcement theory. In D. Levine (ed), Nebraska Symposium on motivation. Lincoln: University of Nebraska Press. 1965. 123–180.

RAPPAPORT, A. F. and HARRELL, J. A behavioral-exchange model for marital counseling. *The Family Coordinator,* 1972, 21, 203–212.

RHEA, B. Department of Sociology, East Carolina University. Personal communication, 1972.

REUBEN, D. *Everything You Always Wanted to Know About Sex but Were Afraid to Ask.* New York: David McKay Co., 1969.

RIMMER, R. *Thursday, My Love.* New York: Norton–New American Library, 1972.

RIMMER, R. *You and I . . . Searching for Tomorrow: The Second Book of Letters to Robert H. Rimmer.* New York: New American Library, 1971.

SATIR, V. *Conjoint Family Therapy.* Palo Alto, California: Science and Behavior Books, 1967.

SEMANS, J. H. Premature ejaculation: A new approach. *Southern Medical Journal* 1956, 44, 353–357.

STEINEM, G. What it will be like if women win. In F. Cox (ed.), *American Marriages: A Changing Scene.* Dubuque, Iowa: Wm. C. Brown Co., 1972.

TURNER, A. J. Couple and group treatment of marital discord. Paper, Association for Advancement of Behavior Therapy, October, 1972.

WALTERS, J. Department of Family Relations and Child Development. University of Georgia, Athens, Georgia. Personal communication, 1972.

WATSON, D. L. and THARP, R. C. *Self-directed Behaviors: Self-modification for Personal Adjustment.* Monterey, California: Brooks/Cole Publishing Co., 1972.

WEISS, R. L., BIRCHLER, G. R., and VINCENT, J. P. Contractual models for negotiation training in marital dyads. *Journal of Marriage and the Family,* 1974, 36, 321–330.

WEISS, R. L., HOPS, H. and PATTERSON, G. R. A framework for conceptualizing marital conflict, a technology for altering it, some data for evaluating it. In F. W. Clark and L. A. Hamerlynck (eds.) *Critical Issues in Research and Practice: Proceedings* of the Fourth Banff International Conference on Behavior Modification. Champaign, Illinois: Research Press Co., 1973.

WOLPE, J. and LAZARUS, A. *Behavior Therapy Techniques.* New York: Pergamon Press, 1966.

WRIGHT, J., JR. Director of Graduate Studies in Criminology, Loyola University, personal communication, 1974.

Index